The Evolution of

NORTH AMERICAN INDIANS

A 31-volume series of outstanding dissertations

Edited by

DAVID HURST THOMAS
American Museum of Natural History

A GARLAND SERIES

Prehistoric Exchange and Sociopolitical Development in the Plateau Southwest

AMY A. DOUGLASS

Garland Publishing, Inc. New York & London 1990

Library of Congress Cataloging-in-Publication Data

Douglass, Amy A.
Prehistoric exchange and sociopolitical development in the plateau southwest / Amy A. Douglass.
p. cm. — (The Evolution of North American Indians)
Originally presented as the author's dissertation (doctoral—Arizona State University)
Includes bibliographical references.
ISBN 0-8240-2500-8 (alk. paper)
1. Indians of North America—Southwest, New—Pottery. 2. Indians of North America—Southwest, New—Commerce. 3. Commerce, Prehistoric—Southwest, New—Case studies. 4. Indians of North America—Southwest, New—Antiquities. 5. Barter—Southwest, New. 6. Southwest, New—Antiquities. I. Series.
E78.S7D73 1991
979'.01—dc20 90-49134

Printed on acid-free, 250-year-life paper.
Manufactured in the United States of America.

Design by J. Threlkeld

ACKNOWLEDGEMENTS

Many people have contributed their knowledge, advice and data to this project and I am deeply indebted to all of them. I would like to thank Jeffrey Hantman for helping me to formulate the basic research questions which ultimately developed into this dissertation. The staff at the Museum of Northern Arizona has been extremely forthcoming in giving me access to the collections, without which this research could not have been undertaken. The collections at the Arizona State Museum and the Western Archeological Conservation Center were also valuable sources of data for my research. I am especially indebted to Peter Pilles for his advice during countless conversations, particularly regarding Little Colorado White Ware design styles, and for generously providing me with information whenever I have requested it.

The sourcing study would have been impossible without the efforts of David Schaller. His commitment to the project is reflected in his thorough and precise analyses. His expertise in mineralogy and petrology has been invaluable. I am also very grateful to Chris Downum for providing me with his data on tree-ring dates and ceramic distributions in the San Francisco Peaks area. Our many discussions concerning the classification and dating of ceramic design styles helped me put these issues in perspective. Steadman Upham's comments on a draft of this dissertation are greatly appreciated.

Many other archaeologists have shared their data and ideas with me, including Robert Euler, Anne Baldwin, Janet Balsom, Michael Bremer, T. Kathleen Henderson, A. Trinkle Jones and Richard Lange. I would also like to thank Dennis Young for his advice concerning the statistical analyses. The production of this manuscript would not have been possible without Marsha Schweitzer's unending patience and attention to detail.

A special thanks goes to my dissertation committee for their support and encouragement during my years at Arizona State University. I owe a great deal to my chairperson, Sylvia Gaines, for her guidance and energetic optimism when I needed it most. Geoffrey Clark and Barbara Stark have been good friends as well as teachers and advisors. I am indebted to Charles Redm for his insight, and for helping me to develop skills in grantsmanship. Reynold Ruppe's unwavering support and wise council since my first days at Arizona State University are difficult to categorize or measure.

This research was supported by funding from the National Science Foundation (Grant No. BBS 8504110), the Wenner-Gren Foundation for Anthropological Research (Grant No. 4617) and the Arizona State University Graduate Student Research Program. Raw material samples were collected in the Hopi Buttes area with the permission of the Navajo Tribe (Permit No. 1986-4) and the Bureau of Indian Affairs (Permit No. NAO ARPA-86-002). Surface collections of sherds at AR-03-04-02-2403 were made with the permission of the Coconino National Forest.

My warmest appreciation is extended to my family for their encouragement throughout my graduate career. My parents, Ralph Douglass and Juanita Walls Douglass, have given me a desire to learn and the freedom to pursue my own interests, without either of which I would not have been able to complete my doctorate. Finally, my mother's grace and fortitude have been a source of inspiration to me which I will always cherish. I would like to dedicate this volume in her memory.

TABLE OF CONTENTS

Chapter Page

Chapter Page

LIST OF TABLES

Table Page

LIST OF FIGURES

Figure | Page

Figure | Page

CHAPTER I

INTRODUCTION

The classification of prehistoric ceramics according to their stylistic and technological characteristics has been an important component of southwestern archaeological research since its inception (Fewkes 1898, 1904, 1909; Nelson 1916, Spier 1917, Kidder 1924). Throughout the first half of the twentieth century, various classes of ceramics were used to define prehistoric cultural units and delineate their boundaries (e.g., Gladwin and Gladwin 1929, Colton 1939, Wasley 1959). With the development of seriation and dendrochronology, certain types of ceramics were designated as temporal diagnostics for constructing regional chronologies. These cultural units and regional chronologies remain essentially intact to the present day.

A great deal of energy has been expended by southwestern archaeologists during the past fifty years in subdividing the ceramic classificatory system into local types and varieties in order to identify local subtraditions and create more detailed chronologies. Despite this great effort, the processes underlying the widespread geographic distributions of many ceramic wares and types are not well understood. Diffusion and migration have been evoked as the major explanatory mechanisms until recently (e.g., Haury 1956, Wasley 1959, Carlson 1970, Martin 1974). In general, exchange has not been considered a significant factor, even though archaeologists have known for decades that it occurred on a relatively frequent basis across long distances (Shepard 1936, Colton 1941, McGregor 1941a).

Theoretical Paradigms and Ethnographic Models

In large part, the lack of emphasis on exchange as an important distributional mechanism was the result of the theoretical context in which southwestern ceramic analysis was conducted during the first half of this century. Research on exchange was not a priority among archaeologists working within a diffusionist/culture area framework. They were interested in tracing the movement of culture traits across space and between cultures. The actual processes involved (i.e., whether people, ideas or goods moved) was less important to them than the outcome.

Exchange continued to be downplayed even after the diffusionist framework lost its prominence in southwestern archaeological thinking because of a long-standing model of prehistoric plateau economic and political organization. The "new archeology" of the 1960s ushered in a dramatically different view of the relationship between the archaeological record and past behavior systems. This new school proposed to reconstruct community social organization and other aspects of culture by examining intra-site artifact distributions, rather than treating material remains as static items on a trait list. However, it perpetuated many of the same views of prehistoric plateau cultures which had been held for decades.

The traditional model of prehistoric plateau cultures used historic Pueblo cultures as analogs, insofar as they were understood through ethnographic studies. It was generally held that prehistoric communities were economically self-sufficient and politically autonomous entities, each representing a microcosm of the culture at large (e.g., Haury 1962). In addition, Puebloan society, both past and present, was believed to be egalitarian.

As a result, exchange was not considered to be an essential component of prehistoric plateau culture since it was not necessary for prehistoric communities to obtain goods or services from one another.

The theoretical paradigms and ethnographic constructs discussed above also had important methodological ramifications which prevented the systematic documentation of prehistoric exchange. Ceramic analyses, whether conducted for the purpose of defining cultural units, establishing chronologies or examining community social organization, relied primarily on attributes which were observable with the naked eye or a hand lens. However, these attributes are not fine-grained enough to measure differences in the raw material constituents of ceramics originating from different geological sources. Chemical and mineralogical analyses which are necessary for sourcing ceramics were not conducted on a regular basis and, therefore, ceramic exchange went largely undetected.

An Alternative Approach to Exchange

During the past decade, some southwestern archaeologists have begun to question the validity of the traditional model of prehistoric economic and political organization on the Colorado Plateaus. The use of historic Puebloan cultures as analogs has been challenged, along with the ethnographic model of these cultures. In addition, archaeological evidence indicates that prehistoric plateau cultures may have been more complex in some cases than their historic counterparts (Upham et al. 1981).

An alternative body of theory has been proposed to explain prehistoric sociopolitical development, which will be referred to subsequently as the developmental model. Briefly stated, the developmental model views agricultural intensification, political leadership beyond the community level, and the development of settlement hierarchies and exchange systems as adaptive responses to the risks engendered by a commitment to an agricultural subsistence pattern within a marginal environment.

The developmental argument can be summarized as follows. As early as A.D. 600 population growth, the colonization of new areas and increasing sedentism began to alter significantly the adaptive strategies of plateau populations. In the centuries that followed, migratory seasonal rounds were replaced by a greater commitment to agriculture and the movement of subsistence goods across environmental zones via exchange (Schoenwetter and Dittert 1968, Braun and Plog 1982). These new subsistence patterns resulted in a greater decision-making load due to the exigencies of managing stored surpluses, organizing inter-community exchange transactions and settling the growing number of disputes generated by increasing population density (Lightfoot 1981, Lightfoot and Feinman 1982).

Such tasks could be handled most efficiently by decision-making specialists. Consequently, communities which developed specialized political leadership would have an adaptive advantage over those which did not (Lightfoot 1981). However, once in place, community leaders would seek to consolidate and legitimize their authority. It is at this point that the process of leadership development takes on a new dynamic, shifting from primarily a "system-serving" to more of a "self-serving" course (Upham 1982:120). According to several ethnographic studies of leadership development in tribal societies (e.g., Leach 1954, Barth 1959, Sahlins 1963, Chagnon 1968), decision-makers would have several means of promoting their leadership including amassing surpluses, increasing the size of their immediate households and communities, and initiating exchange relationships outside their local communities. These strategies would be used by leaders to create obligation on the part of their followers and expand their support bases beyond community boundaries. Exchange would be extremely useful as a source of goods for gift-giving and for establishing cooperative relationships with other leaders. Outside contacts would serve to legitimize decision-makers since their influence beyond the community would set them apart from others. As their authority grew, certain successful leaders might extend their political control over the surrounding area, subordinating decision-makers in other communities. Their exchange ties also would continue to expand outward, extending over increasingly longer distances (Lightfoot 1981, Lightfoot and Feinman 1982).

According to proponents of the developmental model, the process of leadership development would have continued for several centuries in areas on the Colorado Plateaus which experienced sustained population growth, agricultural intensification, and spatial as well as temporal variability in precipitation. By the fourteenth century, the process resulted in the development of various hierarchical political systems, incorporating several settlements, that were engaged heavily in long-distance exchange (Upham 1982).

To summarize, the developmental model presents a very different perspective on exchange, in addition to changing the way in which archaeologists view prehistoric plateau cultures. The movement of goods between communities and settlement systems is no longer an ancillary phenomenon which is of little consequence to the maintenance or change of cultural systems. Instead, exchange has become an essential component of an adaptive strategy. In addition, long-distance exchange has taken on the role of an agent of sociopolitical development since it can be used both to perpetuate and legitimize the authority of decision-making specialists.

The Need for Evidence

The exchange of goods made from clearly exotic raw materials such as marine shell, turquoise and copper throughout the prehistoric Southwest has been known for quite some time (Brand 1938, Colton 1941, Tower 1945). Decorated ceramics were also known to have been exchanged, particularly the distinctive redwares, orangewares and polychromes of the thirteenth and fourteenth centuries (Shepard 1936, 1942; Schaefer 1969). However, it is only recently that the prevailing exchange of more utilitarian items such as plainwares and less exotic lithic materials has come to light. These new data are the result of the rise in sourcing studies during the 1980s. It is becoming increasingly apparent that inter-community exchange at varying geographic scales was prevalent by A.D. 1000 or earlier. However, many questions yet remain concerning the structure of production-distribution systems and the role of exchange in sociopolitical development.

The nature of ceramic exchange is of particular importance because of its crucial role as a source of status and as a legitimizer of political authority within the context of the developmental model. The regional studies of tradeware distributions which have been conducted to date deal with thirteenth and fourteenth century decorated wares such as Jeddito Yellow Ware (Schaefer 1969, Upham 1982), Salado Wares (Lightfoot and Jewett 1984, Crown and Bishop 1987) and White Mountain Red Ware (Lightfoot and Jewett 1984, Upham 1982). However, the major drawback of past regional studies is that they generally do not integrate relatively precise sourcing data with comprehensive distributional data. In other words, they either identify specific geologic sources from which the raw material constituents of the ceramics in question originated, or they are able to characterize the movement of these tradewares between and within settlement systems. However, they rarely accomplish both tasks.

Ceramic production-distribution systems will not be understood adequately until both sourcing and distributional data are brought together. The degree to which tradeware production was restricted to certain communities or areas is not known. Mineralogical and chemical analyses of potential raw material sources need to be conducted in conjunction with comparable analyses on ceramics. The extent to which tradewares were restricted in access to the general population within settlement systems has not been documented for many parts of the Colorado Plateaus. More detailed information is needed on the distribution of these wares in different types of sites and within burial populations. Until the proper sourcing and frequency data are brought to bear, the role of ceramic exchange within the context of hierarchical political organization will remain at issue.

Even less is known about ceramic production-distribution systems prior to ca. A.D. 1200. A regional perspective is lacking from sourcing studies on ceramics produced during earlier centuries. Mineralogical and chemical analyses have been conducted (e.g., Garrett 1979, Crown 1980, Deutchman 1980), but they generally are restricted to samples from one or a few sites in a small area and rarely include the analysis of potential clay or temper sources. In addition, quantitative data on the distribution of ceramics within plateau settlement systems in existence between A.D. 900 and 1100 have yet to be synthesized.

This earlier period should have witnessed the development of long-distance exchange spheres which, according to the developmental model, culminated in systems of prestige exchange in some areas of the plateau Southwest during the thirteenth and fourteenth centuries. Therefore, reconstructing ceramic exchange prior to ca. A.D. 1200 is necessary if the developmental model is to be tested thoroughly. The primary objective of this dissertation is to document the production-distribution system of Little Colorado White Ware, a black-on-white ceramic which was produced between ca. A.D. 1050 and 1250, in order to test expectations derived from the developmental model concerning formative exchange patterns.

Little Colorado White Ware will be used as a case study in order to determine if earlier exchange patterns could have been precursors to the type of prestige exchange which has been proposed for the thirteenth and fourteenth centuries by proponents of the developmental model. In addition, this study was undertaken in order to determine if an earlier perspective can offer additional insights toward the interpretation of the structure and function of later exchange systems.

In order to better understand views on exchange in southwestern archaeological thinking, the following chapter begins with a more in-depth review of the history of ceramic analysis and the theoretical frameworks on which it was based. Past compositional (i.e., mineralogical and chemical) analysis of prehistoric ceramics are discussed and their impact on assumptions concerning ceramic production and exchange are assessed. The developmental model is summarized, along with its criticisms of these long-standing assumptions. In addition, the role of exchange as a dynamic cultural process within the context of this new theory is further developed.

Chapter III presents the evidence for the climatic, demographic and subsistence trends which have been set forth as baseline conditions for sociopolitical development by proponents of the developmental model. Evidence for the development of increasingly centralized and stratified sociopolitical systems on the Colorado Plateaus between A.D. 700 and 1400 is also presented. Chapter IV summarizes and evaluates present data on exchange. The gaps in these data concerning regional exchange systems prior to the thirteenth century are brought out. Finally, this chapter sets forth expectations concerning early (pre-thirteenth century) production-distribution systems in accordance with the developmental model.

Chapter V discusses the research design and data which are used in a case study of early regional exchange. Little Colorado White Ware is presented as a suitable test case. The three goals of the study are introduced: 1) determining the degree of geographic centralization in Little Colorado White Ware production, 2) determining the basic structure of its regional exchange system, and 3) examining stylistic variability within the production-distribution system. The data base also is described. This chapter concludes with a discussion of the limitations of a case study approach.

Each of the next three chapters takes one of the three goals of the case study in turn. Chapter VI deals with the sourcing of Little Colorado White Ware by way of three types of compositional analysis: petrographic analysis, x-ray diffraction and electron microprobe analysis. The data base for the petrographic analysis is composed of thin sections of Little

Colorado White Ware sherds from a core sample of 11 sites in the Hopi Buttes and San Francisco Peaks, the two most likely production areas. Observations of the mineral inclusion in the thin sections and point count data are used to determine whether this ware was produced in one or both areas.

The results of the x-ray diffraction analysis of the clay particles in both fired and unfired Little Colorado White Ware sherds, as well as clay samples from the Hopi Buttes and San Francisco Peaks, are compared in order to identify the geologic formation from which the clay in this ware was derived. The chemical composition of augite crystals in Little Colorado White Ware sherds and volcanic rocks from both areas are examined using electron microprobe analysis. The data from the three types of compositional analysis are brought together in order to delineate the geographic limits of the source area. Finally, the implications of the results of the sourcing study on the issue of community-level production specialization are discussed.

Chapter VII discusses a distance decay analysis which is used to characterize the movement of Little Colorado White Ware within its exchange sphere. The percentages of Little Colorado White Ware sherds in the decorated ceramic assemblages of 40 sites located throughout the Little Colorado River drainage are plotted against the distances of the sites from the source area, as defined in Chapter VI.

Two techniques of exploratory data analysis, resistant line-fitting and smoothing, are used to describe the relationship between Little Colorado White Ware frequencies, a measure of exchange intensity, and distance from the source. These results are used to reconstruct the structure of the Little Colorado White Ware exchange system and hypothesize about its role in inter-community interaction. Contextual data such as intrasite distributions of this ware, topography, vegetation and population densities in various areas within the exchange system are brought to bear on the interpretation of the distance decay patterns. The last section of the seventh chapter compares the results to the expectations set forth in Chapter IV.

Chapter VIII addresses the issue of stylistic variability in Little Colorado White Ware and its significance in terms of the structure of the production-distribution system. An alternative system of classifying this ware based on stylistic criteria, instead of Colton's (1955) typology, is outlined. The temporal relationships between the six styles, based on tree-ring dates and ceramic associations, also are discussed.

The function of style within this ware's production-distribution system is approached by way of three different issues: the relationship between mineralogical and stylistic variability, the distribution of vessel form across style and area, and the geographic distributions of the six styles throughout northern Arizona. The first issue is addressed by a statistical analysis of the petrographic point count data across style. The second issue is examined via a design analysis of 2400 Little Colorado White Ware sherds from 14 sites in the Hopi Buttes, San Francisco Peaks and Chevelon Creek drainage. The third issue is addressed through a survey of unpublished and published sherd counts, as well as personal observations of ceramic collections at various institutions. The temporal placement of the six styles relative to one another is brought to bear on the relationship between mineralogical and stylistic variability, as well as the styles' geographic distributions.

Chapter IX presents a summary of the results of this case study and an evaluation of the expectations of the developmental model with respect to pre-thirteenth century regional exchange. It also advocates more comprehensive compositional analyses of potential exchange goods, as well as regionally oriented studies of exchange.

CHAPTER II

HISTORY OF CERAMIC ANALYSIS IN THE SOUTHWEST

Ceramic analysis always has been an important component of southwestern archaeology's methodology and theoretical interpretation. However, relatively little research has been directed toward explaining prehistoric ceramic distributions in terms of their place within regional socioeconomic systems until recently (e.g., Hantman and Plog 1982, Braun and Plog 1982, Upham 1982). Exchange has been downplayed as an important distributional mechanism because of the theoretical paradigms and attendant methodologies under which southwestern archaeologists have been operating.

In this chapter, I will present a brief history of approaches to ceramic analysis in the Southwest and discuss how theoretical frameworks, particularly as they relate to exchange, have determined analytical methodologies. I will also review compositional analyses of prehistoric ceramics conducted during different periods of archaeological research and their impact on assumptions concerning production and exchange.

The Theoretical Context of Southwestern Ceramic Analysis

In any scientific discipline, methodology is determined by the theoretical assumptions and goals in the context of which it must function. It is therefore necessary to examine both the types of ceramic analysis that have been conducted in the Southwest and the conclusions which have been drawn from them in terms of the theoretical views of the analysts. Throughout the history of southwestern archaeology, there have been several theoretical perspectives or schools of thought which have exerted a strong influence on ceramic analysis. The following three sections will focus on theoretical perspectives which have had a significant impact on views concerning inter-community exchange and, in turn, on the amount of effort that has been expended in sourcing ceramics.

The Culture Area Approach

The description and classification of ceramics has its beginnings in the inception of southwestern archaeology (Fewkes 1898, 1904, 1909; Nelson 1916, Spier 1917, Kidder 1924). Such analyses continued in the 1930s with Kidder and Amsden (1931), Kidder and Shepard (1936), the Gladwins (1930, 1931, 1933), Gladwin et al. (1937) and Haury (1936), among others. The excavations of the 1940s and 1950s explored new areas of the Southwest and consequently the classification system was expanded by the assignment of new geographic type names to what were perceived to be local sub-traditions within broader culture areas. Many of these types turned out to be variants of the same type and were later merged. For example, the first Cibola White Ware seminar merged Cheta and Whipple Black-on-white under Reserve Black-on-white and eliminated McKinley Black-on-white, subsuming it under Puerco Black-on-white. A number of other revisions were also made at this conference (Dittert 1958). The massive amounts of ceramic description which had begun to accumulate were organized into several syntheses such as Mera (1935), Hawley (1936), Colton and Hargrave (1937) and Colton (1955). Thus, during the first half of the twentieth century, a great deal of energy was invested in developing a systematic ceramic typology based on explicit descriptions of stylistic and technological attributes.

Archaeologists were aware that ceramic exchange was a relatively widespread phenomenon as early as the Pueblo II period. Colton (1941:10) states that ". . . small bowls were so widely traded that it is difficult sometimes to locate their home tribe." He speaks of Kayenta Anasazi black-on-white vessels dating between A.D. 700 and 1300 appearing throughout the Salt River Valley. McGregor (1941a:255) states that Black Mesa Black-on-white (or Deadmans, as it was referred to at that time) was "widely traded" and that exchange during Pueblo II and III extended into southern Utah, southern Nevada, California and southern New Mexico (McGregor 1941a:269). Colton even calls for a more detailed study of exchange using the expertise of other disciplines.

> The study of aboriginal trade has just begun. The centers of manufacture of a few objects have been proved above any reasonable doubt. Although we see dimly some of the broad aspects of aboriginal trade we need the aid of the specialist to help us settle the source of manufacture of many objects. We have made a beginning, but thanks to the gracious cooperation among scientific men, the possibility of further contribution to this study of prehistoric commerce appears to have no limit to its horizon (1941:12).

He also mentions Shepard's petrographic studies as a viable means of sourcing ceramics.

It should be pointed out that, although archaeologists were aware of the presence of exchange during Pueblo II and III, there appears to have been a limit in their minds as to the actual volume of exchange. Haury states:

> Exchange of pottery. . .took place on the village-farming community level between neighboring tribes. Again, not until late in prehistory, however - in the fourteenth century - do we see this reaching significant proportions, that is when the volume became large enough to make commerce in pottery appear as an institutionalized activity (Haury 1962:123 as quoted in Breternitz 1966).

Breternitz (1966) is of the opinion that exchange involved transactions between individuals at relatively low volumes before A.D. 1200. In a later edition of his synthetic work, McGregor (1965:381) states that Holbrook and Walnut Black-on-white were found in such abundance in the Sinagua area that they must have been produced locally.

Migration was often invoked as an explanation when exotic ceramic types seemed to suddenly appear in a given area in large quantities. For example, the appearance of Mesa Verde Black-on-white and St. Johns Polychrome in Chaco Canyon was interpreted as the result of a re-occupation of the canyon by Mesa Verde peoples during the thirteenth century (Vivian and Mathews 1965:81). Thus large quantities of exotics seemed to preclude exchange and were perceived as evidence for the actual movement of the potters themselves to a new area.

It is not clear, however, what the quantitative threshold between exchange and local production was in the minds of these archaeologists. No specific figure or rule of thumb is given in the literature as to what percentages of exotic vessels or sherds must be encountered in an assemblage before local production, either by local potters adopting new technologies or immigrant potters, becomes a more viable explanation than exchange.

Nevertheless, archaeologists knew that ceramic exchange occurred during much of the prehistoric period in the Southwest, despite the vagueness of the quantitative boundaries separating exchange and local production. Although sourcing technology was available to document exchange, such studies were not a prevalent part of ceramic analysis until the 1970s. The question remains as to why the vast potential for exploring the nature of exchange in southwestern prehistory was not tapped.

The lack of interest in documenting exchange is due to the fact that such investigations were not a priority within the theoretical framework of southwestern archaeology during the first half of this century. During this period, American ethnologists and archaeologists (including southwesternists) were attempting to describe indigenous cultures and group them according to their locations within certain geographically circumscribed environmental zones: what has come to be known as the culture area approach (Wissler 1917, Kroeber 1939).

Southwestern archaeologists utilizing the culture area model sought to delineate the spatial boundaries of normative "cultures" and describe said cultures according to trait lists composed of their material remains. Important elements of such trait lists were ceramic assemblages whose distinctive technologies and design systems were viewed as manifestations of discrete sets of beliefs and customs. Thus ceramic description and classification were essential components of these prehistoric cultural definitions. A good example of the culture area approach, as Hantman (1983) has pointed out, is the Gladwins' efforts to locate the spatial limits of what they termed "the Red-on-buff culture" (e.g., Gladwin and Gladwin 1929).

The culture area approach, in turn, was an outgrowth of the diffusionist school (Harris 1968:374-377). Following an essentially diffusionist model for culture change, southwestern archaeologists attempted to trace the movements of traits from one culture to the next. In order to do so, it was necessary to determine the "culture center" (Wissler 1926) from which traits originated on the one hand and who the recipient culture was on the other. It mattered little from a diffusionist perspective whether the vessels themselves or the technological and stylistic concepts involved in their production traveled across space. Theoretically, the ultimate outcome was the same: technological and stylistic traits moved from a center of diffusion in one culture to another recipient culture and became part of the latter's behavioral repertoire.

Broad-based reconstructions of southwestern prehistory were based on diffusionist interpretations. In his seminal work *Introduction to Southwestern Archaeology*, Kidder (1924) presented the first comprehensive summary and interpretation of the prehistoric Southwest according to existing archeological data. He viewed the San Juan River basin as the hub of cultural development, from which traits spread to other parts of the Southwest. Kidder saw progressive expansion of the Pueblo sphere of influence throughout its prehistory. This expansion was exhibited in a clinal distribution of Puebloan traits from the San Juan "centre of dissemination" outward (Kidder 1924:47). Thus the most advanced Puebloan traits were to be found in the San Juan and surrounding areas, giving way to less advanced or earlier Puebloan manifestations as one moved outward. The most specialized kivas, highest quality corrugated wares and most characteristic masonry architecture were to be found closest to the San Juan. Farther away, kivas were less specialized, corrugated wares became cruder and pueblo style masonry was less common.

By the mid-1930s, when it became evident that the southern deserts of Arizona were not part of the Puebloan sphere, the Gladwins (Gladwin and Gladwin 1935) were postulating that the Hohokam culture was the source of agriculture and pottery-making in the Southwest. McGregor's (1941a) synthesis of southwestern prehistory is also replete with the movement of traits and the spread and co-mingling of cultures. For example, he speaks of the spread of Mogollon traits northward into the Chaco area and westward along the Little Colorado River to Flagstaff (McGregor 1941a:267). McGregor (1941a:44) even includes a definition of diffusion in his introductory discussion of important archaeological concepts.

One could continue citing instances of diffusionist interpretations of cultural development. However, it is clear from the above examples that southwestern archaeologists at least through the 1950s were interested in sourcing traits, not artifacts. Compositional analysis of ceramics within such a theoretical framework was an unnecessary expenditure of money and effort, even though sourcing techniques such as petrographic analysis and experimental firing were readily available (Shepard 1936). Exchange was significant only in that it served as a mechanism for the diffusion of traits across cultural boundaries.

Archaeologists of this period were also interested in placing trends in cultural development within a chronological framework. Changes in ceramic style and technology observed in stratigraphic sequences (Nelson 1916, Kidder and Amsden 1931) were used to create relative chronologies, which in turn were tied to absolute temporal markers with the development of dendrochronology in the 1920s and 1930s. Colton and Hargrave (1937) incorporated this chronological research into their ceramic descriptions, thus allowing archaeologists to date ceramic assemblages on the basis of the presence/absence of certain temporally diagnostic types. Breternitz (1966) later compiled a more extensive synthesis of dates for ceramic types throughout the Southwest, drawing on data which had accumulated since the 1930s. Needless to say, ceramics are still an important means of dating archaeological remains.

Ceramic analysis within the context of the culture area approach and chronology building focused on attributes which could be detected by visual inspection, that is, with the naked eye or a hand lens. Colton's (1955) type descriptions often include such vague characterizations of temper as "white angular fragments," "opaque fragments" and "crushed rock" which are clearly the product of visual inspection. However, this method of analysis is often not sensitive enough to detect physio-chemical differences between the raw material constituents of ceramics originating from different geological sources. The ability of archaeologists to detect ceramic exchange was thus at a relatively gross level: that is, when exchange involved the importation of ceramics whose construction, color schemes, paint and slip types and/or decorative styles were obviously different.

A few compositional analyses of prehistoric ceramics were carried out during this time period. However, they were rare exceptions to the normal analytical procedures of visual inspection. They had little impact on the general approach to ceramic analysis and its implications for understanding exchange patterns. Shepard's (1936) pioneering petrographic studies of Rio Grande Glaze Wares proved that this type of analysis was a viable means of documenting exchange. She also demonstrated that ceramic exchange was an important factor in the Rio Grande regional system. However, her studies did not affect the normative model of economically self-sufficient prehistoric communities which prevailed in archaeological reconstructions at that time, and which continued to do so until only recently.

Shepard's work remains unparalleled in its scope, both in terms of sample size and geographic scale. She began with the analysis of over 500 thin sections of glaze ware sherds from Pecos (Shepard 1936). Using a combination of petrographic analysis, comparisons of physical properties of pastes and firing experiments, Shepard discovered that Pecos had relied much more heavily on imported ceramics than had been presumed by Kidder. Shepard was able to document the adoption of oxidized firing and glaze paint technology at Pecos at the end of the Glaze I period and the later decline of glaze ware production during Pecos' Glaze IV period. She also was able to locate the sources of wares imported to Pecos and to trace temporal shifts in centers of exchange.

Shepard (1942, 1965) followed up on her work at Pecos by conducting an analysis of 14,700 glaze ware sherds from most of the Rio Grande River valley. She succeeded in shedding light on contemporary exchange relationships between various sectors of the Rio Grande River drainage and shifts in centers of production and exchange through time by examining the geographic distributions of different types of tempering material during each of three time periods. Shepard (1939:249-287) also used petrographic analysis to examine sherds from the La Plata district in southwestern Colorado and northwestern New Mexico, but she could not document exchange within this district. However, Shepard was able to demonstrate that approximately one quarter of the ceramics excavated from stratigraphic tests II and IV at Pueblo Bonito in Chaco Canyon were imported (Shepard in Judd 1954).

Nora Gladwin (1937) used a petrographic analysis of 100 sherds from Snaketown to conclude that Hohokam and Mogollon ceramics were produced in geographically distinct regions. She pointed out that the volcanic rock found in many of the decorated ceramics had to have come from 30 miles east of the site. However, Gladwin did not draw any conclusions concerning the implications of this fact on ceramic production and exchange within the Hohokam regional system. Danson and Wallace (1956) attempted to shed light on the reasons behind the widespread distribution of Gila Polychrome by analyzing petrographically five samples (each containing five sherds) from University Indian Ruin, Casa Grande, Gila Pueblo, Az W:10:50 from Point of Pines and several sites from the Mimbres area. They tentatively concluded on the basis of these small samples that Gila Polychrome was locally made in each area.

In summary, pre-thirteenth century exchange was disregarded as a potentially important distributional process in southwestern prehistory by archaeologists working in the first half of the twentieth century because of the culture area/diffusionist theoretical framework in which they operated and the methods of analysis which they commonly employed. The context of ceramic analysis during this time period also prevented the reconstruction of regional systems of interaction in which the exchange of ceramics potentially played a significant part.

Ceramics and Social Organization

Archaeologists who adopted the "new archeology" in the 1960s began to view artifacts less as traits which could be used to define cultures, and more as the material manifestations of cultural systems. There was great optimism concerning the archaeologist's ability to reconstruct social and ideological institutions which were less directly linked to material culture than subsistence, but which nonetheless awaited discovery in the formal attributes and contextual relationships of artifact assemblages (Binford 1962). As a result of this paradigm shift, the reconstruction of descent and post-marital residence patterns became a major focus of ceramic analysis in the Southwest.

Several interrelated assumptions underlay the social organizational model used in the Southwest, which had a direct impact on analytical methodologies and perceptions concerning exchange. It was assumed that stylistic similarity bears a direct relationship to the degree of social interaction within social units: the more tightly knit the social unit, the more similar would be the designs on vessels used by the members of that unit. The justification for this assumption was derived from ethnographic analogy. Since it had been reported that pottery making was passed on from mothers to daughters among the Western Pueblo in the ethnographic present, it seemed likely that the Mogollon and Anasazi shared similar learning patterns in the prehistoric past. Groups of closely related potters belonging to the same residential group would therefore share a stylistic repertoire that would be distinct from other non-related or less closely related potters. This stylistic sharing would be reflected in spatial clustering of design attributes corresponding to household loci at habitation sites (Longacre 1970).

This approach has been criticized heavily for its assumptions concerning historic Pueblo social organization and ceramic production, as well as its correlation of the spatial clustering of designs with kinship groups (e.g., Allen and Richardson 1971, Stanislawski 1973, Dumond 1977, S. Plog 1976). In addition, it was also necessary to assume that the production of ceramics was a household task and that communities were economically self-sufficient in order for the social organizational model to hold true. In other words, ceramic exchange simply did not fit into this model.

Other archaeologists who did not support this social organizational model also continued to assume that communities were primarily autonomous social and economic units. For example, Dean (1970:150) described Kayenta Anasazi communities in the thirteenth century as being "independent" and "self-contained." Gumerman and Euler (1976) claimed that little if no exchange took place between the inhabitants of Black Mesa and communities in the surrounding areas.

Analytical methodologies were also affected by the new theoretical paradigm, much as they had been in the past. The primary focus of attention during this period was on design attribute analysis, particularly of elements and motifs, since these aspects of design were believed to be most sensitive to social interaction at the household level (Cronin 1962, Longacre 1964, Hill 1970, Tuggle 1970). This emphasis on stylistic analysis meant that technological variability within ceramic assemblages was disregarded and its implications concerning ceramic exchange were ignored.

Fewer compositional analyses of prehistoric ceramics were conducted during the 1960s, especially in Arizona, due mostly to the emphasis at that time on the relationship between stylistic variability and social interaction at the community level. Studies of technological attributes, whether by visual inspection or compositional analysis, were not a priority. Again, the compositional studies that were undertaken had little effect on the prevailing assumptions concerning ceramic production and exchange. Longacre (1964), for example, concluded that all of the ceramics found at Carter Ranch were locally made, based on a petrographic analysis of 20 sherds and his own examination of several hundred sherds under a binocular microscope. However, neither the original petrographer's report nor a subsequent re-analysis of the thin sections substantiated his claim (S. Plog 1980a).

The Rio Grande area was somewhat of an anomaly in that it continued to be the backdrop for petrographic analyses of prehistoric ceramics as a result of Shepard's seminal studies. Warren's (1969b) analysis of Tonque Pueblo ceramics complemented Shepard's earlier work with Rio Grande Glaze Wares. Warren used a combination of petrographic analysis, the geographic distribution of Glaze C and D pottery and the location of temper and clay outcrops to conclude that the inhabitants of Tonque Pueblo were major producers and exporters of ceramics to various sectors of the Rio Grande, west to Zuni and as far east as Kansas and Oklahoma. Warren (1968) also conducted petrographic analyses on sherds from site L.A. 6455 in the Cochiti Dam Project area in order to determine the compositional variability of various ceramic types and locate their temper sources. She isolated three successive ceramic traditions at L.A. 6455, each of which exhibited different proportions of imported and locally made ceramic types.

Once again, compositional analysis did not jibe with the theoretical framework of the time. In many respects, the basic assumptions concerning ceramic production and distribution had changed little since the days of the culture area approach, despite the radical shift in theoretical orientation that had taken place.

More recently, researchers have begun to challenge the long-standing assumptions concerning village economic autonomy in the prehistoric plateau Southwest. They are consequently beginning to apply both petrographic and chemical techniques, such as neutron activation analysis, on a more frequent basis. Several studies have documented the prevalence of ceramic exchange in different areas of the plateau Southwest prior to A.D. 1200. Before discussing these in any detail, however, it is necessary to examine the theoretical developments which have led to a different outlook on exchange and its role as an evolutionary mechanism. The following section will review a current theory which has caused much debate concerning exchange and sociopolitical development.

The Developmental Model

The traditional model of prehistoric societies in the plateau Southwest as aggregates of autonomous, egalitarian and economically unspecialized communities has been called into question for three reasons. First, historic Puebloan societies on which this model is based are no longer regarded as appropriate analogs for the prehistoric period. The impact of Spanish colonization resulted in significant alterations of sociopolitical organization, inter-community economic interaction and subsistence (Cordell and Plog 1979, Wilcox 1981, Upham et al. 1981, Upham 1982, F. Plog 1983). The contact period thus resulted in a disruption of the cultural continuity between the prehistoric and historic Puebloan peoples. Second, there is reason to believe that the perception of historic Pueblo communities as egalitarian and autonomous was inaccurate to begin with (Brandt 1980, Upham 1982). Third, there is archaeological evidence which suggests a break in cultural continuity between the prehistoric and historic periods. During certain time periods in certain parts of the plateau Southwest, population levels were higher than historically recorded levels (Upham 1982); intensive agricultural systems were in operation (Woodbury 1961, Lightfoot 1981,

Upham 1982), as opposed to the extensive systems used historically (Hack 1942); settlement hierarchies exhibiting differential participation of communities in settlement systems had developed (Lightfoot 1981, Upham 1982); and inter-community exchange at both local and long-distance scales were important adaptive mechanisms (Cordell and Plog 1979, Braun and Plog 1982).

A new model, herein referred to as the developmental model, has been proposed by several archaeologists in response to the growing questions concerning the traditional reconstruction of plateau southwestern political and economic organization. Briefly stated, the developmental theory views agricultural intensification, political leadership beyond the community level, the development of settlement hierarchies and exchange systems at varying geographic scales as adaptive responses to the risks engendered by a relatively long-term commitment to an agricultural subsistence pattern within a marginal environment. According to this theory, certain baseline conditions were operative in some parts of the plateau Southwest beginning as early as A.D. 600 which resulted in the process of sociopolitical development (Lightfoot and Feinman 1982). The natural environment throughout this region was, as it remains today, what Upham (1982:113) has characterized as a "high-risk-high-diversity" environment. High risk is a product of significant, frequent and unpredictable fluctuations in environmental factors which are directly linked to subsistence productivity, such as rainfall and temperature. High diversity refers to the spatial proximity of divergent environmental conditions which affect human exploitation of resources (Sanders and Webster 1978). Thus, not only did subsistence productivity vary through time in one particular location, but it also varied across space at any given point in time, posing substantial problems for humans attempting to persist in this environment.

Braun and Plog (1982) have pointed out that successful adaptation involves behavioral responses to perturbations in environmental conditions, rather than to average conditions. An effective means for mobile hunter-gatherers to insure against food shortages in high-risk, high-diversity environments is to exploit a wide range of natural resources in various climatic zones: what Braun and Plog (1982:514) have termed "spatial averaging mechanisms." However, demographic and subsistence changes eliminated this behavior pattern as a viable adaptive strategy in many parts of the plateau Southwest between about A.D. 700 and A.D. 1000 or 1100. Increasing population levels resulted in the year-round occupation of several areas which had previously been exploited seasonally, as will be discussed in Chapter IV. This colonization process and the associated increase in sedentism effectively reduced the exploitation zone of individual groups occupying these areas.

In addition, agriculture took on a greater role in the subsistence regime at this time (Cordell and Plog 1979). Although hunting and gathering still supplied some as yet unknown portion of the diet (which presumably varied from area to area), the implication is that agriculture was an important enough component of the subsistence pattern to cause the most significant adaptive responses in terms of long-term cultural development.

Sedentary agricultural groups would have faced problems not experienced by mobile hunter-gatherers, according to cross-cultural ethnographic evidence. Sedentism usually results in an increase in group size. Reduced seasonal fluctuations in dietary intake associated with agriculture leads to a reduction in infant mortality (Binford and Chasko

1976). Spacing between births is also shortened, resulting in more children per family (Birdsell 1966, Sussman 1972). Population increase is therefore accelerated by sedentism. Larger community size and increased face-to-face contacts on a daily basis also leads to a greater potential for disputes which must be settled if group integration is to be maintained (Lightfoot 1981).

Another important consequence of a greater investment in agriculture is a decrease in the number of food resources which are exploited, most significantly the wild foods which can act as buffers in times of crop failure (Lightfoot 1981, Braun and Plog 1982). In this respect, agriculture would have augmented the risk of food shortage in the plateau Southwest.

To summarize the theory so far, the concomitant population growth, increase in sedentism and greater reliance on cultigens beginning in many parts of the Colorado Plateaus during the eighth century A.D. brought about a new set of adaptive problems which could no longer be solved by mobility. Consequently, new solutions had to be adopted. As will be discussed below, the developmental theory hypothesizes that these new solutions required management by specialized decision-makers. Demographic and subsistence changes within a high-risk, high-diversity environment therefore promoted sociopolitical development.

It should be noted that this rocess of development was not necessarily linear, nor did it occur uniformly throughout the plateau region, according to the proponents of the developmental model. However, they maintain that certain conditions prevailed in some parts of the Colorado Plateaus which ultimately resulted in the formation of stratified societies with relatively centralized political control. The process of sociopolitical development would have been sustained in areas where subsistence risk caused by environmental variability, population growth and a commitment to an agricultural subsistence base continued to apply relatively consistent, long-term adaptive pressure on the local inhabitants. As Braun and Plog (1982:508) have stated, it

is expected that

> sustained increases in the intensity of integration will occur as concomitants of sustained increases in region-wide uncertainty or risks arising from environmental change. The more sustained the environmental change, the more permanent will be the effect on societal organization.

F. Plog (1984:220) also has noted that the process of sociopolitical development would generate a momentum of its own once set in motion as a viable adaptive strategy.

Exchange became one of the risk-minimizing responses engendered by the adoption of a sedentary agricultural existence, according to this theory. Inter-community exchange became an important means of moving subsistence goods from areas of surplus to areas of shortage: an alternative "spatial averaging mechanism" to group mobility (Braun and Plog 1982:514). Surpluses were "banked" by being exchanged for non-perishables which could be stored for longer periods of time. These hard goods could later be reconverted into subsistence goods when the need for supplemental sources arose (Braun and Plog 1982, Upham 1982). In addition, the storage of surplus foods was adopted as a strategy to even out fluctuations in the food supply through time (Braun and Plog 1982).

Between the eleventh and the fourteenth centuries, the subsistence response to ever-increasing population and smaller exploitation zones was agricultural intensification (Upham

1982, Cordell and Plog 1979). The demographic response was population aggregation into larger settlements and the formation of settlement clusters. The resulting increase in the size of the labor force facilitated the building of soil and water control features such as terraces, check dams and linear and grid borders (Upham 1982).

According to the developmental theory, decision-making specialists were needed to meet the increasing demands placed on communities. The sheer volume of managerial problems would have over-taxed the decision-making capacity of an egalitarian political system which operated on community consensus. Such a group decision-making process has the potential of getting bogged down by protracted discussions and stalemates between various factions. Given such issues as allocating productive lands to households or kin groups, arbitrating disputes, redistributing imported foodstuffs, managing and protecting stored surpluses and maintaining exchange ties with other communities, at least one level of leadership above the general population would be a more efficient political system.

Lightfoot (1981) points out that such leadership development may not be the only possible solution to problems faced by sedentary groups. However, the constant demands on the information processing and decision-making capabilities of the political system would select for specialized leadership. In addition, increases in the demands placed on decision-makers by sustained population growth and competition for resources, as hypothesized for the plateau Southwest between A.D. 700 and at least A.D. 1000, would augment the adaptive advantages of a specialized leadership over decision-making by consensus. Once the demands on information processing and decision-making had reached a critical stage, the process of leadership development would have been initiated. Lightfoot and Feinman

(1982, see also Lightfoot 1981) hypothesize that a positive feedback cycle would have developed between leadership development on the one hand and population growth, agricultural intensification and inter-community interaction, including exchange, on the other. Specialized leadership would develop in order to meet the rising tide of decision-making demands. In turn, leaders would themselves increase managerial problems in an effort to secure their control over decision-making.

Individuals interested in acquiring as well as maintaining leadership positions within so-called "tribal" societies must engage in certain activities which promote increases in group size, greater subsistence productivity and inter-community interaction. Lightfoot (1981:54ff) cites many ethnographic studies which demonstrate that three basic tactics are adopted by those aspiring to become, or to remain, leaders in such societies. First, they must amass a surplus of subsistence goods and trade items. These goods can be given as gifts or loans, creating social and economic obligation on the part of the recipients who might be kinsmen, members of the community or individuals in other communities. Second, aspiring leaders must increase the productivity of their respective households in order to accumulate surplus goods. They can do so by intensifying household subsistence production and/or increasing the size of their household and consequently the size of their labor force. Marrying several wives, fathering many children and taking in needy relatives are common means of achieving larger household size.

The third strategy used to obtain and maintain positions of leadership is expanding one's social network outside the sphere of the local community. Aspiring leaders can foster political alliances beyond their own communities through affinal kinship ties and, significantly, exchange relationships. Inter-community exchange provides a medium of interaction which can be used to obtain valued goods for gift-giving and to broaden the support base of leaders. Given attempts to undermine their authority within the community, leaders can draw on outside alliances for political backing. Assuming that political leaders in the prehistoric plateau Southwest used similar strategies to obtain and secure authority, exchange in the current model takes on a dynamic role in sociopolitical development, as well as being an important adaptive strategy for sedentary groups.

Upham et al. (1981, see also Upham 1982) view the hypothesized existence of complex political systems and social stratification in some parts of the plateau Southwest between the twelfth and fourteenth centuries as outgrowths of earlier periods of leadership development. The positive feedback cycle discussed above would increase the demands on leadership. In turn, the political hierarchy would also grow in complexity and extent (cf. Johnson 1978, Wright 1970). For example, when agricultural intensification began to incorporate labor-intensive water and soil control systems (such as terraces, check dams, and linear and grid borders), several communities would have combined their labor forces to undertake such projects. This level of cooperation would have resulted in the development of supra-community leadership. In addition, leaders who controlled the "banking," importation and redistribution of subsistence goods originating outside the local settlement system would be in a position to augment their authority beyond their communities' boundaries, especially during times of critical food shortage. Control over exchange transactions would become a more potent political tool as population levels began to outstrip local potentials for increasing productivity through intensification.

As a result, exchange would shift from primarily a "system-serving" to a "self-serving" mechanism (Upham 1982:120). Nonlocal goods would serve the political ambitions of leaders. The control over the distribution of valued exchange goods, such as ceramics, within the local population would also set up wealth and status differences within the community. The symbolic content of long-distance exchange transactions between decision-makers in different settlement systems would increase: exotic goods would serve more as signals of political alliances between leaders, thus legitimizing their claims to authority, and less as "banked" goods to insure against subsistence shortages.

Certain leaders who were successful in attracting residents, controlling long-distance exchange relations and imposing their authority on several neighboring communities would begin to dominate inter-community political interaction. Part of their success might be due to the fact that they resided in centrally located settlements, thus facilitating information flow between communities, as well as minimizing the costs of transporting exchange goods both within and between settlement systems (Lightfoot and Feinman 1982).

In any event, settlement clusters would become hierarchically organized into bimodal settlement systems, mirroring the development of a supra-community political hierarchy. The resident settlements of supra-community leaders would be larger due to the efforts of these leaders in attracting followers and intensifying subsistence production within their own communities. Such settlements would be centrally located. In addition, they would contain more storage space than other villages since supra-community leaders would control long-distance exchange relations and the distribution of imported goods. Architectural space designed specifically for exchange and/or distribution of exchange goods, such as central plazas or kivas, would also be constructed in the resident villages of supra-community leaders. However, the majority of settlements would be relatively small and would lack such specialized architecture (Upham et al. 1981).

Given the positive feedback cycle between subsistence risk and the organizational solutions posited by the developmental theory, it is valid to ask why the process of sociopolitical development in the plateau Southwest never reached the degree of complexity attained by state-level societies in other parts of the New World. The answer proposed by proponents of the developmental model rests on the same factors of environmental risk and diversity which act as catalysts in the model. Population aggregation, agricultural intensification and increasing centralization of leadership ultimately caused the collapse of the relatively complex systems they had played a part in creating. The energy requirements of these systems generated by population growth and the material demands of decision-makers eventually outstripped the environment's carrying capacity, resulting in system collapse (F. Plog 1978, 1983). There was a ceiling placed on the continued growth and complexity of such regional political and economic systems.

To summarize, the past few years have witnessed a period of re-evaluation and model-building which has had important theoretical ramifications for southwestern archaeology. The perception of prehistoric plateau communities as egalitarian, politically independent and economically self-sufficient entities, derived from ethnographic data on historic Pueblo societies, has been called into question. Several archaeologists have argued that some plateau southwestern societies had begun the process of social differentiation and political centralization as early as A.D. 600, and that many showed marked signs of sociopolitical development by A.D. 1200 in areas where subsistence risk continued over an extended period of time, as discussed above. Differential access to resources, economic goods, status and political authority developed at both the community and settlement system levels. Bimodal settlement systems of inter-related communities formed, which mirrored the two-tiered political hierarchy of community and inter-community leadership.

This developmental model focuses on decision-making institutions as adaptive responses to risks generated by demographic and resource imbalances in a high-risk, high-diversity environment. Yet, such political institutions are perceived as having a dynamic of their own which transcends their adaptive functions. Once obtained, specialized leadership becomes self-serving: those possessing political authority wish to maintain and even augment it, given the proper opportunities and requisite leadership skills.

Exchange at both the local and long-distance scales bridges the gap between organizational responses to subsistence risk and the self-serving dynamic of sociopolitical development. As such, exchange is an important evolutionary mechanism within the context of the developmental model. The concept of prestige exchange as a catalyst of sociopolitical development is not unique to the developmental model, however. For example, Flannery's (1967) interpretations of Olmec interregional interaction incorporated similar ideas concerning the use of long-distance exchange between elite groups as a means of legitimizing their status. Prestige exchange remains an important theoretical issue in Mesoamerican archaeology (e.g., Blanton et al. 1981, Spence 1982, Stark 1986).

However, the developmental model does represent a significant shift in southwestern archaeological thinking concerning sociopolitical organization and inter-community interaction, including exchange. It harkens back to the culture area approach with respect to its emphasis on broad cultural patterns, such as ceramic design styles, over large geographic regions (Hantman 1983). What distinguishes Fred Plog's (1979, 1983) "provinces" and Upham's (1982) "alliances" from culture areas are the dynamic processes which are invoked to explain them. The diffusionist perception of cultures spreading and co-mingling has been replaced in the developmental model by sustained economic and political interaction of different human populations, not necessarily from the same culture or political entity. Similarities in material culture are viewed as active expressions of mutual interdependence and cooperation, instead of as a passive outcome of cultural diffusion (Wobst 1977, Braun and Plog 1982, Hantman and Plog 1982, Upham 1982).

The current developmental model has not been accepted whole-heartedly by many southwestern archaeologists. The primary counter argument to the developmental model has been made by archaeologists involved in research at Grasshopper Pueblo, a fourteenth century settlement containing approximately 500 rooms situated in east-central Arizona between the Salt River and Mogollon Rim. Grasshopper was founded between A.D. 1295 and 1305, and grew to its largest size within the first 30 or 40 years as residents moved into Grasshopper from small dispersed settlements in the surrounding region (Graves et al. 1982).

Years of research by the University of Arizona Archaeological Field School has revealed that exchange became an increasingly important component of the Grasshopper economy through time. This community was part of an extensive exchange network through which it obtained such goods as White Mountain Red Ware from settlements north of the

Mogollon Rim, marine shell probably imported from the Hohokam in the Salt and Gila River valleys, and macaws from Casas Grandes in Chihuahua, Mexico (Graves et al. 1982). Ciolek-Torrello (1978) has presented evidence suggesting that this growing dependence on exchange was matched by an increase in the number of Grasshopper residents who were involved in the specialized manufacture of lithics, pigments and bone tools and ornaments for export to other communities.

Graves et al. (1982) conclude that exchange became the primary means by which the residents of Grasshopper were able to minimize subsistence risk and sustain population growth. This dependence on an exchange economy resulted in

> a system of economically interdependent communities not unlike the settlement system it [the Grasshopper system] had replaced but involving considerably larger, localized populations and exchange as the dominant intercommunity relationship (Graves et al. 1982:116).

To summarize, several factors were operating at Grasshopper Pueblo which are defined as precursors to sociopolitical development within the context of the developmental model: population aggregation into a large settlement, an increasing dependence on intercommunity exchange as a buffer against subsistence risk, participation in an extensive inter-regional exchange system, and increasing craft specialization. However, the archaeologists researching Grasshopper and the surrounding communities have concluded that

> although temporal changes occurred in the production of agricultural and material goods and the organization of exchange relations, the political organization of these communities did not undergo significant development in the direction of increased complexity and differentiation (Graves et al. 1982:117).

Graves et al. (1982) state that there is no evidence for a hierarchical settlement system or differential access to exchange goods by communities within the Grasshopper settlement system. Whittlesey (1978) concludes that there is no evidence for differential access to wealth or, by extension, political power across the burial population at Grasshopper. She attributes status differences (as evidenced in the variability of the size and quality of individual mortuary assemblages) to individual achievements and participation in kin-based groups whose influence would not have extended beyond the immediate community.

These archaeologists have cited Grasshopper Pueblo as a case study of a large pueblo within a settlement system that was heavily dependent on inter-community exchange, and yet which never developed a hierarchical sociopolitical system, thus calling into question the explanatory power of the developmental model. As LeBlanc (1983) has pointed out in his review of one of the few published reports on Grasshopper (Longacre et al. 1982), the theoretical implications of this case study will depend on whether the current interpretations of Grasshopper's development are correct, and how well those interpretations explain the growth of other large settlements throughout the Southwest at about the same time.

The following chapter will outline the supportive evidence presented by proponents of the developmental model, as well as criticisms of the evidence that have been leveled by its opponents. In addition, the current evidence will be evaluated in terms of what it does and does not reveal concerning the structure and development of regional exchange networks.

CHAPTER III

SOCIOPOLITICAL DEVELOPMENT: THE EVIDENCE

As was discussed in the previous chapter, some archaeologists have begun to re-evaluate long-standing assumptions concerning sociopolitical organization, community autonomy and exchange in the prehistoric plateau Southwest. In order for the southwestern developmental model to be credible, its characterization of the plateau environment as well as its claims concerning demographic trends, agricultural intensification, and changes in settlement patterns between ca. A.D. 900 and 1400 must conform to the available archaeological evidence. This chapter will examine the evidence as it relates to the model and will consider alternative explanations of the data, where relevant.

Paleoclimatic Data

Dendroclimatology has provided the most sensitive data on short-term perturbations in climatic conditions in the plateau Southwest for the past 2000 years. Variations in tree ring widths have been used as measures of fluctuations in precipitation and temperature to reconstruct climatic variability through time and across the Colorado Plateaus. Dean and Robinson (1979) employed standardized tree-ring records from 25 stations throughout the plateau Southwest. They were able to document significant decadic variation from average temperatures and precipitation. For example, the decade between A.D. 1090 and 1099 shows negative departures throughout most of the Colorado Plateaus, indicating warmer and drier conditions than the average. However, between A.D. 1110 and 1119, a greater part of the plateau Southwest is characterized by a wetter and cooler than average climate. Their data also exhibit contemporaneous spatial variation in the form of steep climatic gradients separating positive and negative deviations, as existed along the Mogollon Rim between the Salt River and the San Francisco Mountains from A.D. 1120 to 1129. (Refer to Figure 1 for the locations of geographical features and regions discussed in this chapter.)

The most comprehensive studies of environmental variability in the plateau Southwest have been conducted by Euler et al. (1979) and Dean et al. (1985). Both papers present a complex picture of environmental variability in low frequency processes (the aggradation/degradation of floodplain alluvium due to changes in the water table, and relative effective moisture, as measured using the palynological record) and high frequency perturbations (decadal fluctuations in precipitation recorded in tree-ring records) throughout the Colorado Plateaus. These authors note that certain periods were characterized by greater spatial and short-term variability than others. However, the complexity of the paleoenvironmental record leads them to conclude that the most striking feature of the plateau Southwest is its diversity. Dean et al. (1985:542) state:

> Visual comparison of the curves reveals a few regular correspondences between different kinds of environmental variability. . . Just as important as these general correspondences, however, is the diversity of a record in which many patterns of association among environmental variables occurred. This variability of patterning emphasizes that Anasazi adaptation was to environmental diversity as much as to environmental extremes.

Given the comprehensive nature of the paleoenvironmental record and the high degree of resolution of the dendroclimatological data, there is little doubt that the prehistoric plateau Southwest was characterized by a high-risk, high-diversity environment

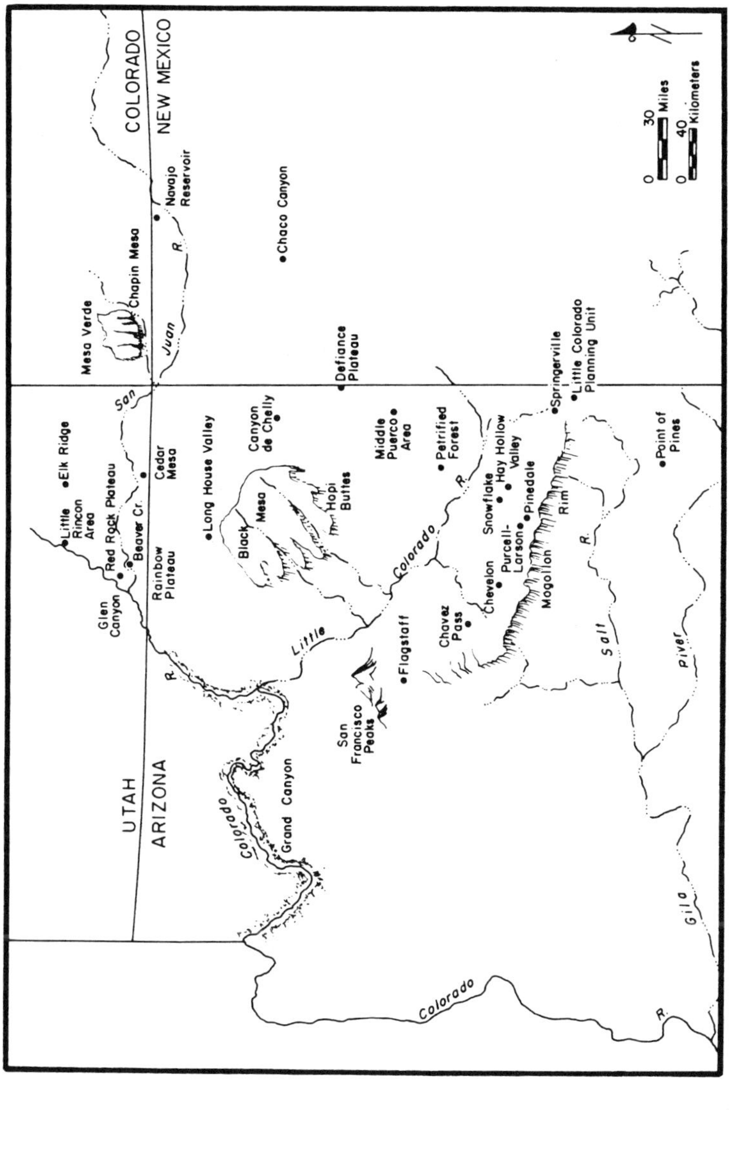

Figure 1. Location of selected geographical features, sites and regions on the Colorado Plateaus.

prehistorically, as it is today. Perturbations in available moisture and temperature were serious enough to warrant adaptive responses on the part of the Colorado Plateaus' inhabitants, as the developmental model claims.

However, the syntheses of paleoenvironmental data presented by Euler et al. (1979) and Dean et al. (1985) show that the risk and diversity factors in the plateau southwestern environment were not constant. Some periods were characterized by greater temporal and/or spatial variability than others. Changes in risk and diversity would have had important consequences for the organizational responses of prehistoric populations. High temporal variability in climatic factors, such as precipitation, which would affect crop yields can be mitigated by storing food surpluses or accumulating other goods whose value can be converted into foodstuffs. The frequency of the variability determines whether direct storage of foodstuffs or "banking" (Braun and Plog 1982) is the most viable approach. High spatial variability in climate can be offset by exchange between communities experiencing different, localized climatic conditions. However, exchange is not an effective adaptive response during periods of low spatial variability since many areas would be experiencing the same types and degrees of subsistence stress (Dean et al. 1985).

Precipitation levels in the period between A.D. 750 and 1000 were characterized by high temporal and low spatial variability. Given these circumstances, subsistence stress would have been reduced most effectively by increasing storage of foodstuffs or "banking". Inter-community exchange would not have been promoted during this time period. Rising water tables after A.D. 900 would have offset the negative effects of unpredictability in precipitation to some degree by increasing ground water storage. Precipitation became more consistent by A.D. 1000. Finally, high spatial climatic variability set in by A.D. 1050. The generally improved climatic conditions, coupled with the high degree of spatial variability between A.D. 1050 and 1150, would have created ideal circumstances for increased exchange and interaction between communities throughout the southern Colorado Plateaus (Dean et al. 1985).

Low spatial and temporal variability persisted between A.D. 1150 and 1300. There was a major drought in the last half of the twelfth century. Conditions improved until A.D. 1275, however, when water tables rose and floodplains aggraded. The period between A.D. 1275 and 1300, which is best known as the Great Drought, saw falling water tables, down-cutting in washes and low precipitation levels. These deteriorated conditions would have had serious effects on the high population levels in many parts of the plateau Southwest at this time. As Dean et al. (1985) point out, even the low temporal and high spatial variability which set in at the beginning of the fourteenth century would not have been enough to sustain the more densely populated settlement systems after this high stress period.

According to the paleoclimatic data, climatic conditions between A.D. 1150 and 1300 would not have encouraged either inter-community exchange and interaction or the accumulation of surplus goods. The two periods of drought between A.D. 1150 and 1300, separated by only a brief 75 year respite, would have taxed the abilities of populations to cope with subsistence stress. Failures to adapt to such long-term stress would have led to the collapse of settlement systems and major shifts in population away from the hardest hit areas.

Demographic and Subsistence Trends: A.D. 700 to 1100

The developmental model sets up three basic preconditions which acted as catalysts for sociopolitical development between the eighth and twelfth centuries: 1) a general increase in population levels, 2) the year-round occupation of areas which had been only sparsely occupied, or had been exploited on a seasonal basis, and 3) an increased reliance on agriculture. In general, the archaeological data substantiate the existence of these three preconditions.

Prehistoric population levels are difficult to estimate with any degree of accuracy. Estimates can be biased by the problems of correlating living space with numbers of occupants, distinguishing seasonal from year-round occupations and controlling for site comtemporaneity when phases are used as the smallest temporal units (F. Plog 1974:88-92, 1975; S. Plog 1980a, Powell 1980, Dean et al. 1985). However, despite the potential sources of bias, corroborative estimates of relative changes in population levels have been obtained from survey data from a number of areas in the plateau Southwest. Together, they indicate a general increase in population beginning ca. A.D. 700 and lasting at least through A.D. 1100 (Braun and Plog 1982, Dean et al. 1985). Table 1 summarizes population trends from several areas in the Colorado Plateaus derived from a number of sources. The dates in this table support the existence of a trend toward increasing population during this time period. In addition, the data show that several areas experienced population maxima at around A.D. 1100. Given the higher population levels at the turn of the twelfth century, a period characterized by much temporal variability in climate (Dean et al. 1985), it is highly likely

Table 1. A Summary of Population Trends for Several Areas Within the Colorado Plateaus.

Area	Initial Occupation	Growth Begins	Population Peak	Abandonment
Grand Canyon	ca. A.D.600	A.D.1000	A.D.1050-1150	A.D.1150
Black Mesa	ca. 700-600	B.C. A.D.800	A.D.1025-1075	A.D.1150 (A.D.600-800?)
Long House Valley	2500 B.C.?	A.D.1000	A.D.1000-1150	A.D.1300
Rainbow Plateau	Pre-A.D.1	A.D.1000	A.D.1000-1225	A.D.700-800 A.D.1270
Glen Canyon	ca. A.D.1	A.D.1050	A.D.1100-?	A.D.?-ca.1050
Sinagua	A.D.500	A.D.1050	A.D. 1150	A.D.1300
Winslow/ Hopi Buttes	ca. A.D.1?	A.D.1050	A.D.1050-1150	A.D.1250
Upper Little Colorado R.	1500 B.C.	A.D.700-900	ca. A.D.1150	A.D.1450
Chevelon	A.D.200	A.D.700-800	A.D.1050-1250	A.D.1300
Canyon de Chelly	200 B.C.	A.D.700-900	A.D.1140-1300	A.D.1300
Defiance Plateau	?	ca. A.D.1050	A.D.1050-1150	A.D.1140
Cedar Mesa	ca. A.D.200	Episodic	A.D.1100-1150	A.D.400 A.D.750 A.D.1200
Elk Ridge	Pre-A.D.700	A.D.700	A.D.700-900	A.D.1260
Red Rock	A.D.200	Episodic	Episodic	A.D.300 A.D.1150 A.D.1260
Mesa Verde	A.D.1-300	ca. A.D.650	?	A.D.1300
Chaco Canyon	Pre-A.D.1	A.D.900	A.D.900-1100	A.D.1150+
Navajo Reservoir	ca. A.D.1	A.D.800	A.D.800-900	A.D.1000
Mid. Puerco	A.D.795	A.D.875	A.D.1100	A.D.1300 A.D.1180 A.D.1225

Note: This table is adapted from Euler 1985 and Dean et al. 1985:Table 1.

that prehistoric populations in the plateau Southwest would have experienced periods ofsubsistence stress which would have necessitated behavioral responses.

The second precondition, namely the colonization of new areas, also can be substantiated by the archaeological record. Areas which had been exploited only peripherally, such as Red Rock Plateau (Lipe 1970), Cedar Mesa in southeastern Utah (Matson and Lipe 1978) and Black Mesa in northeastern Arizona (Powell 1980), were inhabited on a year-round basis by A.D. 1100. Many of these areas, such as Black Mesa (Powell 1980), the Springerville area in east-central Arizona (Lightfoot 1978) and the Little Rincon area of the Colorado River in southwestern Utah (Sharrock et al. 1961), were agriculturally marginal.

As Braun and Plog (1982) have pointed out, it is not clear exactly what proportion of the diet was supplied by cultigens, and whether per capita consumption of domesticated foods actually increased during this period. However, there is evidence for the development of strategies which reflect attempts to increase total agricultural yields, the third precondition set forth by the developmental model. Water and soil control features such as check dams, terraces, linear and grid borders, reservoirs and irrigation ditches appear ca. A.D. 900 and become quite common in many parts of the plateau Southwest by 1100 (Schoenwetter and Dittert 1968, Vivian 1974). Such features have been recorded at Beaver Creek (Lindsay 1961), Chapin Mesa (Rohn 1963), the Little Rincon area (Sharrock et al. 1961), the Walhalla Glades in the Grand Canyon (Jones 1983), Point of Pines (Woodbury 1961), and Pinedale and Hay Hollow Valley in the upper Little Colorado River drainage (Lightfoot 1981), among other localities.

Strategies for trapping or dispersing runoff and reducing soil erosion were opportunistic in the sense that features or systems of features in any given locality were designed to meet the needs of local microenvironmental conditions and landforms (Vivian 1974, Woosley 1980). As a consequence, they exhibit a great deal of variability in their design and relative complexity. However, they all required an investment of labor, regardless of their form, which signals a commitment to a sedentary agricultural way of life.

Settlement Patterns: A.D. 900 to 1100

The developmental model posits leadership development and increasing political complexity as organizational responses to decision-making problems engendered by a sedentary agricultural subsistence pattern in a high-risk, high-diversity environment. As discussed above, a consequence of increasing political complexity was the development of settlement hierarchies, according to the model. Specifically, the model predicts that clusters composed of at least two different types of settlements would have developed. In their simplest form, such systems would possess one large, centrally located settlement (the locus of political leadership for the cluster as a whole) which would be surrounded by several smaller communities. Ideally, each large settlement would possess a central plaza, a kiva and/or a community room with associated storage rooms: features associated with exchange and redistribution. Such communities also would contain burial populations which had been accorded differential treatment with respect to associated burial goods, reflecting the status differences between decision-makers and their followers. Finally, the large settlements would possess greater amounts of imported goods relative to their population sizes than the smaller surrounding villages (Lightfoot 1981, Lightfoot and Feinman 1982). More complex systems might contain secondary centers, creating a third tier in the hierarchy. Such centers would possess at least some of the specialized characteristics of the primary centers, although they might be smaller and less centrally located.

However, the evidence supporting the existence of such two-tiered settlement hierarchies is mixed. Settlement patterns throughout the plateau Southwest exhibit a great deal of variability at this time. Some areas contained settlement hierarchies as characterized by the developmental model while other areas did not. The hierarchical settlement patterns that were in existence varied among one another in a number of respects.

One of the most often cited cases for settlement hierarchies is the upper Little Colorado River region. Longacre (1970) observed a two-tiered settlement pattern in the Hay Hollow Valley. According to Longacre, it was characterized by relatively large settlements containing great kivas which were surrounded by small villages lacking such structures. He hypothesizes that this pattern was the result of a system of "multicommunity solidarity" which integrated several communities "by creating mutual interdependence among social groups through reciprocal exchange of goods and services" (Longacre 1970:17).

In contrast to Longacre's claim, F. Plog (1974) states that it is not possible to associate large sites or great kivas with site clusters in the Hay Hollow Valley. Plog also found variability in settlement patterns when he compared the Hay Hollow and Purcell-Larson areas. Purcell-Larson sites tend to exhibit more clustered distributions than those in Hay Hollow valley. Site clusters in the former area are characterized by a single large site which is surrounded by several smaller sites, and a great kiva, thus matching the expectations of the developmental model. Hantman and Jewett (1978) also found a great deal of variability between the Purcell-Larson, Pinedale, Little Colorado Planning Unit and Hay Hollow localities in terms of site densities, clustering and the percentage of limited activity sites.

Lightfoot (1981) used survey and excavation data to evaluate the structure of settlement systems in the Pinedale, Snowflake and Hay Hollow localities of the upper Little Colorado. He concludes that the development of settlement hierarchies began in the region at about A.D. 700. Several settlement clusters composed of large centrally located sites and smaller surrounding communities developed between A.D. 700 and 1100. The larger sites were associated with greater per capita storage space, exchange goods and high status burials than the smaller sites, according to the author.

However, when one examines the data from each of the three areas individually, the variability in settlement systems during this time period is quite apparent. These three areas differed in terms of the number of levels within their settlement hierarchies (ranging between one and three) and the size of the communities within each level. The small communities were not necessarily clustered around a larger settlement. There is little evidence from the survey data to suggest that the larger settlements functioned as political centers since they are not always associated with great kivas or concentrations of exchange goods. Lightfoot (1981:243) also states that restricted access to mortuary offerings in the excavation data "was most evident after A.D. 1100". However, the ratio of storage space to habitation space in large excavated communities jumped markedly after A.D. 700, suggesting an accumulation of surplus goods which might have been used for sociopolitical transactions

(Lightfoot 1981). Putting all these data together, it is clear that the evidence for hierarchical political systems in the upper Little Colorado River drainage before the twelfth century is equivocal.

Before the eruption of Sunset Crater (ca. A.D. 1066), the San Francisco Peaks area was characterized by scattered villages composed of between two and five pithouses. These small communities were probably tied to larger villages which contained community rooms believed to have functioned as loci for some type of inter-community interaction (Pilles 1976). It therefore appears as if this area was developing some form of bimodal settlement systems before the eleventh century.

Current survey data indicate that certain areas did not have settlement hierarchies between A.D. 900 and 1100, such as the Grand Canyon (Janet Balsom, personal communication 1987), the Hopi Buttes (Gumerman and Skinner 1968) and the Petrified Forest (A. Trinkle Jones, personal communication 1987).

Summary: A.D. 700 to 1100

Overall, the environmental conditions and cultural trends taking place during these centuries are in line with the prerequisites for the developmental model. The period between A.D. 700 and 1100 was a time of growth and transition, presenting new adaptive challenges and decision-making needs concerning agricultural intensification, the management of stored surpluses and the negotiation of inter-community exchange transactions. It is conceivable that such needs could have been met by an emerging leadership and there is some evidence to suggest that such leadership was developing in certain parts of the Colorado Plateaus.

Climatic conditions generally were improving throughout this period, promoting a further reliance on agriculture. Storage of foodstuffs would have increased during the low spatial and high temporal environmental diversity between A.D. 750 and 1000. The subsequent period of high spatial environmental variability between A.D. 1050 and 1150 would have encouraged inter-community exchange.

Population increase was widespread in the plateau Southwest between A.D. 700 and 1100, as demonstrated in Table 1. Population maxima were reached in many areas by A.D. 1100. Many new and often marginal areas had become year-round habitation zones by the twelfth century. Such demographic trends put greater pressure on increasing subsistence productivity. An increasing investment of labor into agricultural practices is attested to by the diverse, opportunistic water and soil control systems found throughout the Colorado Plateaus.

Settlement patterns were characterized by a great deal of diversity between A.D. 900 and 1100. Some areas lacked any type of settlement hierarchies, while other areas had developed two or more types of settlements which were integrated into a single multi-community system. Hierarchical systems varied as to the spatial distribution of their settlements, the number of levels they possessed and the range of site sizes within each level. The larger settlements were not always associated with specialized architectural features such as great kivas. Nor did they necessarily possess greater concentrations of exchange goods or storage space.

However, such variability is to be expected during the tenth, eleventh and twelfth centuries when settlement systems were changing in response to widespread demographic and subsistence pressures. Not all areas would have experienced these pressures to the same degree, nor would they have changed at the same rate, even though population increases and greater reliance on agriculture were widespread throughout the plateau Southwest. F. Plog (1984:223) has postulated that highly integrated systems arose in areas experiencing high spatial and/or temporal variability in rainfall. Aside from these climatic factors, some areas may never have been populated densely enough or permanently enough to develop settlement hierarchies at all.

Demographic and Subsistence Trends: A.D. 1100 to 1400

The period between A.D. 1100 and 1400 was characterized by a complex pattern of population dislocations due to the abandonment of several parts of the plateau Southwest and aggregation in other areas (refer to Table 1). Dean et al. (1985) correlate major population shifts with two episodes of significant environmental stress during this period: the drought and low temporal and spatial variability in climate which occurred in the middle of the twelfth century, and the co-occurrence of a major drought with a lowering of the water table and soil degradation between A.D. 1275 and 1300. The combination of low temporal and spatial climatic variability with drought and lowering water tables would have rendered both agricultural intensification and exchange ineffective in alleviating subsistence stress. If exchange and intensification were no longer viable adaptations, the only alternative might have been the abandonment of the agriculturally more marginal areas and resettlement in areas with more optimum conditions.

On the one hand, major population dislocations would have seriously disrupted the process of sociopolitical development in many parts of the plateau Southwest. On the other hand, population aggregation into fewer areas would have resulted in significant increases in both the number and complexity of decision-making tasks at the community and inter-community levels. The organizational demands created by more people living together and attempting to subsist off less land would have promoted the continuing development of decision-making hierarchies, if one follows the reasoning of the developmental theory. As Upham has stated,

> [T]he existence of large population centers not only requires an increase in the investment of agricultural labor but necessitates a more complex organizational system to manage that labor, to settle disputes, and to systematize the daily activities of large numbers of people. In short, a relationship exists between population aggregation, agricultural intensification, the organization and management of labor, and increasing sociopolitical complexity (1982:110-111).

Therefore, although the developmental process shifted spatially, the overall effect of population aggregation would have been a net increase in sociopolitical complexity in those areas occupied during the thirteenth and fourteenth centuries.

Nearly 80% of the sites containing architecture around Nuvaqueotaka in the Anderson Mesa area were related to agriculture during this time period. These sites included systems of terraces placed perpendicular to small drainages, reservoirs intended to catch surface runoff and single-room field houses (Upham 1982).

Extensive water and soil control systems composed of check dams, terraces and field houses were in operation in the Mesa Verde area (Rohn 1977). Chaco Canyon had a complex agricultural system consisting of terraces, grid borders, diversion dams, canals and reservoirs by some time after A.D. 1000 (Vivian 1970, 1974).

Such extensive and, in some cases, relatively complex soil and water control systems brought many additional acres under cultivation, thus increasing the food supply in relatively densely populated areas. There is no question that these systems, when viewed in their completed form, represent large amounts of labor input. However, the actual size of the labor force is dependent on the length of time it took to build one of these systems. It is conceivable that at least some of them grew accretionally. If this were the case, small work parties composed of individual household or kin groups could have constructed facilities such as check dams on a small scale with little outside supervision. Likewise, the same groups could have been in charge of maintaining them (Woodbury 1961, Rohn 1977).

In addition, the nature of the water source would determine whether a centralized form of authority was needed to apportion the water supply to agricultural fields. Fields watered directly by runoff or rainfall would necessitate little centralized management. The diversion of water from watercourses or bodies of water such as reservoirs would require more centralized control since irrigation ditches would have to be built in order to transport the water to the agricultural fields of an entire community, or several communities (Vivian 1974). With the possible exception of such facilities as the Mummy Lake reservoir on Chapin Mesa (Rohn 1977), the vast majority of the soil and water control features in the plateau Southwest did not rely on diverting permanent sources of water. As a result, the need for centralized management of agricultural intensification in most areas between A.D. 1100 and 1400 can be called into question.

Settlement Patterns: A.D. 1100 to 1400

Settlement hierarchies become more discernible in many parts of the Colorado Plateaus during this period, although some areas experience disruptions in settlement systems and abandonment by the second half of the thirteenth century. Elden phase (ca. A.D. 1130 to 1210) settlements in the San Francisco Peaks area exhibit a three-tiered hierarchy. Gratz and Pilles (1979) distinguish among primary, secondary and tertiary sites. Primary sites such as Ridge Ruin, Juniper Terrace and Three Courts Pueblo, are relatively large and possess community rooms, compound walls and courtyards. They are all associated with ballcourts. Primary sites also contain more trade goods than tertiary sites. Secondary sites, such as Elden Pueblo, contain about twenty rooms, some of which are community rooms. However, they lack the formal architectural layout of the primary sites and are not associated with ballcourts. Tertiary sites are the smallest category, having between seven and 15 rooms. Sites in the San Francisco Peaks area do not cluster consistently, although tertiary sites seem to be located within a two-mile radius of secondary sites. Most of the population seems to have abandoned the San Francisco Peaks area during the thirteenth century. A large proportion of the inhabitants of this area moved southeast to Anderson Mesa, founding Kinnikinick, Nuvaqueotaka, the Pollock site and Grapevine Pueblo (Pilles 1976).

Between ca. A.D. 1100 and 1250, two inter-community centers developed for the first time in the Hopi Buttes area (the Plaza site) and near Holbrook (the Sundown site) respectively. Each of these sites contained walled-in plazas, storage rooms along one side of the plaza, small kivas and one great kiva. The remainder of the sites in the area are small villages consisting of pit houses, surface rooms with masonry foundations and jacal superstructures, and kivas (Gumerman and Skinner 1968, Adams 1985). However, the ratio of centers to small communities was very small and it seems unlikely that the Plaza and Sundown sites could have serviced all the settlements in the entire central Little Colorado valley. Smaller settlements do not cluster around the centers. Instead, they are scattered throughout the area, suggesting that communities were not organized into well-integrated settlement systems.

The Hopi Buttes area was largely abandoned by A.D. 1250 and present data indicate that population from this area moved north to the Hopi Mesas and southeast to the Homolovi settlements on the Little Colorado River (Gumerman and Skinner 1968, Adams 1985). Both the Hopi Mesas and the Homolovi areas underwent a similar process of initial rapid population growth due to immigration. This growth was followed by population aggregation into larger settlements and a decline in the hierarchical nature of the settlement pattern after A.D. 1350 (Adams 1985).

The Pinedale, Snowflake and Hay Hollow localities were characterized by hierarchical settlement patterns between A.D. 1100 and 1250. Pinedale settlements systems exhibited a two-tiered hierarchical structure. Each system contained a large settlement which was associated with a great kiva, and which also contained significantly greater amounts of polychrome ceramics. Each large site was surrounded by six to eight smaller settlements. The Snowflake area settlements contained three discrete size categories of settlements. Only one of these systems exhibits clear hierarchical organization within the boundaries of the survey area. Great kivas and polychrome ceramics are associated with large and medium settlements in this latter system.

Hay Hollow Valley, on the other hand, experienced the abandonment of many of the smaller villages and the aggregation of its inhabitants into a few large settlements. The large settlements appear to be composed of primary and secondary settlements: the primary settlements are larger and contain kivas and enclosed plazas. In addition, the primary and secondary settlements are clustered together, suggesting that they were politically linked (Lightfoot 1981).

As mentioned above, preferential access to mortuary goods is particularly evident in the burial populations of these areas after A.D. 1100. Storage space remains higher for large and medium sites, as it had during the earlier period, while storage space at small sites remained more constant. After A.D. 1250, storage space at large and medium settlements doubled in volume (Lightfoot 1981). Unfortunately, the volume of space designated for storage at smaller sites during this later period is not available. As a result, it is difficult to say whether this marked increase in storage space was due to the greater needs within the community for stored goods (particularly since populations began to aggregate after A.D. 1250), or an increase in exchange activity.

Between ca. A.D. 1250 and ca. 1400, all three areas experienced significant disruptions in their settlement systems. Many small communities in the Pinedale area were abandoned and their inhabitants aggregated into Pinedale Ruin and its immediate hinterland, forming a small two-tiered settlement system. Likewise, many of the small villages in the Snowflake area were abandoned. The total population of the area decreased significantly and the sociopolitical organization of the settlement system was reduced to a one-tiered system. The Hay Hollow settlement system also underwent a period of abandonment, with only three small- to medium-sized communities dating to this period (Lightfoot 1981).

Three-tiered settlement systems were operating within the Mesa Verde area between ca. A.D. 1100 and 1300. Laczko (1979) correlates this settlement pattern with two levels of political organization above the general population. The large sites, ranging in size from 70 to 150 rooms, are located on mesas with water control systems. The large site on Chapin Mesa is close to the largest great kiva found at Mesa Verde dating to this time period, suggesting that it was involved in some form of redistribution or inter-community ceremonial activity (Laczko 1979, cf. Vivian and Reiter 1960).

The transition from Pueblo II to Pueblo III in the Mesa Verde area witnessed a decline in the number of sites with a concomitant increase in site size. It is possible that population aggregation into larger sites was related to the need for organizational mechanisms to coordinate and supervise larger labor forces related to agricultural intensification, according to Laczko (1979). Ultimately, efforts at intensification and increased organizational input were unsuccessful and the Mesa Verde area was largely abandoned by A.D. 1300.

Chaco Canyon represents the clearest evidence of sociopolitical development in the plateau Southwest. The developments in Chaco Canyon are somewhat problematical in that they bridge what is traditionally considered the transition between Pueblo II and Pueblo III at ca. A.D. 1100. Excavations suggest that major building activity at the large settlements began after A.D. 1000 (Vivian 1974). However, the Chacoan system as a whole was probably not fully developed until the twelfth century (Cordell 1979).

Vivian (1970) has described the two basic types of settlements within the Chacoan system as "towns" and "villages". The towns are large multistoried pueblos with an average of over 200 rooms. They are characterized by planned layouts. Masonry work is of the highest quality known from the Colorado Plateaus, suggesting specialized labor. The central plazas contain great kivas which also possess a number of formalized features such as antechambers, square raised fireboxes and deflectors. The towns contain large quantities of non-utilitarian exchange goods such as macaws from Mexico, as well as copper bells [which might have come from Mexico (McGuire 1980)], turquoise inlays, mosaics, pendants and beads. Ceramic forms such as cylinder jars and effigy vessels are also unique to the towns and in turn are suggestive of specialized production.

In contrast, villages are single-story pueblos with an average of 20 rooms. Their masonry construction is of a lower quality than that of the towns and they do not contain great kivas, although some villages might have used isolated great kivas such as Casa Rinconada (Vivian 1974, Cordell 1979). Roads radiating out from Chaco Canyon represent a significant labor investment, particularly since some of them are lined with masonry curbs or are built of raised roadbeds (Cordell 1979). Since they were probably used by all travelers coming in and out of the canyon, it seems reasonable to assume that they were built by labor parties under the direction of some form of centralized inter-community leadership. In addition, the connectivity between canyon settlements and Chacoan outliers suggests a high level of integration for the Chacoan system as a whole.

The actual temporal relationships between large and small settlements in the Anderson Mesa system is still a matter of controversy. The interpretation of this particular system is essential to the evaluation of the developmental model since it served as the primary test case upon which the model was built. Upham (1982) maintains that the large settlement of Nuvaqueotaka and surrounding smaller communities were roughly contemporaneous, placing Nuvaqueotaka in the role of a sociopolitical center and port of trade. He cites the fact that the small settlements and Nuvaqueotaka have ceramic assemblages that are stylistically similar, although they are composed of different wares. Since style is temporally diagnostic, Upham (1982:192) concludes that "the occurrence of particular ceramic styles tends to indicate contemporeneity between the occupation of many settlement system sites and Nuvaqueotaka". Upham (1982:168-169) also argues for a substantial amount of temporal overlap between the three roomblocks at Nuvaqueotaka. He treats the site as a contemporaneous unit in his discussions of the Anderson Mesa settlement system, except for an earlier occupation at the north pueblo between ca. A.D. 1100 and 1215.

Upham views the distinct distributions of ceramic wares as a function of differential access to exchange goods across the settlement system, rather than as temporal markers. He states that Nuvaqueotaka seems to control access to certain wares at different points in time. For example, when Cibola White Ware was prevalent at Nuvaqueotaka between A.D. 1100 and 1150, Tusayan and Little Colorado White Ware were more common throughout the rest of the settlement system. Likewise, as Cibola White Ware was replaced at the large center by polychromes, red wares and orange wares ca. A.D. 1250, it increased in frequency at the smaller sites (Upham 1982:193). Upham interprets this pattern as evidence that Cibola White Ware was more highly valued before A.D. 1150 and thus remained at the center. Later on, its preferred status was superceded by the polychromes, orange wares and red wares.

Upham further supports this conclusion with a discussion of the co-occurrence of black-on-whites with later decorated wares, such as polychromes, black-on-reds and black-on-oranges, in a "deep, unmixed" stratigraphic column at 33.8S-295.0 E at the North Pueblo of Nuvaqueotaka (Upham 1982:193). He interprets this co-occurrence as an indication of the continued demand for black-on-whites and their possible curation for subsequent distribution to the smaller communities (Upham 1982:193). Upham therefore calls into question the traditional interpretation of black-on-whites as pre-dating the later polychromes and decorated red wares and orange wares (e.g., Colton 1946, Breternitz 1966).

Upham's interpretations of the variability in ceramic assemblages within Nuvaqueotaka and throughout the Anderson Mesa settlement system have been contradicted or criticized by other researchers who have examined the data. Henderson (1980a) has developed a chronology for the Anderson Mesa settlement system based on a multivariate seriation of temper types within Alameda Brown Wares from 260 sites. She defined four temporally distinct plainware groups on the basis of the multivariate analysis. Henderson was able to confirm her seriation by comparing it against the sequence of plainwares in six stratigraphic test units from Nuvaqueotaka, including 33.8S-295.0E. Significantly, however, Henderson (1980a:17) also concluded that "the overlap between the [three] pueblos [at Nuvaqueotaka] is relatively small," and that "certain caution must be exercised in viewing them as a contemporaneous occupation."

Henderson (1980b) used her plainware chronology to reconstruct the settlement history of the Anderson Mesa area between A.D. 700 and 1400. She found that there was a general trend of population aggregation through time, particularly after A.D. 1150. On the basis of site density, room density and agglomeration measures, Henderson concluded that greater numbers of people were living in increasingly fewer sites throughout the occupation span of the Anderson Mesa area.

In addition, she noted that the structure of the settlement system changed through time. Hierarchical settlement systems had replaced widely dispersed settlements by A.D. 1150, one being centered around Nuvaqueotaka and another around Kinnikinick and Grapevine. However, Henderson contends that these systems were no longer in operation by the fourteenth century. The population had aggregated into three large settlements by A.D. 1300: Nuvaqueotaka, Kinnikinick and Grapevine. Hinterland sites consisted of field houses and terraced fields (see also Henderson 1979). Therefore, according to Henderson's reconstruction of the Anderson Mesa settlement system, the hinterland habitation sites and the fourteenth century components of the large ruins are not contemporaneous, as Upham (1982) has suggested.

Coinman (1984) has examined additional ceramic data from the North Pueblo, as well as the two southern pueblos at Nuvaqueotaka. She concludes that the mean ceramic dates calculated by Upham (1978:22-26) from the deposits in 33.8S-295.0E, and subsequently used to formulate the temporal sequence at Nuvaqueotaka, are not valid because the underlying assumptions of the mean ceramic formula (South 1972) concerning ceramic production through time cannot be substantiated for prehistoric plateau pottery. Coinman also questions the use of the mean ceramic dates from this stratigraphic sequence as "independent" dates for placing ceramic distributions from other parts of the site in time.

Coinman reviews the distribution of different decorated wares across the site and between stratigraphic contexts (subfloor, floor, fill and surface). She finds that *both* white and non-white wares increased in frequency in the upper strata at the North Pueblo and that the relative frequencies of the different wares remained consistent throughout all strata, in contrast to Upham's (1982) claims concerning relative changes in ware frequencies through time.

Downum (1986) claims that the stratigraphic sequence at locus 33.8S-295.0E has been disturbed significantly by pothunting, rodent burrowing and other pits whose dates are unknown. In addition, the sequence includes a 25 cm stratum of slopewash, among other "questionable stratigraphic contacts" (Downum 1986:7). Downum also points out that only four Sosi style sherds were found throughout the entire stratigraphic sequence. Such a low frequency could be due to intrusion by slopewash or any of the other types of disturbance present in the unit.

It is clear that many disagreements remain concerning the internal structure and dating of Nuvaqueotaka, as well as its role within the Anderson Mesa settlement system. Specifically, these controversies revolve around the validity of the stratigraphic sequence at 33.8S-295.0E, the use of South's (1972) mean ceramic formula to derive date ranges, and the interpretation of the variability in ceramic assemblages within Nuvaqueotaka and the settlements throughout Anderson Mesa. Until these issues are resolved, the explanatory power of the developmental model with respect to fourteenth century political and economic organization will remain in question, at least for this important test case.

Summary: A.D. 1100 to 1400

The period between the twelfth and the fifteenth centuries witnessed the culmination and dissolution of many of the cultural trends which had begun in the earlier period. Population growth was followed by dislocation and the abandonment of many areas due to adverse climatic conditions for most of the period between A.D. 1150 and 1300. Populations aggregated into a few areas with greater agricultural potential.

Water and soil control features dating to this time period attest to further agricultural intensification and a greater labor investment in elaborate systems, as compared to the earlier period. However, it is not clear whether such systems are the result of cumulative construction activity over an extended period, or whether they were planned and built as complete systems. The actual building sequence bears directly on whether or not managerial supervision was necessary in their construction.

Settlement hierarchies continued to develop in many parts of the plateau Southwest, exhibiting more levels than previously in some cases and greater differentiation between the higher order and lower order settlements. However, many of these systems experienced collapse and abandonment beginning in the second half of the thirteenth century.

The proponents of the developmental model view the continuation of earlier demographic and subsistence trends, at least in some parts of the Colorado Plateaus, as sources of increasing decision-making pressures which would have promoted the development of centralized political control. They point to increasingly complex settlement and water and soil control systems as evidence for this process of sociopolitical development. However, the internal structure of such systems and their degree of complexity has been questioned by some researchers.

Another line of evidence has been cited in support of the developmental model,and has become a key issue in the controversy surrounding Nuvaqueotaka, as discussed above. It involves the formation of regional exchange networks and the differential distribution of exchange goods within settlement hierarchies at least between A.D. 1100 and 1400. The following chapter will discuss the evidence for exchange between A.D. 900 and 1400, gaps in the data and the controversies surrounding the interpretation of some of this evidence.

CHAPTER IV

EXCHANGE: THE EVIDENCE

Exchange is an important evolutionary mechanism within the context of the developmental model, as discussed in Chapter II. According to this model, it functioned both as an adaptive response to subsistence risk by sedentary populations and as a means of reinforcing leadership development. The following two sections will discuss the evidence for exchange between A.D. 900 and 1400, as well as gaps in the data and the controversies surrounding the interpretation of some of this evidence. The final section will present a short summary of the evidence presented in the Chapter III and this chapter. Expectations concerning pre-thirteenth century exchange will be set forth according to the developmental model.

I will begin by discussing the evidence concerning exchange between A.D. 1100 and 1400 for a number of reasons. First, more is known about exchange between the twelfth and fourteenth centuries, primarily because of the highly distinctive decorated wares and exotic goods that exhibit widespread geographic distributions after A.D. 1200. Second, the nature of exchange during these centuries has a more direct bearing on the existence of hierarchical political systems in the later periods of plateau southwestern prehistory, as proposed by the developmental model. Finally, the evidence for regional exchange prior to the twelfth century is important from the standpoint of examining the development of the later regional networks. This evidence will be presented last and will set the groundwork for a discussion of research into the structure of pre-thirteenth century regional exhange.

Exchange: A.D. 1100 to 1400

Studies of exchange during this period have concentrated primarily on the distinctive decorated wares which exhibit widespread geographic distributions. Findlow and Bolognese (1982) have conducted one of the few studies of exchange in non-ceramic goods. They used trend-surface analysis and linear regression to document the structure of prehistoric and historic obsidian exchange from five major sources in New Mexico. They concluded that most obsidian procurement was by direct access, with the exception of the Red Hill-Mule Creek and Antelope Wells sources.

Between ca. A.D. 1100 and 1300, the Red Hill-Mule Creek source exhibited an exponential fall-off pattern which is characteristic of a down-the-line exchange system in which goods flow through a chain-like series of transactions from the source, to increasingly distant loci. The Antelope Wells source had developed a hyperbolic pattern of fall-off by A.D. 1100, which presumably lasted until the advent of the historic period ca. A.D. 1600. The authors correlate a hyperbolic fall-off pattern with a system that is intermediary between down-the-line and more directional exchange, where transactions are targeted at certain relatively distant loci even though other potential exchange loci are located closer to the source.

Long-distance exchange of exotic goods such as turquoise, copper bells, macaws and shell have been known for quite some time. Copper bells and macaws were imported from Casas Grandes in northwestern Chihuahua, Mexico (DiPeso 1974, McGuire 1980). Marine shell ornaments were manufactured by Hohokam craftsmen from shells originating on the Pacific Coast and the Gulf of California. These goods were transported north into the San

Francisco Peaks area (Fish et al. 1980). Some shell also may have been reaching the San Francisco Peaks from the Gulf of California (Colton 1941). McGuire (1980) states that Casas Grandes was also a major exporter of shell goods into the Rio Grande, northeastern Arizona and the San Francisco Peaks area. Finally, turquoise found in the Valley of Mexico has been traced to the Cerrillos source in New Mexico by neutron activation analysis (Weigand et al. 1977).

Some archaeologists have regarded exchange with Mesoamerica as evidence of sustained interaction between the two regions. They have claimed that culture change within the Southwest was in large measure a response to developments in mesoamerican culture. The most extreme proponents of this view regard the Southwest as a colony of Mesoamerican state-level societies which was exploited by groups of pochteca (long-distance traders) both as a market for their goods and as a source of valuable raw materials such as turquoise (DiPeso 1968, Kelley and Kelley 1975). The Chaco Canyon settlement system is cited as a pochteca outpost because of its early development in relationship to other systems in the plateau Southwest, as well as its great kivas and stockpiles of exchange goods (Kelley and Kelley 1975).

McGuire has effectively criticized this theory by addressing the four points which have been used to support it:

> (1) the presence of Mesoamerican-derived traits in the Southwest, (2) the identification of presumed pochteca burials in the Southwest, (3) the identification of presumed pochteca outposts in the Southwest, and (4) the presumed missionization of the Southwest by Mesoamerican cults (1980:4).

McGuire demonstrates that there is no solid evidence for direct mesoamerican intervention in the Southwest. Many of the traits attributed to mesoamerican intervention, such as kivas and lavish burials, can be more parsimoniously explained as manifestations of indigenous cultural developments. Mesoamerican symbols, in his view, were most probably the result of widespread interaction because of the significant stylistic differences exhibited in their southwestern counterparts. McGuire proposes that exchange and interaction with the hinterland in northwestern Mexico was a more important mechanism of mesoamerican influence on the Southwest than the direct intervention of state-level societies from the Valley of Mexico.

Finally, Plog et al. (1982:232) have proposed what they term a world systems model of southwestern-mesoamerican interaction which focuses on "an elite based exchange in which regional centers in both the Southwest and Mesoamerica were linked." According to the authors, this model avoids the extremes of either the isolationist or the imperialist views of southwestern-mesoamerican interaction, which are based on unwarranted interpretations of the data. However, their world system model is based on the theory that there were stratified, politically centralized societies in the Southwest, whose elites were exchanging both goods and ideas with Mesoamerica as early as A.D. 1150. Therefore, this world system model is closely linked to the developmental model and must rely on the same evidence for sociopolitical complexity in the Southwest.

Although ceramic exchange has not been used as a major line of evidence for interaction with Mesoamerica, it is one of the principal components of the argument for elite exchange in the Southwest (Upham et al. 1981). Shepard (1942, 1965) must be credited with undertaking the first study explicitly directed at examining the development of regional ceramic production-distribution systems. She divided her sample of sherds into three time periods: Glaze I Red was designated the Early group; Glazes I Yellow, II and III were designated the Intermediate group and Glazes IV, V, and VI were labeled the Late group.

Shepard was able to reconstruct the development and spread of glaze paint technology through her compositional analyses. Beginning about A.D. 1250, redwares with the glossy glaze paint were first exchanged into the Rio Grande area from the Little Colorado River valley in east-central Arizona. Exchange began with communities in the western sector of the Rio Grande but soon spread east until all the larger settlements in the Rio Grande valley were obtaining glaze-painted redwares. There seems to have been a period of local experimentation in an attempt to reproduce the glaze paint. However, this experimentation met with little success until inhabitants of the Albuquerque district were able to produce a glaze paint with minerals derived from the Ortiz Mountains. In the Intermediate period, settlements in the Galisteo area gained control over the ore outcrops and thus began to monopolize the production of glaze wares, using a lighter colored slip which was locally available. Although the Galisteo area was able to control the production and exchange of glaze wares for an extended period of time, other areas such as the Zia and Pecos districts began producing their own. It is not clear whether they had ores locally available for the glaze paint, or if they obtained the ore through exchange. However, the Late period was marked by local production and greater diversity in style, reflecting both economic and sociopolitical independence of the various districts within the Rio Grande drainage.

Schaefer (1969) has recorded the distribution of Jeddito Yellow Ware (which was produced between ca. A.D. 1325 and 1600) throughout Arizona, New Mexico, Colorado, Utah and California. He divided this ware's distribution area into one degree latitude and longitude map quadrats. Schaefer found the highest densities of sites containing Jeddito Yellow Ware in the quadrats encompassing the Hopi Mesas, the presumed production area of Jeddito Yellow Ware. The next highest densities were found in the Verde Valley, the San Francisco Peaks and along the San Juan River in southern Utah. Schaefer postulated that the residents of the Verde Valley and San Francisco Peaks were exchanging with the Hopi, while the occurrence of this ware along the San Juan was the result of Hopi occupation of the area. He also attributed the lower densities in the Show Low-Springerville area to exchange with the Hopi. The lowest densities occurred in the peripheries of Jeddito Yellow Ware's distribution; despite the distances between these peripheral areas and the Hopi Mesas, Schaefer envisioned direct exchange with such distant peoples as the Mohave by means of traders traveling to Hopi, or Hopi traders traveling out to these remote areas.

Schaefer anticipated the developmental theory in his explanations for the exchange of Jeddito Yellow Ware. He postulated that this ware served as a means of gaining prestige by allowing individuals to establish outside contacts through exchange with distant peoples. Schaefer hypothesized that this ware also could have served as a medium for alliance formation and as a means of fascilitating the exchange of subsistence or utilitarian items.

Lightfoot and Jewett (1984) used x-ray diffraction analysis and distributional studies to demonstrate that Cibola White Wares and White Mountain Red Wares were produced above the Mogollon Rim in east-central Arizona and were exchanged into the Tonto Basin between A.D. 1100 and 1400. They noted changes in access to Cibola White Ware with increasing distance from its source. This ware was found at both large and small sites in the Pinedale and Snowflake areas, indicating that it was readily available to all households within the production area. In fact, the mean percentage of Cibola White Ware on small sites was greater than the mean percentage at large sites in the Snowflake area.

In the Tonto Basin, the mean frequency of Cibola White Ware was not significantly different between the large and small sites. However, 83.3% of the sites with 20 or more rooms contained this ware, as opposed to only 33.3% of the small sites, suggesting a more directional form of exchange targeted at the larger settlements. The authors suggest that access to this ware was restricted to decision-makers. Cibola White Ware thus appears to have changed function from a household decorated ware in its area of manufacture, to a more highly valued and perhaps status-laden tradeware in the Tonto Basin.

In contrast, White Mountain Red Ware seems to have functioned as a highly valued commodity whose access was restricted both within and outside its production zone. It is found primarily at large sites both above the Mogollon Rim in the Pinedale and Snowflake localities, and below the Rim in the Tonto Basin. Salado Wares were most likely produced above and below the Mogollon Rim, although their locus of production below the rim is not known. In any event, their access also seems to be restricted to large sites, suggesting that they were highly valued commodities, as was White Mountain Red Ware.

Crown and Bishop (1987) have attempted to determine whether or not Salado polychromes were manufactured throughout the widespread geographic area in which they are found. The authors analyzed 179 Gila Polychrome sherds from sites throughout Arizona and southern New Mexico by instrumental neutron activation analysis. Multivariate statistical analysis sorted the sherds from 18 sites into 12 compositionally distinct, internally homogeneous groups. When two sites were included within a single group, they were located no more than 60 km from one another, indicating that the groups were geographically restricted. Three sites had such compositionally heterogeneous samples that the authors could not place them in any of the statistical groups.

Although Crown and Bishop were not able to correlate the groups with geologic sources, they were able to conclude that Gila Polychrome was produced throughout its area of distribution. The existence of multiple production loci suggests that long-distance exchange was not as important a distributional mechanism for Gila Polychrome as it was for such wares as Jeddito Yellow Ware and White Mountain Red Ware. In addition, the production system of at least one type of Salado polychrome crosscuts the traditional boundaries assigned to the Anasazi, Mogollon and Hohokam. Interestingly, the three sites exhibiting the greatest amount of compositional heterogeneity are located within the Salado heartland. It appears as if at least some of the Salado vessels were brought into the heartland from various locations, and may not have been produced locally at all.

Upham (1982) has examined the structure of the long-distance exchange of Jeddito Yellow Ware, Winslow Orange Ware, White Mountain Red Ware and Zuni Glaze Ware. He used the percentages of these wares found at large sites in nine settlement clusters occupied during the fourteenth century: Verde, Anderson Mesa, Middle Little Colorado, Hopi, Puerco, Silver Creek, Upper Little Colorado, Zuni and Acoma. By constructing

Lorenz curves (Upham 1982:140) and falloff plots for each of the four wares, Upham was able to demonstrate that none of them were evenly distributed throughout the nine settlement clusters, nor did their frequencies exhibit a simple negative correlation with increasing distance from their respective sources. In fact, all the wares except for Zuni Glaze Ware exhibited greater than expected frequencies in certain settlement clusters which lie 100 km or more from their postulated sources.

According to Upham, these data indicate that the settlement clusters did not participate equally in the exchange networks of the four ceramic wares, nor were the exchange systems operating through a simple down-the-line mechanism. Instead, Upham concludes that exchange was directional, being targeted at specific settlement systems which were tied together sociopolitically into what Upham has termed alliances.

Finally, Toll et al. (1980) have presented evidence for a shift in control of ceramic exchange from Chaco Canyon to the San Juan Basin during the latter half of the thirteenth century. The authors employed clay firing experiments, the microscopic examination of temper inclusions and design attribute analysis to show that there was not an abrupt change from Chacoan to Mesa Verde ceramics in Chaco Canyon after the Classic Bonito phase, as one would expect if immigrants from Mesa Verde had re-occupied the canyon after the collapse of the Chacoan system (Vivian and Mathews 1965). Instead, they found a complex mixture of locally made ceramics, ceramics manufactured in the Chuska Valley and ceramics imported from the Mesa Verde area at 29SJ633, a small site in Chaco Canyon dated at ca. A.D. 1250. In addition, the Mesa Verde Black-on-white found here fell stylistically between the Chacoan and Mesa Verde traditions. These data indicate a gradual transition in economic relations from within the Chacoan sphere, including the former supply area in the Chuska Valley, to increasing connectivity with the San Juan Basin.

The general picture of ceramic exchange that emerges from these studies is that several regional exchange networks were operating by ca. A.D. 1200 or 1250, within which distinctive decorated wares were circulating. Some of these networks shifted geographically through time. In some cases, large settlements were playing a pivotal role in these exchange systems by creating a demand for the ceramics and acting as major loci of exchange. It is not clear, however, what the nature of the demand was, or the means by which such settlements were able to obtain ceramics from long-distant production areas.

Proponents of the developmental model see the large settlements as nodes in elite exchange networks. According to this model, decorated ceramics functioned as status markers which were circulating among allied decision-makers residing in these settlements. However, the extent to which tradewares were restricted in access to certain groups within the resident population of the large settlements is not known.

Alternatively, it is possible that the observed concentration of tradewares at large settlements is the product of demographic and economic factors such as levels of demand and transport costs. It is possible that, because of their large population size, these settlements were able to generate a high enough volume of demand to make worthwhile the transport of such breakable and cumbersome goods as ceramics over long distances. If this were the case, one would expect the larger settlements to possess higher concentrations of the ceramics even if they were not prestige items slated for an elite group of consumers. Smaller communities surrounding the large settlements would receive such tradewares indirectly because of their relatively low levels of demand for these goods. One would therefore expect the small communities to have fewer vessels per capita as a result of the additional frictional effects introduced by their indirect channels of access.

Whether observed patterns of tradeware distributions are the result of elite exchange or supply and demand cannot be sorted out given the nature of currently available data. Upham (1978) documents the differential distribution of Jeddito Yellow Ware within the burial population of Nuvaqueotaka. He also demonstrates that this ware would have been available to only a small percentage of the households at Nuvaqueotaka, given its frequency within the total decorated ceramic assemblage. These data support his argument that Jeddito Yellow Ware was a status-laden exchange good. However, comparable data are not available for other sites and settlement systems. It is not possible to determine whether Nuvaqueotaka is representative of the intrasite distributions of this ware at other large settlements throughout the plateau Southwest. More detailed information on the distribution of tradewares in different types of sites within several settlement systems, and within the burial populations of the large settlements themselves, must be gathered before the hypothesized structure and function of long-distance exchange within this period can be confirmed.

In addition, extant studies of regional exchange between A.D. 1100 and 1400 generally fall short when it comes to integrating relatively precise sourcing data with comprehensive frequency distributions of the ceramics in question. Shepard (1942, 1965) and Toll et al. (1980) present data which link the non-plastic inclusions of particular ceramics to specific geological sources. However, neither study is able to characterize the movement of these ceramics between and within settlement systems encompassed by regional exchange networks.

Schaefer (1969) presents only a crude quantitative measure of the amount of Jeddito Yellow Ware exchanged in the various quadrats in his sample; no site-by-site frequencies are given. Upham (1982) uses only the large sites within the nine settlement clusters. Again, there are no data presented on the occurrence of the tradewares at smaller contemporaneous settlements within these clusters, except for Anderson Mesa. As a consequence, one is unable to determine whether or not the tradewares were concentrated at the larger sites in all the settlement clusters he examined. Upham's study also lacks conclusive sourcing data. The results of petrographic analyses are presented, but no effort is made to match any of the wares' constituents to provenienced geological sources.

Upham relies heavily on the occurrence of high concentrations of each ware within specific settlement clusters as a means of identifying their production areas. However, the marked positive deviations from the exponential functions on his own fall-off graphs indicate the danger of such assumptions: high concentrations of a tradeware within a particular settlement system can be the result of directional exchange, not local production. Jeddito Yellow Ware and Winslow Orange Ware are sufficiently uniform in terms of their mineralogical composition to suggest that they were manufactured within a geographically restricted production zone and transported over long distances. However, White Mountain Red Ware exhibits greater variability in its mineral inclusions. Fourmile Polychrome, Pinedale Polychrome and Showlow Polychrome (three types of White Mountain Red Ware) may have been produced in more than one locality (Upham 1982:132). It is not clear at this point exactly where these types were made and to where they were transported.

Lightfoot and Jewett (1984) come closest to achieving a balance between sourcing and distributional data. However, their proveniencing of raw clays is weak since they classify their sherds into different groups on the basis of the abundance of feldspar. Their classification is tenuous at best since feldspar is found in virtually all clays, and since the abundance of feldspar may be a function of the amount of temper in the sherds, rather than the mineralogical composition of the paste (David Schaller, personal communication 1986).

In conclusion, many issues remain unresolved concerning the structure of exchange between A.D. 1100 and 1400, as well as its role in sociopolitical development. It is clear, however, that exchange of exotic goods and some decorated ceramics was occurring between different regions and cultural groups. Plateau southwestern peoples also maintained contacts (albeit indirect ones) with state-level societies such as Casas Grandes in northwestern Mexico through long-distance exchange and therefore could have been exposed to concepts of hierarchical political organization. Given the fact that climatic conditions in the period between A.D. 1150 and 1300 were not suited to subsistence exchange, widespread exchange networks were probably the result of some type of social or political forces. By the thirteenth century, access to certain widely exchanged goods was greater at large settlements which may have been centers within hierarchical settlement systems. The frequencies of such commodities was low enough, at least in some cases, to indicate restricted access even within these larger communities. What remains at issue is first, how widespread these patterns were and second, whether or not they were tied into hierarchical, centralized political leadership.

It is not the aim of the present research to resolve these issues, important as they are for evaluating the explanatory value of the developmental model. Instead, the major goal of this dissertation is to examine the eleventh and twelfth centuries which pre-dated the proposed culmination of centralized leadership and prestige exchange. The earlier perspective is being taken as a point of comparison with what is known of exchange during the thirteenth and fourteenth centuries in order to further the understanding of the role of exchange in culture change. A test case will be used to determine if the earlier patterns indicate a trend toward the type of prestige exchange postulated for the fourteenth century by proponents of the developmental model.

The next section will present the data which is currently available on exchange between A.D. 900 and 1100. The unanswered questions concerning exchange in this earlier period will be discussed. Implications for exchange patterns during the development of sociopolitical complexity will be presented in light of the expectations of the developmental model. In the final section of this chapter, the need for compositional analyses conducted at a regional scale will be addressed.

Exchange: A.D. 900 to 1100

Even less is known about the structure of exchange systems in general, and ceramic production-distribution systems in particular, during this earlier period. However, due to the increasing number of sourcing studies, there is conclusive evidence that exchange of utilitarian items was both common and occurred over relatively long distances, contrary to Haury's (1962) and Breternitz' (1966) contentions that such exchange involved primarily neighboring villages and low volumes of goods.

Shell from the Pacific Coast, the Gulf of California and the Gulf of Mexico was transported throughout the Southwest by early Puebloan times, although it was not as common on the Colorado Plateaus as it was in the Hohokam area (Brand 1938, Tower 1945). McGuire and Downum (1982) discovered that shell tended to concentrate in larger sites between Snaketown and the San Francisco Peaks. Its frequencies were less affected by distance from Snaketown (chosen as an arbitrary starting point due to its central role in shell ornaments manufacture) than they were by site size, according to the authors.

Recent studies have demonstrated that utilitarian goods such as lithic raw materials and ceramics were also exchanged on a regular basis. They were exchanged over shorter distances, but in greater volumes, than shell. For example, basalt was extensively used in the Chevelon drainage although it is not indigenous to the area (Green 1975).

Findlow and Bolognese (1982) also examined obsidian procurement in New Mexico between A.D. 900 and 1100. The major form of procurement was through direct access, as was the case in later centuries. However, the distribution of obsidian from the Red Hill-Mule Creek and Antelope Wells sources displayed an exponential fall-off, indicating a down-the-line form of procurement during this period.

By A.D. 1000, communities on Black Mesa were participating in an exchange network of imported lithic raw materials. These materials were from relatively distant sources in many cases, such as obsidian from Government Mountain, creamy opaque silicified claystone from southeastern Utah, Owl Rock chert from near Moenkopi Wash and Chinle chert from the Gray Mountain area. In addition, most of the settlements examined from this period contained lithic raw materials from several sources, often originating from opposite directions (e.g., obsidian from the southwest and creamy opaque silicified claystone from the northeast). This pattern indicates that Black Mesa settlements were redistributing imported lithic materials among themselves (Green 1985). The fact that imports appear in varying combinations at different sites might be the result of reciprocal exchange relationships participated in by individual households through exchange partnerships or kinship ties [cf. Pires-Ferreira and Flannery (1976) on Formative mesoamerican obsidian exchange].

As was mentioned in Chapter II, increasing interest in exchange as a component of sociopolitical development has resulted in a greater emphasis on compositional analysis of ceramics, employing both petrographic and chemical techniques. Several studies have documented cases of ceramic exchange in various parts of the Colorado Plateau prior to the development of such well-known tradewares as White Mountain Red Ware.

Garrett (1979) conducted a petrographic analysis of 116 sherds from Black Mesa, Long House Valley, Cow Springs and the Middle Chinle Valley in northeastern Arizona. She discovered a complex intermixture of local production, local exchange within Black Mesa and more far-flung exchange networks which incorporated Black Mesa and the other three areas included in the analysis. Garrett concluded that exchange was more prevalent on Black Mesa during the twelfth century than previously had been believed. In another study, Sosi Black-on-white and Dogoszhi Black-on-white sherds from five Pueblo II sites on Black Mesa, the adjacent Klethla Valley, the Kaibito Plateau farther to the west and the

Navajo Mountain area were subjected to neutron activation analysis (Deutchman 1980). Differences between the chemical composition of the two types suggested that ceramic exchange was occuring among the Black Mesa sites, as well as between Black Mesa and the Kaibito Plateau.

Garrett, as reported by S. Plog (1980a), also conducted petrographic analysis on 18 Little Colorado White Ware and 18 Cibola White Ware sherds from sites dating between ca. A.D. 1092 and 1281, situated in the Purcell-Larson area of east-central Arizona. Their distinct mineralogy indicates that they were not produced in the same area. The most notable difference lay in the presence of igneous rock fragments in the Little Colorado White Ware thin sections. Plog concluded that this ware was not locally produced because of the absence of volcanic materials in the Purcell-Larson area. Comparative petrographic analyses showed that Little Colorado White Ware sherds from Purcell-Larson were most like sherds from an area just north and northeast of Winslow.

Garrett also has performed a petrographic analysis of 22 Lino-Kana'a style sherds from the Apache-Sitgreaves National Forest and Black Mesa. She concluded that all the sherds originated from a common source since there were few significant differences in the mineral inclusions. In contrast, 44 Sosi style sherds from the same two areas were quite different in terms of their mineral inclusions, suggesting that the samples of Sosi sherds were not from the same production locality (Hantman 1983).

Crown (1980) reported the results of a petrographic analysis on 60 sherds from six transitional Pueblo II/Pueblo III sites in the upper Little Colorado River drainage of east-central Arizona. The sherds consisted of both brown and grey corrugated utility wares. The results of the analysis showed that, while the grey wares were locally produced, the brown wares were most probably being traded into the area.

Schwartz et al. (1980) summarized the results of a limited petrographic study of ceramics from Unkar Delta in the Grand Canyon which was conducted by Warren. These results indicated that only slightly over 10% of the pottery found at Unkar Delta was locally made. The mineral constituents in the Little Colorado White Ware sherds were uniform enough to suggest that they originated from a fairly restricted geographic area. Balsom (1984) has used heavy mineral analysis of crushed sherds from Unkar Delta and the Walhalla Glades to compare the mineralogy of the ceramic assemblages from the two areas. She concludes that ceramics from Unkar Delta and the Walhalla Glades were the product of a single ceramic producing population since there was very little difference between the mineral distributions of either assemblage.

Hantman and Plog (1982, see also S. Plog 1980b) have argued that there was a reduction in the geographic scale of exchange networks between ca. A.D. 900 or 950 and 1100, as witnessed by the increasing number of wares and more localized distribution of design styles during this period. The authors point out that, prior to this time period, ceramic design styles were spread over large portions of the Southwest, as has been recognized by a number of archaeologists (e.g., Roberts 1931:133, 134; Colton 1939:59, Danson 1957:92). In addition, there is a return to regional distributions of style and tradewares after A.D. 1100, although at a smaller geographic scale than prior to A.D. 900.

Observations of stylistic distributions alone do not provide sufficient evidence for shrinking exchange networks between the tenth and twelfth centuries. Compositional analyses have demonstrated that style can vary independently of production technology so that different wares often possess the same design styles (F. Plog 1976, Deutchman 1980, Hantman and Plog 1982, Hantman et al. 1984). Therefore, homogeneity of design is not necessarily indicative of the number of ceramic production loci operating at any given period of time.

There are some petrographic data which indicate that this trend toward more localized exchange of ceramics may have occurred. Petrographic analysis of Lino-Kana'a style sherds (pre-dating A.D. 900) from Black Mesa and the Apache-Sitgreaves National Forest are enough alike mineralogically to suggest that they originated from a common source. In contrast, Sosi style ceramics (post-dating A.D. 1000) from these two areas are markedly different in terms of their mineral inclusions and probably were manufactured in different loci. It appears that Black Mesa and the Apache-Sitgreaves area were participating in different ceramic exchange networks at least by A.D. 1000. Petrographic data also indicate that Sosi and Dogoszhi style ceramics were being produced in separate loci on Black Mesa and exchanged between settlements on the mesa. Similarly, Sosi and Reserve-Tularosa style vessels were produced in different parts of the Apache-Sitgreaves area (Garrett 1979, as reported in Hantman and Plog 1982 and Hantman 1983).

Compositional, stylistic and frequency data on San Juan Red Ware and Tsegi Orange Ware have been used in order to document changes in the exchange of red wares on Black Mesa through time. The data suggest that San Juan Red Ware was imported into Black Mesa from the Four Corners area some 110 km to the northeast, while Tsegi Orange Ware was probably produced in northeastern Arizona closer to Black Mesa (Hantman and Plog 1982).

San Juan Red Ware exhibited its highest frequencies on Black Mesa between A.D. 800 and 950 and then decreased in abundance through time. At the same time as San Juan Red Ware frequencies were decreasing, Tsegi Orange Ware frequencies were increasing. Since the latter ware was produced closer to Black Mesa, it would appear that ceramic exchange networks in this area were indeed diminishing in spatial extent (S. Plog 1980b, Hantman and Plog 1982).

However, not all of the data for the A.D. 900 to 1100 period indicate shrinking exchange networks. Green (1985:156) found that "[i]t was only after A.D. 1000 that sites on Black Mesa shared widely in the exchange of rare [lithic raw material] imports, in most cases available only at great distances." Tusayan White Ware has been found in the San Francisco Peaks area (e.g., Colton 1946) and the Hohokam sphere at least as far south as Snaketown between A.D. 750 and 1150 (Haury 1976, McGuire and Downum 1982). Light firing clays from which Tusayan White Ware were made outcrop in the Klethla Valley, Long House Valley, the Chilchinbito area and on Black Mesa, all in northeastern Arizona (Geib and Callahan 1985). Therefore, this ware was being traded over considerable distances during a time period when ceramic exchange networks on Black Mesa were decreasing in size. It is possible that the diminution of Black Mesa ceramic exchange networks was not a plateau-wide phenonenon and had more to do with the impending breakdown of the Black Mesa settlement system.

To summarize, several observations can be made concerning exchange between A.D. 900 and 1100:

1. exchange was a prevalent phenomenon in many parts of the plateau Southwest, as expected for a period of high spatial climatic variability, at least between A.D. 1050 and 1150;
2. exchange occurred at varying geographic scales, from inter-community exchange at the local level, to inter-regional exchange between different cultural systems;
3. lithic raw materials, as well as decorated and plainware ceramics were exchanged at different geographic scales simultaneously;
4. different exchange goods underwent distinctive changes in their distribution at the same time (e.g., lithic raw materials from long-distant sources were being exchanged to Black Mesa while the importation of ceramics from long distances was attenuating).

Many basic questions still remain unanswered concerning the exchange of goods during this period, however. The organization of production-distribution systems, in particular, is not well understood. The degree of production specialization at both the community and supra-community level is unclear. It is not known whether exchange goods, particularly nonexotics such as ceramics and lithics, were manufactured by specialists, or whether they were made by unspecialized household producers. The geographic scale of production is unclear as well: that is, whether one community, a group of neighboring communities, or an entire area or region was involved in the production of exchange goods. In addition, the nature of exchange transactions are poorly understood: were they reciprocal and egalitarian, or was access to goods restricted to certain groups? Did the structure of exchange for certain goods change with increasing distance from their sources? These are only a few of the relevant issues which need to be addressed concerning the structure and function of exchange prior to the twelfth century.

Conclusions and Implications

The data show that cultures on the Colorado Plateaus were undergoing major changes between A.D. 900 and 1400 which would have presented considerable adaptive challenges. Population growth, increasing reliance on a sedentary agricultural way of life and the development of hierarchical settlement patterns occurred, at least in some areas, throughout this entire period. These changes were concomitant with prevalent exchange activity inolving many different types of goods and operating at various geographic scales, from local to regional. According to the developmental model, the increased decision-making load was met by the rise of leaders who eventually extended their authority over entire settlement systems. The proponents of the developmental model also propose that exchange functioned initially as an averaging mechanism to minimize fluctuations in subsistence stress. Through time, however, it was transformed from an adaptive strategy to a political tool used by leaders to consolidate and legitimize their authority, according to this theory.

If the developmental model is correct in its interpretations of sociopolitical development and the role of exchange in this process, then certain expectations can be set forth concerning the structure of production-distribution systems during the formative stages of development, prior to the culmination of hierarchical sociopolitical systems in the thirteenth and fourteenth centuries:

1. The exchange goods should occur in relatively high frequencies outside their production zones; they should be found in exchange contexts at relatively long distances from their sources, at least far enough away to cross settlement system boundaries.
2. Areas with hierarchical settlement patterns should have concentrations of long-distance exchange goods at the larger sites with specialized architecture such as kivas, ballcourts or community rooms; smaller sites lacking such specialized architecture should have relatively lower frequencies of the exchange goods (Lightfoot 1981, Lightfoot and Feinman 1982).
3. Such long-distance exchange goods should occur in small enough quantities that they would have been available to only a small percentage of the community (Upham 1982).
4. There should be an uneven distribution of the exchange goods within the larger sites' residential areas and/or burial population, signaling differential access to the goods within the community (Upham 1982).

Having set forth these expectations, the next chapter will outline a case study and research design to test their validity with respect to pre-thirteenth century exchange.

CHAPTER V

DETERMINING THE STRUCTURE AND FUNCTION OF A PRODUCTION-DISTRIBUTION SYSTEM

A review of the archaeological evidence has demonstrated that the baseline conditions set forth by the developmental model were in place on the Colorado Plateaus between A.D. 900 and 1100. The combination of spatial and temporal environmental perturbations, increasing population sizes, sedentism and an increasing commitment to agriculture significantly augmented subsistence risk and necessitated a behavioral response. According to the developmental model, the response was the development of increasingly complex and more centralized sociopolitical systems, which were controlled by high status leaders, and spanned several communities within individual settlement clusters. The archaeological record also shows that hierarchical settlement systems were operating, at least in some parts of the plateau Southwest, and that many of the larger central settlements were the loci for some type of economic distribution. Compositional analyses have documented both localized and long-distance exchange of a variety of goods such as lithic raw materials, ceramics and shell ornaments.

However, many questions remain concerning the nature of production-distribution systems operating between the tenth and twelfth centuries. It is necessary to begin addressing these issues with a research design which examines a whole production-distribution system. This chapter will outline such an approach. The following section will present a case study and will discuss why it is appropriate to the research. The second section will discuss a research design aimed at addressing these critical issues. The data base and the criteria used in its selection will be described in the third section. Finally, a discussion concerning the problems of generalizing from a single case study will be presented.

Little Colorado White Ware as a Case Study

The decision was made to focus on a ceramic tradeware for a number of reasons. First, ceramics appear to have been a common exchange good which is ubiquitous throughout the archaeological record. Second, they were exchanged both locally and over long distances and are therefore amenable to the study of exchange networks operating at different geographic scales. Third, ceramic exchange is used as a major line of evidence for leadership development and legitimization by the proponents of the developmental model. Finally, ceramics can be sourced through a number of petrographic and chemical analytical techniques.

Ceramic wares are an appropriate unit of analysis for sourcing studies in particular because they are defined according to technological attributes which have direct bearing on manufacturing technology and mineralogical composition. Types, on the other hand, are subdivisions of wares based on stylistic differences which can vary independently of technology (F. Plog 1976, Deutchman 1980, Hantman and Plog 1982, Hantman et al. 1984).

The fourth reason for selecting a ceramic case study is that ceramics can be utilitarian and/or ceremonial goods. As a result, their exchange can be related to economic factors such as production specialization and subsistence risk minimization (i.e., the banking of foodstuffs) on the one hand, and sociopolitical factors such as prestige exchange on the other. Therefore, ceramics have the potential of functioning within very different types of exchange networks. Fifth, most of the data on fourteenth century exchange pertain to ceramic tradewares. An earlier ceramic case study would therefore serve as a direct comparison. Finally, the designs on decorated ceramics can provide additional data concerning production specialization, the structure of exchange networks and the ideational context of their exchange.

Little Colorado White Ware (subsequently referred to as LCWW) was constructed by coiling and was fired in a reducing atmosphere. It is characterized by a dark to light grey core and typically has abundant grey or tan angular sherd temper. Quartz and volcanic rock fragments are also common inclusions. Both surfaces of bowls and jar exteriors are coated with a chalky white to light grey slip, which is often quite thickly applied. Decorated surfaces are moderately polished and display geometric designs painted with black carbon paint (Colton 1955, Ware 9B). This ware has been divided into six types by Colton (1955), based on stylistic criteria: St. Joseph, Holbrook, Padre, Chevelon, Walnut and Leupp Black-on-white. Detailed discussions of the types and their corresponding design styles can be found in Chapter VIII and Appendix C.

The Chevelon Archaeological Research Project (CARP) developed an alternative classification scheme to Colton's ware/type system for black-on-white ceramics. The CARP classification focuses on combinations of technological attributes to create descriptive designations for classes of ceramics which are roughly comparable to Colton's ware designations. The three technological criteria used in this system are surface finish, temper and paint type (F. Plog 1976). Under the CARP classification scheme, LCWW is designated as SShO (*S*lipped surfaces, *Sh*erd temper and *O*rganic paint). The SShO label has also been employed by Stephen Plog (1980a) and Hantman et al. (1984). However, this ware will be referred to herein by its traditional name which is more widely accepted.

There are four reasons why LCWW is an appropriate case study for this research. First, it was manufactured at least between the eleventh and thirteenth centuries, placing it in the proper time frame for examining the development of regional ceramic exchange systems and the potential beginnings of prestige exchange during the eleventh and twelfth centuries.

Colton (1955) dates this ware between A.D. 1000 and 1375. He lists earlier dates for St. Joseph Black-on-white (A.D. 700 to 900). However, it is only represented by a single sherd. It has not been demonstrated that this type is a valid classificatory unit. Breternitz' (1966) "best" indigenous tree-ring dates for the various types of LCWW fall between A.D. 1075 and 1250.

This ware became the dominant white ware in the central Little Colorado River valley at the beginning of the Holbrook Phase (ca. A.D. 1025 to 1050). It continued to be the most abundant white ware in this area until it was largely abandoned in the late MacDonald Phase ca. A.D. 1250 (Gumerman and Skinner 1968). Putting all the evidence together, this ware would appear to date between ca. A.D. 1025/1050 and 1250 (S. Plog 1980a).

The second reason why LCWW is an appropriate case study is that it has an extensive geographic distribution. Remains of this ware have been identified in archaeological contexts throughout the Little Colorado River drainage. It also occurs in smaller quantities in the Verde River valley as far west as Perkinsville, the Tonto Basin and as far north as Page (Douglass 1982). Third, the middle and upper Little Colorado River drainage has been one of the most intensively surveyed and excavated parts of the Southwest (e.g., Colton 1946, Martin et al. 1962, 1964; Gumerman and Skinner 1968, F. Plog 1974, 1981; F. Plog et al. 1976, Lightfoot 1981). There is thus a large body of published frequency data on this ware, as well as extensive sherd collections and archival site records that are available for study. The frequency data will be essential for carrying out the second goal of the research design to be described in the next section.

Some disagreement exists concerning the production source of LCWW, providing a fourth reason for using this ware as a case study. The different theories concerning its production source have rested mainly on observations of the frequency distribution of LCWW across space. Stephen Plog's (1980a) hypothesis that it was produced somewhere north or northeast of Winslow is the only one which is based on comparisons of the mineral inclusions of sherds found in different areas. However, his samples were small, precluding any assessment of mineralogical variability, or a determination of whether more than one geologically distinct area was producing LCWW.

Colton (1955) describes the production area of LCWW as the Little Colorado River valley between the Petrified Forest National Park on the east and the San Francisco Peaks on the west. McGregor (1937) initially placed the production center of Holbrook Black-on-white just south of Joseph City approximately 60 miles east of the San Francisco Peaks. He later states, however, that this type eventually became established and was made in the San Francisco Peaks area (McGregor 1941a, 1965). Breternitz (1966), following Colton, lists

Walnut Black-on-white as indigenous to the area just east of the San Francisco Peaks between Padre and Diablo Canyons. Fred Plog (1983:314, personal communication 1984) has concluded that this ware was made "somewhere in the vicinity of Flagstaff," based on his examination of the results of Garrett's petrographic analysis for Stephen Plog (1980a).

Gumerman and Skinner have designated what they call an area of "pure" LCWW sites, as shown in Figure 2. Wilson (1969) believes that this ware was produced in the area from Holbrook and the Petrified Forest National Monument to Leupp, which coincides with Gumerman's and Skinner's "pure" region to some degree. He also states that LCWW may have been produced in the MacDonald Canyon locality south of the Little Colorado River and east of Chevelon Creek (Wilson 1969:348).

The general disagreement therefore rests on whether or not LCWW was produced as far west as the San Francisco Peaks area. I have conducted a preliminary distance decay study on the distribution of this ware in the upper and middle Little Colorado River drainages (Douglass 1982). This analysis revealed a bimodal distribution in the frequencies of LCWW sherds with increasing distance from Winslow. The two modes correspond to sites in the Hopi Buttes and San Francisco Peaks area respectively. The bimodal distribution may be due to the existence of two sources, if high concentrations of this ware were caused by production activity.

Frequency data have been used to designate production loci in the absence of compositional and geological data to source ceramics. However, Upham's (1982) study of fourteenth century tradewares has suggested that relatively high concentrations of these goods can be the result of exchange rather than production. The only way to distinguish

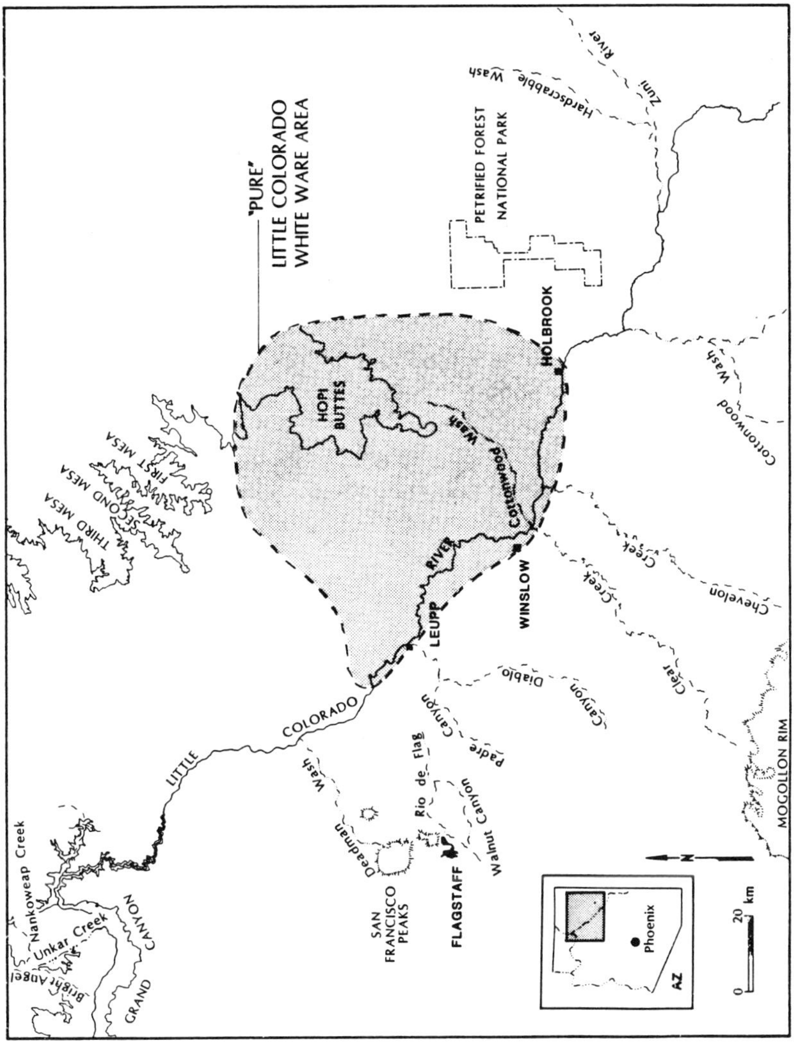

Figure 2. Location of area containing "pure" LCWW sites designated by Gumerman and Skinner (1968:Figure 1).

between these two processes is to provide independent sourcing data through compositional analyses of the ceramics and potential raw material sources.

The final reason in support of LCWW as a case study is its ease of identification. Swarthout and Dulaney (1978) have demonstrated that it is difficult to arrive at a consensus in the classification of prehistoric southwestern ceramics among analysts with diverse backgrounds and training. However, LCWW can be distinguished readily from contemporary Cibola and Tusayan White Wares by surficial inspection due to its distinctive heavy white slip, light-colored sherd temper, grey paste and organic paint. There is thus a good chance that this ware has been consistently identified, even by the large number of ceramic analysts who have worked with assemblages from the Little Colorado River drainage. As a result, frequency data in published site reports and archival site records can be employed with a reasonable amount of confidence.

The Research Design

The general aim of the research is to examine the production-distribution system of a single exchange good which was in operation before the thirteenth century, during which time the developmental model posits that regional exchange networks were developing in the context of increasingly hierarchical sociopolitical systems. The basic structure of the research design described in this section can be applied to the study of any prehistoric good which was exchanged on a regional scale and whose production source can be identified.

The research design must be contextual in the sense that it should address not only the organization of the production and distribution of exchange goods, but the broader context of such activities within the cultural system in which they operated (Hodder 1982). It has been recognized widely that exchange involves more than the transfer of material goods between individuals and social groups. The exchange of material goods is carried out in the context of social, religious and political interaction, within whose dynamics it must function (Mauss 1954, Schneider 1974, Earle 1982, Hodder 1982). Alliance formation, marriage agreements, exchange partnerships, patron-client relationships and inter-community ceremonials are only a few examples of such types of interaction.

The developmental model views exchange as a political tool used by decision-makers to establish obligation on the part of the general population, maximize their status and legitimize their authority (Lightfoot 1981, Upham 1982). Exchange cannot be understood in a vacuum; nor can the developmental model be tested in this earlier time period unless the research design includes methods for relating the manufacture and distribution of goods to sociopolitical organization.

Three broad areas of research need to be pursued in order to test the developmental model: the organization of production, the types of inter-community exchange mechanisms operating at various geographic scales, and the social and political context of exchange. The research design has been organized according to these three objectives, each with its own attendant set of methods, as discussed below.

Determining the Degree of Geographic Centralization in Production

The degree of community-level specialization in the production of LCWW lies somewhere along a continuum which ranges from centralized production by a single community or center, to widespread production by each community which possessed vessels of this ware. The system probably lies at some point between these two extremes, with several (but not all) communities within the San Francisco Peaks area and/or the Hopi Buttes area manufacturing this ware. The degree of community-level specialization can only be determined once the geographic context of production has been documented more precisely. Therefore, the location and spatial extent of this ware's raw material source(s) must be determined. The precision with which the source(s) can be pinpointed is dependent on the sensitivity of the sourcing techniques which are used and the degree of compositional heterogeneity in the raw material source(s). Before outlining the methodology for sourcing LCWW, a brief discussion will be presented concerning the necessary components of sourcing studies used to reconstruct the organization of a ceramic production-distribution system.

Sourcing studies should be an integral part of research aimed at understanding prehistoric exchange networks. There are four criteria necessary for compositional analyses specifically targeted at ceramics. They must utilize:

1. a sample derived from a single ceramic ware
2. a regional scale, the limits of the project area being defined by the distribution of the ware in question
3. a sample size large enough to allow for the measurement of the mineralogical variability within the ware in question
4. a geological reconnaissance of the potential source area(s) and a complementary compositional analysis of potential raw material sources.

First, more understanding can be gained by focusing on a single ware than can be derived from fragmentary information on a variety of different ceramic types. The appropriateness of using a ceramic ware as a unit of analysis has been discussed above. Second, focusing on the ceramics from a single site or a relatively small project area prevents one from gaining a regional perspective on the distribution of ceramics made from particular clays and non-plastic inclusions. A small-scale approach is adequate for distinguishing between locally produced and imported ceramics found in a restricted geographic area. However, it is insufficient for answering questions concerning the number of source areas specializing in the manufacture of certain ceramics or the structure and scale of ceramic exchange networks. Such issues can be addressed more effectively by using the spatial distributions of the ceramics themselves rather than the boundaries of specific excavation or survey project areas.

Third, small sample sizes can compromise the results of a sourcing study by limiting its ability to measure the degree of compositional variability within the ceramic ware in question. Finally, it is not possible to locate the production source of ceramics unless the constituents present in them can be related to geologic deposits. Without such geological evidence, it is difficult to determine if the compositional variability observed between different ceramics is the product of intra- or inter-source variability. That is, are they compositionally different because they originated from different sources, or because they were made from a single source which varies in its mineralogical and/or chemical composition?

It is admittedly difficult for a compositional study to meet all four criteria when it is ancillary to another project. The present study was undertaken in part to demonstrate how compositional analysis can be accomplished within the context of a research design explicitly directed toward answering questions about the organization of prehistoric ceramic production and distribution. Therefore, the sourcing of LCWW is accomplished by using a combination of petrographic analysis, x-ray diffraction and electron microprobe analysis on sherds and potential raw material sources. A total of 269 sherds from 11 sites in the two most likely source areas (the Hopi Buttes and San Francisco Peaks) were selected for analysis.

It is not possible to distinguish ceramics which were made in different localities within a geologically uniform region using any of these techniques. However, the two most likely production localities are characterized by geologic formations containing rocks with distinctive minerals. Therefore, it is highly probable that sherds produced in one of these two areas can be distinguished from sherds produced in the other area on the basis of their constituents. It will be assumed for the purpose of the sourcing study that finished LCWW vessels were being transported between communities and settlement systems, instead of the raw materials from which they were made. This operating assumption is basic to any form of technical analysis which uses mineral or chemical constituents in ceramics to determine the provenience of production sources.

Although it is an important component of the production-distribution system, determining the actual mode of production is beyond the scope of this research for reasons which will be discussed in Chapter VI. In addition, this study is regional in scope. It focuses on inter-site interaction, and thus emphasizes exchange over production. Determining the geographic context of LCWW's production is therefore undertaken primarily as a prerequisite to the second goal, and not as a means of fully reconstructing this ware's production system.

Determining the Basic Structure of Exchange

The main objective of this part of the research is to characterize the movement of LCWW throughout its exchange system. The two primary variables considered are: 1) how far the vessels traveled to reach their various exchange contexts (distance from the source) and 2) relative volume of LCWW exchange activity at each locus (herein expressed as the percentage of LCWW sherds of the total decorated ceramic assemblage for each site in the sample). These variables are utilized in a distance decay study which is divided into two parts, each of which will use a different technique of exploratory data analysis (Tukey 1977).

First, a linear function which best characterizes the relationship between the volume of LCWW exchange and distance from the source is calculated using resistant line-fitting, a technique analogous to linear regression. As Hodder (1974) has pointed out, the relationship between interaction (exchange being a particular type of interaction) and distance from the source of the interaction is best described by a curve which can be linearized by transforming the interaction and/or distance variables using logarithms and exponents. Five linear distance decay models of exchange systems (Hodder 1974, Hodder and Orton 1976, Renfrew 1977), each requiring a different set of transformations, are applied to the data. Each model is evaluated in order to determine if it provides a satisfactory representation of the relationship between frequency of LCWW exchange and distance form the source.

Insight can be gained concerning the movement of LCWW between settlements by expressing the relationship between these two variables in the form of a linear function. For example, down-the-line exchange produces a distinct linear relationship as compared to directional exchange. In down-the-line exchange, goods are passed on from one community to the next. Each community retains a certain proportion of what it receives and passes the rest onto its neighbor further away from the source. In the case of directional exchange, higher order centers within a hierarchical settlement system have preferential access to the exchange good due to the greater drawing power of their relatively larger populations, their role as redistributive centers and/or the greater drawing power of high status groups living in such centers (Renfrew 1977).

In the second part of the distance decay study, a graphical technique called smoothing used in order to highlight any perturbations in the overall distance decay trend in LCWW exchange. The purpose of this part of the study is to determine if certain areas within the LCWW exchange system experienced relatively more or less intense exchange activity than would be expected for their distance from the source. Such departures from the general distance decay trend may indicate that different exchange mechanisms were operating in different parts of the exchange system. The distance decay study will be discussed in detail in Chapter VII.

Examining Stylistic Variability within the Production-Distribution System

The relationship between stylistic and mineralogical variability has important implications for understanding both the structure and the ideational context of LCWW production and exchange. From the standpoint of production, this relationship can reveal whether different production areas manufactured vessels decorated with distinct styles, or whether different production areas shared the same set of styles. From the perspective of exchange, the spatial distribution of the various styles relative to one another must be examined in order to determine whether or not they were slated for different exchange spheres. Style might have signalled function if different styles, whether produced in one or more areas, were transported to the same communities. However, different styles might have operated within separate exchange networks, regardless of who was producing them. In this context, design styles might reflect inter-community political and economic cooperation rather than vessel function.

Of course, it is possible that LCWW styles will exhibit a combination of the circumstances discussed above. Some styles might be universally produced and consumed, while others might be more restricted in terms of who was producing them and/or the types of contexts in which they are found. Changes in style through time must also be considered as they affect the organization of production and distribution throughout the two hundred year period in which LCWW was made. However, the process of analyzing these factors can be initiated by plotting the geographic distributions of the various styles relative to each other and by measuring their degree of covariation with mineralogical attributes. The design analysis is discussed in Chapter VIII.

To summarize the research design, a contextual approach has been outlined with the overall objective of examining the production-distribution system of LCWW from a regional perspective. Intra-site data are considered where necessary to aid in the interpretation of the results and to provide independent corroborative evidence. Three goals have been outlined briefly, along with their corresponding methodologies. The following section discusses the site data used to address each of the three goals.

The Site Sample

The site sample can be divided into three parts, each of which corresponds to one of the three goals of the research design: a core sample for the compositional analyses, an extended sample for the distance decay study and the design analysis sample. Refer to Table 2 for a summary of the site sample and Figure 3 for their geographic locations.

The Core Sample

The core site sample was obtained from the site files at the Museum of Northern Arizona in Flagstaff. LCWW sherds from these sites were selected from the museum's excavation collections. A total of 11 sites were selected for the sourcing study. Both higher order settlements and small villages were included in order to determine how LCWW production and/or exchange was organized within bimodal settlement systems.

Between 30 and 50 sherds were selected from each of three approximately contemporaneous centers: Winona Village and Juniper Terrace in the San Francisco Peaks area, and the Plaza Site in the Hopi Buttes area. These sites were defined as higher order

Table 2. The Site Sample.

Site	Area	Reference	Core	Extended	Design
Winona Village	S.F.[a]	McGregor 1937 McGregor 1941a Colton 1946	X	X	X
NA 10 779	S.F.	MNA site files	X		X
NA 10 803	S.F.	Hudgens 1974	X	X	X
Rincon Pueblo (NA 7432)	S.F.	Kelley 1969	X	X	X
Juniper Terr. (NA 1814)	S.F.	Colton 1946	X	X	X
NA 680	S.F.	Smith 1952	X	X	X
AR 03-04-02-2403[b]	S.F.	Coconino Nat. Forest Survey Files	X		
Plaza Site (NA 9400)	H.B.[c]	Gumerman 1969	X	X	X
NA 9183	H.B.	Gumerman 1969	X	X	X
NA 10 757	H.B.	Trott and McPherson 1984	X	X	X
NA 7806	H.B.	Olson 1963	X	X	X
NA 103	S.F.	Ritchie 1970		X	
Tse Tlani (NA 8762)	S.F.	Ward 1969		X	
Hibbard Pueblo (NA 1140)	S.F.	Colton 1946		X	

Table 2. The Site Sample (continued).

Site	Area	Reference	Core	Extended	Design
Turkey Tanks (NA 2098)	S.F.	Colton 1946		X	
Metate House (NA 1764)	S.F.	Colton 1946		X	
Crack-in-Rock (NA 537)[b]	S.F.	Colton 1946		X	
AZ I:10:30 (ASM)	S.F.	Tagg and Layhe 1985		X	
NA 7817	S.F.	Olson 1963		X	
NA 7818	S.F.	Olson 1963		X	
NA 9182	H.B.	Gumerman 1969		X	
NA 9192	H.B.	Gumerman 1969		X	
NA 9165	H.B.	Gumerman 1969		X	
NA 12 574	Leupp	Keller 1979		X	
Grand Falls (NA 1292)	G.F.[d]	Colton 1946		X	
CS 690	Chev.[e]	S. Plog 1980a		X	X
CS 43	Chev.	S. Plog 1980a		X	X
CS 731	Chev.	S. Plog 1980a		X	X
CS 900	Chev.	S. Plog 1980a		X	X
CS 503	Chev.	S. Plog 1980a			X
CS 412	Chev.	S. Plog 1980a			X

Table 2. The Site Sample (continued).

Site	Area	Reference	Core	Extended Design
NA 17 271B	Snow.[f]	Hartman et al. 1985		X
NA 17 282	Snow.	Hartman et al. 1985		X
Agate House[b]	P.F.[g]	Cosgrove 1951		X
DoBell Site (Az Q:1:7 ASM)	P.F.	Harrill 1973		X
Nankoweap[b] (sev. sites)	G.C.[h]	Schwartz 1963		X
Unkar Delta (sev. sites)	G.C.	Schwartz et al. 1980		X
Bright Angel	G.C.	Schwartz et al. 1979		X
AZ Q:7:26	Z.R.[i]	Westfall 1981		X
AZ Q:3:63[b]	Z.R.	Beeson 1966		X
AZ Q:3:8[b]	Z.R.	Beeson 1966		X
AZ Q:4:50[b]	Z.R.	Beeson 1966		X
AZ Q:7:14[b]	Z.R.	Beeson 1966		X
AZ Q:7:9[b]	Z.R.	Beeson 1966		X

[a] San Francisco Peaks area
[b] surface collections
[c] Hopi Buttes
[d] Grand Falls area
[e] Chevelon Drainage
[f] Snowflake area
[g] Petrified Forest National Monument
[h] Grand Canyon
[i] Zuni River drainage

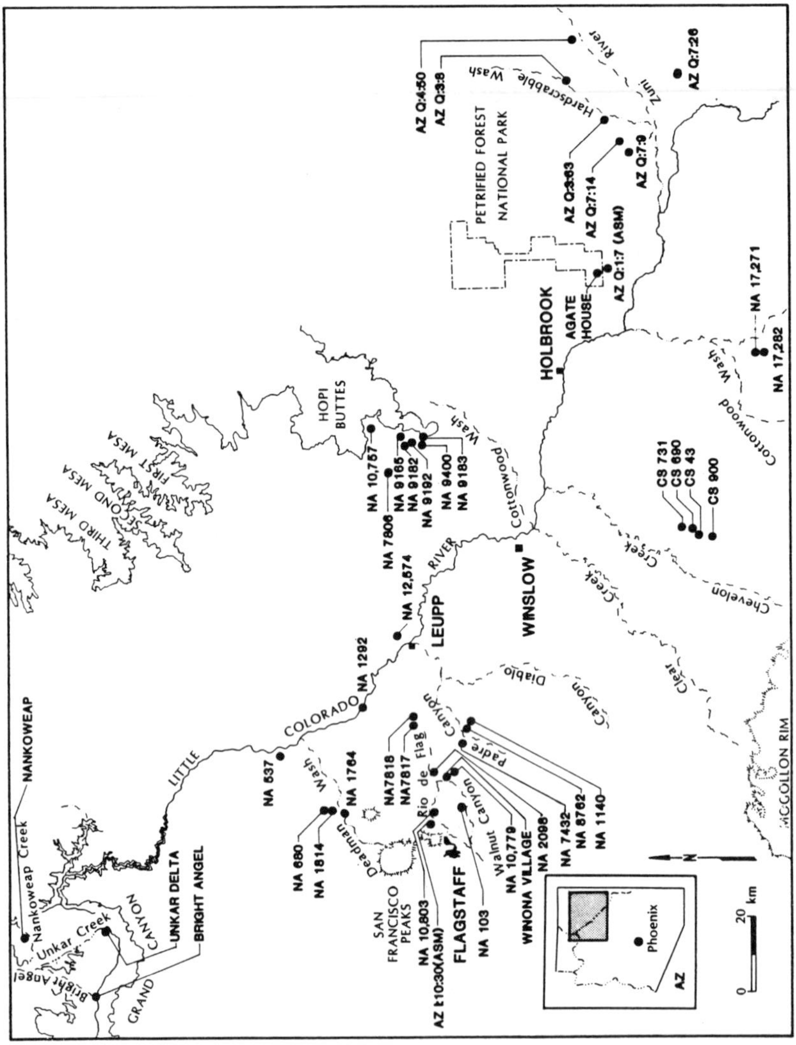

Figure 3. Location of sites used in this study.

settlements and potential production-distribution centers of this ware for the following reasons:

1. They were all occupied at some time between A.D. 1050 and 1250.
2. They are located in one of the two areas in which Little Colorado White Ware most likely was produced.
3. They are larger than surrounding sites.
4. They possess one or more features, such as plazas, ballcourts and/or great kivas, which may have been used for the distribution of exchange goods.
5. They contained relatively large Little Colorado White Ware assemblages.

Winona Village and Juniper Terrace are located near two separate tributary systems of the Little Colorado River which lie at opposite ends of the San Francisco Peaks. Winona Village is in close proximity to Padre and Youngs Canyons in the southeast, while Juniper Terrace is near Deadmans Wash to the north. Therefore, it may be possible to detect mineralogical differences in the sherds from these two sites if both locales were producing LCWW.

Juniper Terrace was not the only potential production-distribution center extant during this time period in the Deadmans Wash drainage. Wupatki, for example was a large multi-storied pueblo with a ballcourt which had a sizable LCWW assemblage and which was occupied from the early twelfth century to the mid thirteenth century. However, as Robinson et al. (1975:95) have stated,

> "[d]ates from individual rooms are difficult to interpret as they sometimes have considerable range either as a result of mixing of material during collapse, reuse of material prehistorically, or contemporary clerical confusion."

It was therefore not possible to date the LCWW assemblage of this site with greater than a 150 year time span, or to relate it temporally to Winona Village. Its temporal relationship to the latter site was deemed especially important since it was located within the same potential production zone. Mixing of the fill during the collapse of the upper levels of the structure and "contemporary clerical confusion" also have led to the loss of provenience information for portions of the sherd collection from this site. Juniper Terrace was selected because of its tighter dating, partial contemporeneity with Winona Village and better provenienced collections. In addition, it possesses all the characteristics of a center which could have participated in the production and distribution of exchange goods indigenous to the area.

The issue of dating these sites deserves some further comment. Winona Village and Juniper Terrace are among the best dated sites in the San Francisco Peaks area. Winona Village, however, is a complex site composed of seven clusters of pithouses with associated trash middens and a ball court. One of the clusters (NA 2131) also contains a three-room masonry structure. Interpretations of numerous tree-ring dates have placed the occupation of Winona Village between ca. A.D. 1086 and 1145 (Robinson et al. 1975, Downum 1984). However, not all of the pithouse clusters were constructed or occupied contemporaneously. Sherds for the sourcing study were selected from pithouse clusters which span the entire occupation period of the site as it is presently understood. Some portions of the sherd sample from Winona Village are therefore more contemporaneous with the Juniper Terrace sample than others. This fact was taken into consideration when evaluating the differences in the components of LCWW sherds from the two centers. (Refer to Appendix B for details on the dating of the pithouse clusters.)

Juniper Terrace has a strong cluster of cutting dates between A.D. 1129 and 1139. These dates are primarily from structure E. The provenience for some of the dates have not been established (Ahlstrom 1985). Unfortunately, Structure E did not have enough LCWW sherds for the petrographic sample. As a result, sherds were selected from Structure A and the assumption was made that this structure dates to approximately the same time period as Structure E. This assumption is based on the fact that both 1814A and 1814E are located within the west compound, and that both structures share similar ceramic assemblages (Colton 1946).

No absolute dates exist for the Plaza site. Gumerman and Skinner (1968) have assigned this site to the MacDonald Phase based on its ceramic assemblage, thus placing its occupation somewhere between A.D. 1100 and 1250. As far as dating is concerned, it is no better than Wupatki. However, the Plaza site is the only presently known settlement which qualifies as a potential production-distribution center in the Hopi Buttes area, thus necessitating its inclusion in the sourcing study.

An attempt was made to select three smaller sites in the area surrounding each of the three centers. (This was not entirely possible in the case of Juniper Terrace, as will be discussed below.) Sites were selected if they met the following criteria:

1. They were occupied at some time between A.D. 1050 and 1250.
2. They are relatively small (less than ten rooms).

3. They lack specialized architectural features such as open plazas, ballcourts and great kivas.
4. They are no more than 25 km away from one of the centers. [Fred Plog (1979:121) has argued that a distance of 25 to 30 km provides a reasonable "territorial radius" within which communities would have interacted, and thus exchanged goods, on a regular basis.]
5. They were year-round habitation sites; field houses and seasonal camps, for example, were excluded from consideration.
6. They contained at least 20 LCWW sherds in the collections stored at the Museum of Northern Arizona.
7. They were excavated.

The decision was made to use excavated sites whenever possible in the sourcing study in order to minimize the problem of sample bias. It was felt that a reasonably representative sample of sherds from a site would in turn yield a more representative range of compositional variability in LCWW than would a biased sample.

Potential biases can be introduced into surface assemblages by non-random (i.e., "grab sample") surface collection strategies and the casual collection of surface sherds by the lay public. Grab samples are generally biased toward cultural and temporal diagnostics or anomalous appearing sherds which cannot be identified readily in the field. As a result, one would expect such samples to contain primarily those LCWW sherds which closely matched Colton's (1955) description, with perhaps a few odd specimens being included. There is therefore no assurance that the full range of compositional variability would be represented in the sample, particularly if such variability was not visible with the naked eye. Casual collection is heavily biased toward decorated wares and would result in the elimination of such ceramics from subsequent archaeological sampling. Such activity also would tend to narrow the range of mineralogical variability represented in the LCWW left behind on the site.

Excavated assemblages also can be biased toward diagnostics by the non-random collection and curation of sherds, although the biases are probably less severe than in the case of surveyed sites. Non-representative samples are a particular problem for excavations which were conducted prior to the introduction of random sampling procedures and the routine screening of fill in the 1960s. Many of the sites included in the core sample were excavated prior to this time. However, it was felt that such biases could at least be minimized by selecting sites in which all or most of the cultural features at the site had been excavated. Surveyed sites were avoided whenever possible in order to circumvent the potential interpretive problems of attempting to compare excavated and surface-collected ceramic assemblages which possessed different degrees and types of bias.

Juniper Terrace presented a problem in this regard because little excavation has been done in the Deadmans Wash area near where the site is located. As a result, only two smaller sites were selected from the area around Juniper Terrace, one of which had not been excavated, thus violating the seventh criterion. However, it was deemed more beneficial to have lower order sites whose assemblages could be compared to that of Juniper Terrace, instead of abiding strictly by the site selection criteria and thus precluding such comparison.

The possibility exists that not all of the smaller settlements were occupied contemporaneously with the corresponding center. It is difficult to narrow occupation periods down sufficiently in the absence of tree-ring dating to assure contemporaneity. Therefore, differences between sites in terms of the mineralogical or chemical composition of their LCWW assemblages would have to be interpreted in the light of possible changes in production source(s) or technology through time.

The Extended Sample

The distance decay study involved an extended site sample composed of the original 11 sites and an additional 29 sites. The additional sites were selected from published site reports, cultural resource management reports, and the site files at the Museum of Northern Arizona. The following criteria were employed in the selection process:

1. The site was occupied between ca. A.D. 1050 and 1250.
2. The site is located in the Little Colorado River drainage between the Grand Canyon and the Arizona/New Mexico border.
3. The site was a year-round habitation.
4. The site contained LCWW.
5. Ceramic frequencies were available in published site reports or archives.
6. The site was excavated.

Priority was given to excavated sites for the reasons discussed above. However, it was necessary to use surveyed sites from the Zuni River drainage and the Deadman's wash area in order to fill substantial gaps in the distance measurements and include sites from as many parts of the Little Colorado River drainage as possible. The only reported frequency data for Agate House in the Petrified Forest were based on surface collections, even though the site was excavated. Again, it was felt that a violation of the sixth criterion was preferable to employing a data set containing gaps in the distance increments which would adversely affect the statistical procedures of the distance decay analysis. The Chevelon sites were selected on the basis of those excavated sites which had large enough sherd collections for the design analysis.

The size of the geographic area needed for the extended sample resulted in a wide potential date range for site occupations. Hantman (1983) has demonstrated that the average occupation span of tree-ring dated sites in the plateau Southwest with less than 10 rooms is 34 years. Given the 200 year time span of the extended sample, it is highly unlikely that all 40 sites were occupied at the same time. Even if all the sites had associated absolute dates, it would have been impossible to find a large enough sample of sites dating within a 34 year period throughout such an extensive region. As a result, variation in the structure of the LCWW exchange system as revealed by the distance decay study must be interpreted in light of the potential for changes in inter-community exchange relationships through time.

It was not possible to select a random sample of sites since most of the available sites meeting the criteria had to be used in order to have a sufficiently large sample. Neither can it be demonstrated that the extended site sample is representative of the regional production-distribution system of LCWW. The sample is simply the best that is available given the excavation projects which have been undertaken in the Little Colorado River drainage to date. It is possible that some areas which participated in the production and/or exchange of this ware are not adequately represented because they have not been subject to archaeological excavations. However, every effort was made to seek out all available sources of information at the Museum of Northern Arizona, Northern Arizona University, Arizona State University and the University of Arizona. The distance decay study was conducted under the assumption that the extended site sample is representative of the production-distribution system of LCWW. However, the possibility of bias in the site sample was taken into account both in the choice of statistical methods used and in the evaluation of the results.

The Design Analysis Sample

The site sample for the design analysis was composed of ten of the core sample sites from the Hopi Buttes and the San Francisco Peaks area (excluding the surveyed site, AR 03-04-02-2403, for which there was not a sufficiently large LCWW assemblage available), and six sites from the Chevelon area. This sample was used for an in-depth analysis of the stylistic composition of LCWW found in the two likely source areas, as well as an exchange locus in which this ware occurs in relatively large quantities. As discussed earlier, petrographic analysis of LCWW sherds from the Chevelon area revealed igneous rock inclusions which are not found in this area, indicating that this ware had to have been imported (S. Plog 1980a).

In addition, extensive sherd collections from these three areas were available for analysis. Sherds from the core sites were drawn from excavation collections at the Museum of Northern Arizona, as was done for the petrographic analysis. The Chevelon sherds were obtained from the CARP collection housed in the Department of Anthropology at Arizona State University.

Limitations of a Case Study Approach

LCWW has been selected as a case study for examining the organization of production and exchange systems of ceramics in the plateau Southwest prior to the thirteenth century A.D. It must be kept in mind that this ware is only one of many commodities which were being exchanged between ca. A.D. 1050 and 1250. Certain limitations of a case study approach must be considered when evaluating the results of the present research.

First of all, it is difficult to generalize from one particular production-distribution system to another. Different goods circulating during the same period of time, even in the same area, could have been manufactured via different modes of production. In addition, contemporaneous distribution systems may have been characterized by distinct structures, functions and mechanisms of exchange (Pires-Ferreira and Flannery 1976).

It is also necessary to use caution when employing cultural evolutionary schemes such as Service's (1971) or Fried's (1967). One should therefore avoid assigning such typological rubrics as "redistribution" or "reciprocity" in a simplistic manner which colors the way in which one views the parts of the system which are not directly observable through the case study in question. Once such a label has been applied to a particular system of exchange, it is tempting to assume that other goods and types of transactions operated in the same manner as the case study. It is conceivable that a society could have many types of exchange, depending on the type of good, the sociopolitical context of the transaction and/or the nature of the relationship between the participants (Price 1978, Hirth 1984).

Following this same line of reasoning, it is equally undesirable to reconstruct political organization directly from a particular type of exchange system without independent evidence, as would be the case if one assumed that a redistributive exchange network had to have operated in the context of a chiefdom. Such a procedure could also become tautological if one used the proposed economic/political link to argue for a developmental relationship between regional exchange and sociopolitical organization.

Finally, one should avoid generalizing from one particular culture, settlement system or region to another. Contemporary cultural systems did not necessarily develop at the same pace or through the same set of developmental stages. As a consequence, developmental relationships between political organization and regional exchange may have differed. For example, Drennan and Nowack (1984) have pointed out that there was little sociopolitical change in the Tehuacan Valley in Mexico during the Early and Middle Formative when there was open interaction beyond the valley, particularly with Oaxaca. Instead, the most rapid change occurred during the Late and Terminal Formative when the Tehuacan Valley was relatively isolated from the outside. This pattern is in direct contrast to evidence from other parts of Mesoamerica, such as the Valleys of Mexico and Oaxaca, where sociopolitical development and regional exchange occurred conterminously (Blanton et al. 1979, 1982; Blanton and Feinman 1984, Charlton 1984, Santley 1984).

Despite these limitations, LCWW, once better understood, can serve as a point of comparison for investigating other exchange goods. The conclusions drawn from this study can be used as a guide for constructing hypotheses and corresponding test implications concerning the operation of other production-distribution systems. The current project is only one of many studies which need to be conducted on the development of exchange networks in the pre-thirteenth century prehistoric plateau Southwest.

The following three chapters will deal with each of the stated goals of the research design in turn. Finally, the results of the three phases of research will be summarized and their implications concerning the nature of pre-thirteenth century exchange, as it impacts the developmental model, will be discussed.

CHAPTER VI

THE GEOGRAPHIC CONTEXT OF LITTLE COLORADO WHITE WARE PRODUCTION

The first goal of the present research is to determine the degree of geographic centralization in the production system of LCWW. In order to accomplish this goal, it is necessary to establish first whether LCWW was produced in more than one locus. Second, the production locus/loci must be provenienced as precisely as possible. Finally, the potential size of each production locus must be determined, based on the geographic extent of the geologic deposits from which the constituents of this ware were derived. Ultimately, the size and provenience of the source area(s) will shed light on the degree of community-level specialization of LCWW production. That is, it will be possible to determine whether any single community could have controlled access to the raw materials, and thus monopolized the production of this ware, given the spatial extent and location of the necessary resources.

I hypothesized in the previous chapter that the production system involved several communities within the San Francisco Peaks area and/or the Hopi Buttes based on the relatively high frequencies of LCWW found in these two areas. The precision with which the location and size of the raw material source(s) can be ascertained is dependent upon the sensitivity of the sourcing techniques to mineralogical variability and the actual degree of such variability in the raw material sources themselves.

A basic assumption underlying the sourcing study is that LCWW vessels were exchanged, rather than the raw materials from which they were produced. Not only is this a necessary operating assumption in any ceramic sourcing study (Shepard 1936, 1942), but there is supportive ethnographic evidence to lend it credence. Arnold (1981) performed a survey of 85 ethnographic cultures in which 82% obtained clay from 7km away or less and 96% obtained tempering material at a maximum distance of 8km. Thus, in the greater majority of ethnographic cases for which raw material procurement data are available, raw clays and temper are locally procured. This practice seems reasonable for prehistoric plateau southwestern potters as well, given the ubiquity in this region of both clay and non-plastic raw materials which are suitable for temper.

As also mentioned in Chapter IV, the research design does not include a determination of the mode of LCWW production. Establishing whether production was carried out by part-time household potters, full-time individual specialists or full-time workshop industries (van der Leeuw 1977) at the intrasite level is beyond the scope of the present research. Distinguishing between different types of productive units would require detailed intrasite analyses. Data on intra-site variability in mineralogical and stylistic attributes of this ware (such as types of design elements, their composition and articulation with one another) would be necessary, as well as the identification of activity areas connected with the production of ceramics.

These data are not available for the site sample utilized in this research. Many of the sites were excavated before the advent of statistically oriented artifact sampling strategies and the routine testing of extramural areas in which ceramic production could have taken place. Ethnographic studies have documented outdoor ceramic building, drying and/or firing for many parts of the world in which ceramic production is a household task, such as the Southwest (Lambert 1966, Harlow 1973), the Great Plains (Newman 1955), Mesoamerica (Reina and Hill 1978, Coe and Diehl 1980), South America (Litto 1976), Africa (Nicholson 1929, David and Henning 1972) and the Philippines (Longacre 1981). If LCWW had been produced in an analogous fashion, the lack of data on extramural areas would preclude locating evidence of its production.

Since this study is regional in scope, it focuses on inter-site interaction and thus emphasizes exchange over production. Sourcing LCWW is necessary in order to determine to where it was exchanged and in what quantities. Documenting the geographic context of this ware's production is therefore undertaken as a prerequisite to the second goal, and not as a means of fully reconstructing this ware's production system.

The sourcing study will be presented in this chapter. First, the geology of the two likely source areas, the Hopi Buttes and the San Francisco Peaks area, will be described. The distinctive mineralogy of their volcanic deposits will be emphasized since this bears directly on the possibility of distinguishing between ceramics produced in each area. This discussion will be followed by sections presenting the results of the petrographic analysis, x-ray diffraction and microprobe analysis respectively. Finally, conclusions will be drawn concerning the source area(s) of LCWW. David Schaller performed the compositional analyses. The sections on regional geology, petrographic methodology, the qualitative assessment of the petrographic analysis, x-ray diffraction and electron microprobe analysis have been abstracted from Schaller (1987).

Geology of the Potential Source Areas

The geology of the two potential source areas, the Hopi Buttes and San Francisco Peaks area, is quite distinct with respect to the types of sedimentary and volcanic rocks present in each. Since the two areas are situated on opposite sides of the Little Colorado River drainage, sand deposits formed by the weathering of the rocks from each area are not found together, except along the river. As a result, it should be possible to determine which of the two areas was producing LCWW by examining the petrology and mineralogy of sherds. If both areas prove to be production sources for this ware, it also should be possible to distinguish between the remains of vessels made in either area.

The sedimentary rocks occurring in the San Francisco Peaks area are predominantly from the Permian Kaibab and the Triassic Moenkopi Formations. The Kaibab Formation is made up of silty dolomite and dolomite sandstone. Minor sandstone and dolomitic limestone occur in lesser quantities (Ulrich et al. 1984). The Moenkopi Formation consists of mudstone, siltstone, silty sandstone and sandstone. The sedimentary rocks present in the Hopi Buttes area are composed of several Triassic, Jurassic, Cretaceous and Tertiary formations listed in Table 3.

Many of the sedimentary rocks on the Colorado Plateaus contain deposits of clay (Patterson 1969). The Moenkopi Formation is the major source of clay located in the San Francisco Peaks area. The Chinle Formation is the largest source of clay on the Colorado Plateaus. It outcrops in a continuous band between the San Francisco Peaks area and the Hopi Buttes. The Bidahochi Formation is a major source of clay in the southwestern portion of the Hopi Buttes, where the sites used in this study are located.

Table 3. Mesozoic Rock Units in Northeastern Arizona.

TERTIARY
Bidahochi Formation
Upper Member
Lower Member: calcareous mudstone, siltstone, sandstone and volcanic ash

CRETACEOUS
Mesa Verde Group
Yale Point Sandstone
Wepo Formation
Toreva Formation
Mancos Shale: claystone and siltstone
Dakota Sandstone: sandstone, conglomeratic sandstone and conglomerate

Morrison Formation
Brushy Basin Member
Westwater Canyon Member
Recapture Member
Salt Wash Member
Cow Springs Sandstone

JURASSIC
San Rafael Group
Bluff Sandstone
Summerville Formation
Todilto Limestone
Entrada Sandstone: siltstone and sandstone
Carmel Formation: siltstone and sandstone

TRIASSIC?
Navajo Sandstone
Kayenta Formation: mudstone, siltstone and silty sandstone
Moenave Formation
Springdale Sandstone
Dinosaur Canyon Member: sandstone and silty sandstone

TRIASSIC
Windgate Sandstone
Lukachukai Member: sandstone
Rock Point Member: siltstone and mudstone

Table 3. Mesozoic Rock Units in Northeastern Arizona (continued).

TRIASSIC (continued)
Chinle Formation
Owl Rock Member: interbedded limestone and calcarous siltstone
Petrified Forest Member: claystone, siltstone, and minor sandstone
Sandstone and Siltstone Member
Monitor Butte Member
Mesa Redondo Member
Shinarump Member: sandstone and conglomerate
Moenkopi Formation

Note: This table was adapted from Wilson 1974. Hopi Buttes formations are shown in *italics*.

Although illite, montmorillonite and kaolinite are present in most of the sedimentary rocks in both areas, the relative proportions of each vary significantly between geologic formations (Schultz 1963). Moenkopi Formation clay is predominantly illite, although kaolinite and clorite also occur in much smaller quantities. The Shinarump Member of the Chinle Formation (refer to Table 3), which outcrops parallel to the east bank of the Little Colorado River, is dominated by kaolinite. This member usually has considerable amounts of sand mixed in with the clay, making it less suitable for ceramic production than some of the other clay deposits in the area. The Petrified Forest Member of the Chinle Formation is almost pure montmorillonite. According to Shepard (1980), montmorillonitic clays characteristically suffer from severe shrinkage upon drying and firing. Therefore, they cannot be used in their pure form for ceramic manufacture. Little has been published concerning the composition of the clay deposits in the Bidahochi Formation. However, it has been mined for commercial sources of clay in the recent past. The commercial deposits contain abundant amounts of calcium-rich montmorillonite (Kiersch and Keller 1955). Clays associated with the formations which outcrop on Montezuma's Chair and Round Top (i.e., the Kayenta Formation, Entrada Sandstone, the Carmel Formation, Dakota Sandstone and Mancos Shale) will not be discussed here since it seems unlikely that prehistoric potters would have taken the trouble to climb the buttes when abundant clay sources lay within easier reach.

The volcanic rocks of the Hopi Buttes and San Francisco volcanic field are very distinct petrographically from one another. The San Francisco volcanic field is characterized primarily by basaltic cinder cones with associated lava flows. O'Leary Peak is the only silicic volcanic deposit in the area (Moore et al. 1974). In contrast, the Hopi Buttes volcanic field is dominated by lava-capped mesas and the chimney-like volcanic necks from which it has derived its name (Williams 1936).

Schaller (1987:3) describes the petrology of the San Francisco volcanics, based on Moore et al. (1974):

> Olivine occurs in all of the basaltic rocks in the form of groundmass grains and is also common as phenocrysts. . .The presence of euhedral [having a perfect crystal form] plagioclase grains in the groundmass distinguishes San Francisco Peaks basaltic rocks from those of the Hopi Buttes. Phenocrysts of plagioclase also occur in all of the San Francisco Peaks volcanics. . .Pyroxene is also very common as both a groundmass phase and as phenocrysts. . .The alkali-rich high-alumina basalts and basaltic andesites contain pigeonite or orthopyroxene in addition to augite. Opaque phases present in the basaltic rocks include ilmenite and titaniferous magnetite. The basaltic andesites also contain a silica mineral, probably cristobalite, as a late crystallizing phase. The mineralogical assemblage of the rhyodacite found at O'Leary Peak includes sanidine, plagioclase, amphibole, biotite, quartz and orthopyroxene.

The volcanic rocks in the Hopi Buttes are predominantly basalts which differ in their texture and chemical composition from the San Francisco volcanic field basalts. They have a distinctively porphyritic texture (that is, having large crystal inclusions set in a fine-grained matrix) and chemically are classified as alkalic lamprophyres. One of the most distinctive characteristics of the Hopi Buttes volcanic rocks is the predominance of augite phenocrysts (Williams 1936). The modal abundance of augite in the basalts usually ranges between 5 and 10 percent. However, since these phenocrysts are more resistant to weathering than the volcanic matrix in which they are found, many of the sand deposits in washes in the area contain much larger amounts of augite crystals. In some washes, the concentration of augite crystals is so high that the sand appears black. The augite crystals are a pale brown to green color in thin section and are typically fresh and unaltered.

Many of the volcanic rocks also contain altered olivine phenocrysts. Another distinctive feature of the Hopi Buttes volcanics is the scarcity of hornblende, biotite and feldspar. Feldspar, when it does occur, is in the form of small sanidine crystals.

The unique groundmass texture of the rocks in the Hopi Buttes volcanic field makes possible the identification of volcanic rock fragments from this area. The groundmass consists of a randomly oriented aggregate of augite, granular titaniferous magnetite, and acicular apatite. Figure 4 illustrates the differences between the Hopi Buttes and San Francisco volcanic rock textures.

The sand-sized portion of mineral inclusions are the most diagnostic for proveniencing a ceramic ware's production source. Sand deposits provide a mineralogical cross-section of the area from which they have been extracted, since they are formed by the weathering of indigenous geologic formations. Since the formations in the San Francisco Peaks area and the Hopi Buttes are so distinct from one another, it follows that the sand deposits from these two areas would also be quite different. In turn, the sand-sized mineral grains used as temper by prehistoric potters in the two areas should be distinguishable from

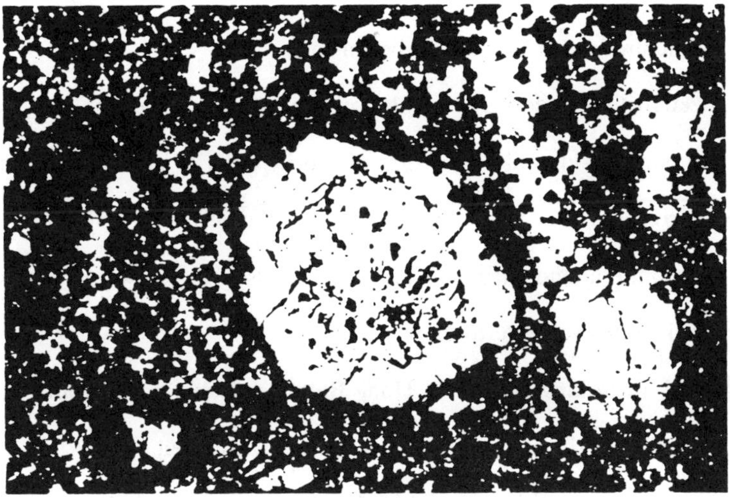

a. Hopi Buttes volcanic rock.

b. San Francisco volcanic rock.

Figure 4. Photomicrographs of volcanic rocks from the two potential production areas under plain polarized light.

one another. Therefore, certain expectations concerning the sand-sized inclusions in ceramics manufactured in each area can be set forth.

Sand-sized inclusions derived from the volcanic cinders of the San Francisco Volcanic field would contain considerable quantities of blocky laths of plagioclase feldspar in the groundmass of volcanic rock fragments. Olivine, orthopyroxene, amphibole, biotite and quartz would be quite abundant in San Francisco sands. Augites would be less abundant than in the Hopi Buttes volcanic rocks.

Sand-sized inclusions from the Hopi Buttes volcanic field would contain rock fragments with the distinctive groundmass texture discussed above. They would be characterized by large quantities of augite with lesser amounts of olivine, orthopyroxene, amphibole, biotite and quartz than the San Francisco sands. To summarize, sand-sized particles from the two potential source areas should be distinguishable because of the distinctive groundmass texture of the volcanic rock fragments incorporated in them. In addition, the San Francisco volcanics contain predominantly feldspars while the Hopi Buttes volcanics contain mostly augites.

Petrographic Analysis

The primary purpose of the petrographic analysis is to identify the mineral inclusions of LCWW sherds collected from the Hopi Buttes and San Francisco Peaks core sites. First, the petrographic data are compared to the mineralogy of the geologic deposits in the two areas in question in order to establish if one or both of them were production sources for this ware. Second, a quantitative analysis is used to compare the mineralogical inclusions of sherds found in the two potential source areas to each other in order to determine whether or not they came from distinct sources.

Petrographic analysis is an essential first step in any ceramic sourcing study, whether or not it is the only technique to be employed. Much information can be gained by observing thin sections of sherds in addition to the identification of mineral inclusions. The shapes, sizes and distributions of non-plastic inclusions can be noted, as well as characteristics of the clay matrix itself such as texture and porosity. All of these factors can be used to identify the geologic source more accurately (Williams and Jenkins 1976; Shepard 1980; Lemoine et al. 1982). In addition, basic information concerning mineralogical composition provided by petrographic analysis is often essential in relating chemical data derived from such compositional techniques as neutron activation analysis back to particular inclusions within the ceramic (Arnold 1981).

Methodology

A total of 269 LCWW sherds were selected for the petrographic analysis from the core site sample. Refer to Table 4 for a listing of the sites and their individual sherd sample sizes. Ideally, an equal number of bowl and jar sherds were to be selected from each design style present in the LCWW assemblage of each site in the core sample. However, it was not possible to carry out this sampling procedure in every case due to the fact that some styles were only present in bowl or jar form, or because one of the forms was under-represented among the sherds which met the necessary size and shape criteria.

Table 4. Petrographic Sample Sizes from the Core Sites.

Core Site	Area	Sample Size
Winona Village	S.F.[a]	30
NA 10,779	S.F.	20
NA 10,803	S.F.	21
NA 7432	S.F.	19
Juniper Terrace	S.F.	30
NA 680	S.F.	20
AR 03-04-02-2403	S.F.	18
Plaza Site	H.B.[b]	50
NA 9183	H.B.	19
NA 10,757	H.B.	22
NA 7806	H.B.	20

[a] San Francisco Peaks Area
[b] Hopi Buttes Area

The petrographic sherd sample was not collected in a statistically random fashion because of the restrictions placed on sherd selection by the requirements of thin sectioning. Minimally, the sherds had to be $6.5cm^2$ (2.5cm x 2.5cm) so that they could be sliced and cut down to the proper size for mounting on a slide. Sherds less than approximately 3mm thick are too susceptible to breakage during the slicing procedure and were consequently excluded whenever possible. The sherds also had to be relatively flat in order to produce a thin section with enough surface area. In some cases, these strictures were relaxed when more satisfactory examples of a particular style and/or vessel form were not available. However, they resulted in inferior quality thin sections (e.g., ones which were too small or of uneven thickness) in some cases. Finally, only sherds with identifiable design elements were chosen in order that they could be classified stylistically with a reasonable degree of confidence.

Although it was not possible to randomly select sherds for the petrographic sample, a conscious effort was made to collect the most representative sample in terms of style, vessel form and compositional attributes such as paste color, texture and temper types. Therefore, it was assumed for the purposes of the sourcing study that this sample is representative of the range of variability in the mineral composition of LCWW found in the Hopi Buttes and San Francisco Peaks area.

The thin sections were cut from slices parallel to the surface of the sherds, rather than employing the more common practice of cutting slices parallel to their cross section. This procedure was undertaken in order to maximize the surface area from which point counts were to be taken. In addition, it minimized the effects of weathering processes which may have altered the mineralogy of the interior and exterior surfaces of the sherds. The sherds slices were reinforced by vacuum impregnation with clear epoxy before being ground into thin sections. The thin sections were prepared and mounted onto glass slides by commercial petrographic laboratories.

Polarized-light microscopy was used to characterize the mineralogy and petrology of the 269 LCWW sherds used in the compositional study. The petrographic analysis was performed with a Zeiss Large Universal petrographic microscope equipped with a Zeiss mechanical stage using a magnification of 100x.

Point counting was performed on all of the thin sections in order to obtain a quantitative measure of the modal abundance of the non-plastic inclusions in the LCWW sherds (Glagolev 1934; Chayes 1956). During this procedure, the mechanical stage is moved at a fixed interval and each grain which falls under the cross hairs of the microscope is identified and tallied. The mechanical stage is moved in this fashion until the predetermined point count total is reached. A random sample of the types of constituents present in the thin section is obtained in this manner, assuming that the thin section is representative of the ceramic vessel from which it came. It must be kept in mind, however, that not all of the types of constituents present in the thin section will be tallied since rare and relatively small grains are less likely to be encountered under the cross hairs. The thin sections were scanned visually for such constituents after the point counting was completed since rare elements are often diagnostic with respect to the geologic source of a sample.

The point count scanning interval was set at 1.0mm horizontally and vertically. The point count traverse was made with the horizontal interval set at 0.5mm in a few cases where the small size of a particular thin section made it impossible to obtain the necessary total number of point counts with the 1.0mm interval. This modification was made only in those cases where the original size of the sherd prevented the preparation of a standard size thin section between 10 and 11cm^2. The scanning interval should be larger than the largest grain size in the sample in order to obtain the best results, according to Van Der Plas and

Tobi (1965). Grains in excess of 1.0mm are quite rare in LCWW. Therefore, this criterion has been satisfied in the present analysis.

A total of 300 point counts were made for each of the 269 thin sections. This figure was chosen as the best compromise between achieving an accurate quantitative measure of the mineralogical composition of the thin sections on the one hand and operating within a reasonable time frame on the other. For example, the accuracy of 300 point counts is not much greater than the accuracy achieved with 500 point counts (Van Der Plas and Tobi 1965:Figure 1). Therefore, the additional time invested in counting more than 300 points per thin section becomes a matter of diminishing returns.

The point count data for the 269 thin sections are listed in Appendix B. Pore spaces and unidentifiable grains which were encountered under the cross hairs were not counted as part of the 300 point count total. However, their presence was recorded. It is often difficult to distinguish between true pores and cavities which have been induced artificially by the removal of a grain during sample preparation. However, secondary minerals were found lining the walls of many of the pores which were counted, suggesting that the recorded porosity is very close to the true porosity of the samples.

Grains with diameters smaller than 0.06mm were defined as matrix for the purposes of the point counting. This arbitrary value corresponds to the division between sand and silt on the Wentworth (1922) scale. It is usually impossible to identify minerals smaller than this size. Grains were assigned to the following constituent categories during the point counting: clay matrix, quartz, sherd temper, albite-twinned feldspar, cross-twinned feldspar, untwinned/ other feldspar, volcanic rock fragments, ferromagnesium minerals, opaque minerals, cryptocrystalline quartz, and secondary or other unidentified minerals.

In many cases, the color and/or texture of the sherd temper very closely resembled the surrounding clay matrix. As a consequence, some sherd grains may have been identified erroneously as clay matrix. However, use of the substage condenser on the Zeiss microscope resulted in a discernible contrast between sherd temper grains and the background matrix which minimized such errors. Some sandstone fragments may have been misidentified as sherd temper, but this is probably a small source of error since sherds generally contain more clay matrix than sandstone.

Monocrystalline and polycrystalline quartz were not counted as separate categories. Assigning quartz grains to one or the other category was made very difficult by their small size. Arbitrary assignments would have to have been made in many cases, which could have biased the point count data. The greater majority of the quartz grains in this ware do appear to be monocrystalline, however.

Grains were defined as quartz if they appeared colorless under the crossed polars and did not exhibit the cleavage or cloudy brown color which is characteristic of slightly altered feldspar. Orthoclase (an unaltered, untwinned form of feldspar) in particular may have been confused with quartz. However, a concerted effort was made to apply consistent, objective criteria for classifying grains as either quartz or feldspar. All of the rock fragments observed in the thinsections appeared to be basalts. Ferromagnesium grains were identified by their bright first or low second order interference colors under the crossed polars. Grains which appeared opaque under plane polarized light were tallied under the opaque category.

Chalcedony, opal and all other varieties of cryptocrystalline quartz make up the tenth category. Secondary minerals found lining pores in the clay matrix, alteration products (either found separately or acting as cement between mineral grains, as in the case of sandstone) and unidentifiable minerals were subsumed under the secondary mineral category.

Such rare minerals as zircon, tourmaline, rutile and epidote were identified in only a few samples. However, their small size and scarcity precluded their being included in the point counting. As is almost always the case in petrographic analysis, some grains were unidentifiable, either because they had been altered drastically or because of some imperfection in a thin section. Unidentified grains were noted on the tally sheet but were not included in the 300 point total.

Qualitative Assessment

The petrographic analysis has shown that LCWW is remarkably uniform with respect to its mineralogy and the structural relationships of its various constituents, which indicates that this ware was made in a single geologically uniform region. In addition, the mineralogy of the sand-sized inclusions in LCWW closely matches the mineral composition of the geologic formations in the Hopi Buttes area. This section will present conclusive evidence that the Hopi Buttes was the sole production source of LCWW.

Both the average grain size and the amount of sand-sized grains display a wide range of variability from one specimen to another. However, the relative abundance of the different types of inclusions are relatively constant throughout the entire petrographic sample. In decreasing order of abundance, the sand-sized grains present in LCWW are quartz, crushed sherds, feldspar, chert, volcanic rock fragments, augite and opaque oxide minerals.

The sherd temper ranges in size from 0.2 to 2.5mm, although it usually does not exceed 0.7mm in diameter. Most of the sherd fragments are subangular to subrounded, which is expected since they were crushed mechanically (cf. Powers' 1953 roundness terms). In a few rare instances, slip is visible on a grain of sherd temper as a contrasting layer along one edge of its cross section. Therefore, at least some decorated wares were used as temper in LCWW.

Quartz is the most abundant non-plastic inclusion present in LCWW. Quartz grains are usually subangular to subrounded, although angular and rounded grains are also present. Most of the quartz grains are between 0.1 and 0.3mm in diameter. Some are as large as 1.2mm, but they rarely exceed 0.5mm in diameter. The size range of the quartz grains suggests that most of the sand was extracted out of stream beds, and that the potters were selecting for the coarser deposits. Monocrystalline quartz is by far more common than polycrystalline aggregates.

Quartz could have been incorporated into this ware via three separate processes. First, a small amount of quartz was probably already present in the clay. Second, a significant proportion of the quartz could have been derived from the sherd temper since many of the sherd grains have quartz temper in them (Figure 5a). Much of this quartz temper would have broken free during the process of grinding up the sherds. Finally, quartz is so abundant in many specimens that it appears to have been added deliberately as temper. Sherd temper is present in the greater majority of these specimens as well. In a few rare instances, specimens which match the definitional criteria of LCWW in every other respect lack sherd temper altogether and are tempered with quartz-rich sand instead (Figure 5b).

The major types of feldspar present in LCWW are orthoclase (untwinned), plagioclase (albite-twinned) and microcline (cross-twinned). The feldspar grains are comparable in size to the quartz grains, although they can be as large as 1.0mm in diameter. The most common grain shape is subrounded with low sphericity. The orthoclase and plagioclase grains tend to be altering to clay, while the micro-cline is relatively unaltered (Figure 6a). These size, shape and alteration characteristics match those of feldspars found in sandstone deposits, indicating that the feldspars in LCWW probably originated from weathering sandstone which found its way into local washes.

A few microcrystalline quartz grains are present. They appear to be composed primarily of detrital chert and are comparable in size to the rest of the sand temper. The chert grains are usually of moderate sphericity and are subrounded. Opaque grains are relatively rare and generally are no larger than 0.1mm in size. All the opaques appear to be iron-titanium oxide minerals, mostly magnetite, based upon the examination of several uncovered thin sections under reflected light. Opaque oxides are widely distributed in many different types of geologic deposits and are therefore not diagnostic for the purposes of sourcing LCWW.

The pyroxene grains and basaltic rock fragments are the most diagnostic in terms of proveniencing the production source of LCWW because they vary from one geologic deposit

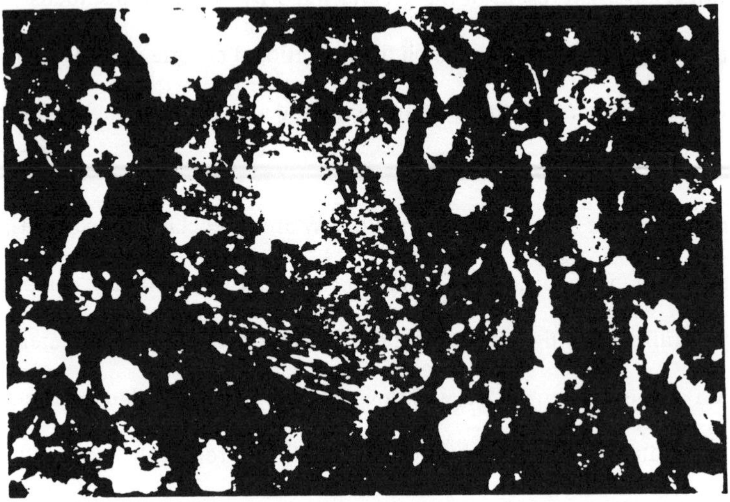

a. Quartz grains inside sherd temper (PPL).

b. Quartz grains without sherd temper (XPL).

Figure 5. Photomicrographs of LCWW sherds in plain polarized light (PPL) and cross polarized light (XPL).

to another, unlike quartz and feldspar which are widely distributed. No orthopyroxene has been observed in the petrographic sample, while orthopyroxene is commonly found in the San Francisco volcanic deposits. The pyroxene grains present are of the clinopyroxene variety. Their optical properties suggest that they are augite (Figure 6b), although this identification had to be confirmed by using the electron microprobe to determine their chemical composition. (Refer to the results of the electron microprobe analysis below.)

The ratio of augite to volcanic rock fragments in the thin sections closely matches the ratio found in Hopi Buttes sand deposits. The augite grains are generally between 0.5 and 1.0mm in diameter, making them distinctly larger than the average quartz or feldspar grain. Since augite is much less resistant to erosion than quartz, the size differential would indicate that the augite is entering stream deposits from a different source than the quartz. The augite crystals are typically subrounded to angular and of moderate to low sphericity. Indications of alteration, particularly oxidation, are almost completely absent. Hopi Buttes augites are characteristically unaltered, whereas San Francisco augites are typically quite altered and have opaque oxide rims. The crystals in the petrographic sample are usually unzoned like Hopi Buttes augites, although some zoned crystals are present. Some thin sections lack augite. However, its absence in a particular thin section does not necessarily indicate that the vessel from which the thin section originated was not produced in the Hopi Buttes, due to the generally very small abundances of augite across the sherd sample.

All of the volcanic rock fragments found in LCWW appear to be basalts (Figure 7a). They display a distinctively uniform groundmass texture, suggesting that they all originated from the same volcanic field. All of the phenocrysts are pyroxene. The groundmass is made

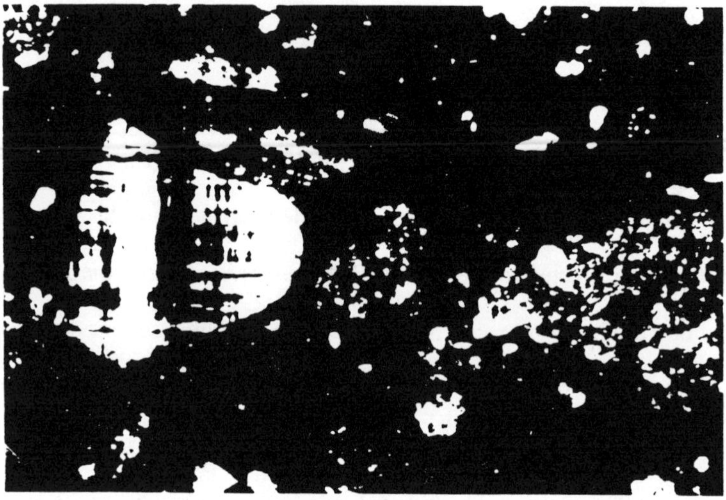

a. Unaltered microcline.

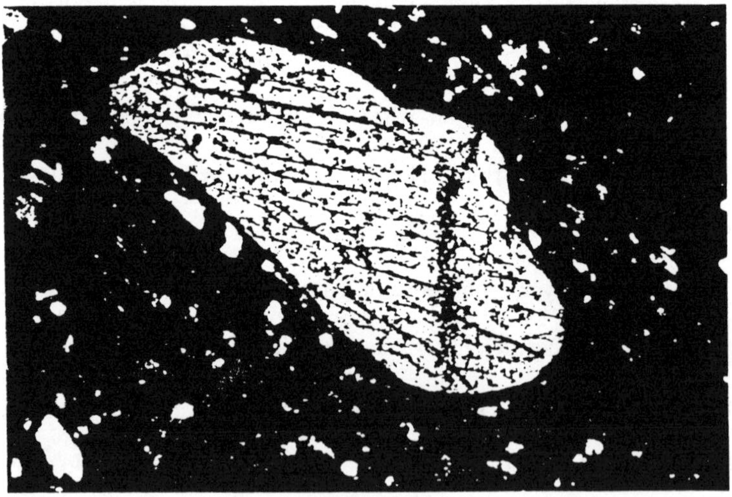

b. Augite crystal.

Figure 6. Photomicrographs of LCWW sherds in cross polarized light.

up of an interwoven aggregate of pyroxene, granular opaque grains, acicular apatite and analcime which is identical to the distinctive texture of the Hopi Buttes volcanics. Significantly, none of the volcanic rock fragments in the LCWW thin sections contain plagioclase feldspar, one of the distinguishing characteristics of the San Francisco volcanic field.

Many of the pore spaces are lined with secondary minerals, probably mostly clays, which also can be found in discrete masses in the matrix. Several specimens have discrete clots of secondary minerals associated with relatively coarse sand temper. These samples are 2133T.1, 2133T.4, 9400.17, 9400.37, 9400.38 and 9400.49. It appears as if the secondary minerals have formed around the sand grains, cementing them together in a manner which resembles sandstone (Figure 7b). However, there is a very high abundance of the yellow matrix relative to the encased sand grains. In addition, there is also a high abundance of what appears to be the yellow matrix in isolated clots without associated sand grains. These relationships are not characteristic of sandstone. The secondary minerals are probably due to post-depositional processes which are as yet undetermined. Therefore, these minerals are not diagnostic with respect to sourcing.

The heavy mineral suite found in LCWW is composed of zircon, biotite, tourmaline, garnet, rutile, epidote and hornblende. Zircon is the most abundant heavy mineral by far (Figure 8). A large proportion of the sand found in LCWW seems to have been derived from mature sandstones, based on the fact that the heavy mineral suite is dominated by stable minerals such as zircon, tourmaline and rutile, and the relatively low ratio of feldspar to quartz (since feldspar weathers more readily than quartz).

a. Basalt fragment (PPL).

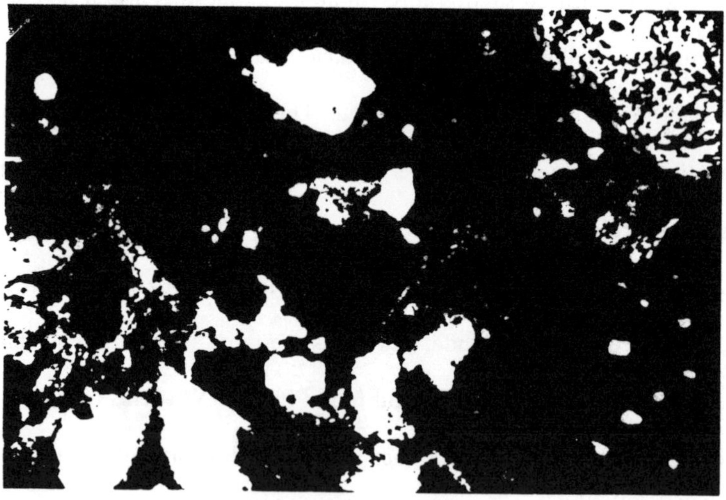

b. Secondary mineral (XPL).

Figure 7. Photomicrographs of LCWW sherds in plain polarized light (PPL) and cross polarized light (XPL).

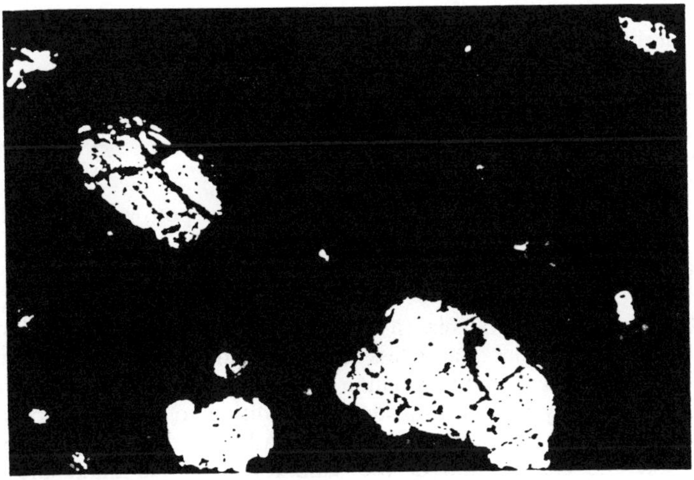

Figure 8. Photomicrograph of LCWW sherd with zircon in cross polarized light.

Biotite is extremely rare in the petrographic sample. The scarcity of biotite, together with the relative abundance of zircon and the size range of the quartz grains, suggests that the quartz in LCWW was probably derived from the Wingate Sandstone Formation. This sandstone is distinctive among the Colorado Plateaus sedimentary formations for its almost complete lack of biotite. In contrast, the Moenkopi Formation, which is the principal sedimentary formation in the San Francisco Peaks area, is characterized by much larger concentrations of biotite. No silicic volcanic rock fragments have been found which would tend to rule out the Chinle Formation as a source for the quartz and other sand-sized inclusions in LCWW.

There is a relatively wide range of textural diversity in LCWW, in contrast to its mineralogical uniformity. Textural variability is determined by the amount of quartz temper added by the prehistoric potters, the ratio of sherd temper to sand temper and the size of the temper grains. These variations are thus due to differences in production technology which can exist within a single production source.

On the basis of his qualitative assessment of the petrographic analysis, Schaller (1987:19) concludes:

> The sand-sized fraction of mineral grains present in the vast majority of the LCWW samples includes quartz, less abundant feldspar, and ultra stable heavy minerals such as zircon and tourmaline which were probably derived from the weathering of fairly mature sandstone in addition to pyroxene crystals and volcanic rock fragments derived from the weathering of volcanic rocks. This is precisely the composition of the sand found in the many dry washes traversing the Hopi Buttes area. Since this mineralogical assemblage is so distinctive, the petrographic evidence overwhelmingly supports the conclusion that the sand present in LCWW was originally obtained from the Hopi Buttes area.

Petrographic analyses of LCWW sherds found in other areas provide corroborative evidence for this conclusion. Warren (1969a; Schwartz et al. 1980:132) states that "[t]he physical properties of the Little Colorado White Ware pottery were so consistent that a source of limited geographic area must be assumed." She describes one type of inclusion as a "greenish black, vitreous, medium grained pyroxene" (Warren 1980:352) which closely matches the characteristics of the augite weathering out of volcanic rocks in the Hopi Buttes. Warren (1980:353) also states that mica (i.e., biotite) is rare in the Grand Canyon LCWW paste, as it is in the current sample, and mentions "occasional yellowish calcite fragments" which might be the same secondary minerals described above.

Garrett's petrographic analysis of LCWW from the Chevelon drainage yielded point count frequencies which are similar in certain constituent categories to those discussed in the following section (see S. Plog 1980a, Table 5.1). Some variability does exist between the point count data from the current analysis and Garrett's study. However, it is difficult to evaluate the significance of this variability because of the disparate sample sizes (Garrett only examined 18 LCWW sherds) and the potential differences in the classificatory criteria used by Garrett and Schaller. Nevertheless, Stephen Plog (1980a:68) points out that the presence of volcanic rock fragments in LCWW suggests that the Hopi Buttes is the production source, since both volcanic rock fragments and "pure" LCWW sites occur in this area.

Given the evidence from Warren's and Garrett's studies, as well as the uniform mineralogy and nature of the inclusions of LCWW examined in the current analysis, I have concluded that this ware was produced solely in the Hopi Buttes area. LCWW found elsewhere, including the San Francisco Peaks area, had to have reached its destination via direct transport from the Hopi Buttes, or indirectly through some form of exchange network. The statistical analysis of the point count data further substantiates this conclusion, as discussed in the following section.

Statistical Analysis

A quantitative analysis of the point count data was undertaken in order to measure the degree of mineralogical differences between the sherd samples from the Hopi Buttes and San Francisco Peaks area. The purpose of this analysis was to test the proposition that both samples came from the same production source. In addition, the statistical tests were used to determine if more than one production locus within the source area could be detected by differences in the mineralogy of the sherds in the petrographic sample. Several univariate and multivariate statistical procedures were used in order to make these comparisons.

The first step involved the use of basic exploratory techniques in order to determine the parameters and shapes of the frequency distributions for the point count data from the two areas in question. Descriptive statistics, frequency histograms and bivariate plots were generated using BMDP2D, 5D and 6D respectively. Descriptive statistics for all 11 constituent categories for the Hopi Buttes and San Francisco samples are listed separately in Table 5. Overall, they reveal a remarkable degree of similarity between the two areas. However, the descriptive statistics show that the San Francisco sample has larger standard deviations for all constituent categories, except for volcanic rock. In addition, this sample has wider ranges of values for all categories except twinned feldspar and volcanic rock. These differences probably are due in large part to the greater size of the San Francisco sample.

The histograms also show a great deal of similarity in the frequency distributions of all 11 mineral categories between the two areas. The greater ranges of values for the San Francisco sample are reflected in maximum outliers for the quartz, sherd, untwinned feldspar, opaques and cryptocrystalline quartz categories. This sample also possesses a greater concentration of matrix values in the lower range than does the Hopi Buttes sample. Again, the greater number of outliers in the San Francisco sample is due in large part to

Table 5. Descriptive Statistics (in Percentages) for the Eleven Constituent Categories from the Hopi Buttes (H.B.) and San Francisco (S.F.) Samples.

Category	H.B. Mean	H.B. S.D.[a]	H.B. Min.[b]	H.B. Max.[c]	S.F. Mean	S.F. S.D.	S.F. Min.	S.F. Max.
Clay Matrix	88.6662	5.1007	72.0	98.3	86.9146	5.8431	68.0	98.0
Quartz	5.3216	3.0187	0.3	16.3	5.9436	3.6846	0.7	23.3
Sherd Temper	4.2360	3.3085	0.0	13.3	5.2576	4.2426	0.0	20.3
Untwinned Feldspar	0.5513	0.8532	0.0	7.0	0.7766	1.2518	0.0	11.7
Secondary/ Other	0.8441	0.9080	0.0	4.3	0.6867	0.9858	0.0	5.3
Albite Twinned Feldspar	0.0937	0.1686	0.0	1.0	0.1114	0.2147	0.0	1.0
Cross Twinned Feldspar	0.0387	0.1287	0.0	1.0	0.0759	0.1923	0.0	1.3
Volcanic Rock	0.1288	0.3331	0.0	2.3	0.1203	0.2301	0.0	1.0
Ferro-magnesium	0.0613	0.1658	0.0	0.7	0.1127	0.2043	0.0	1.0
Opaques	0.0486	0.1413	0.0	0.7	0.0816	0.1692	0.0	1.0
Crypto. Quartz	0.1856	0.2760	0.0	1.0	0.2158	0.3563	0.0	2.0

[a] Standard Deviation
[b] Minimum Value
[c] Maximum Value

its greater sample size (since the larger the sample, the greater the probability of the occurrence of extreme values).

The categories can be divided into two groups, based on their frequency distributions. The first group contains categories with relatively continuous though non-normal distributions and the second group is composed of categories with discrete distributions. The matrix histograms (Figure 9) are illustrated as examples of the five continuous categories which also include sherd temper, quartz, untwinned feldspar and secondary/other minerals. The ferro-magnesium histograms (Figure 10) are representative of the balance of categories with more discrete distributions. The discrete distributions are a reflection of the fact that some of the constituents are present only in very minute quantities, resulting in a very few or no point counts per specimen. The distinction between discrete and continuous frequency distributions was used in the statistical comparisons of the point count data discussed below.

The final exploratory procedure involved generating 55 bivariate plots consisting of all possible combinations of the 11 constituent categories. Two representative bivariate plots are illustrated in Figure 11. None of the 55 bivariate plots display discrete clusters of the Hopi Buttes or San Francisco samples. Instead, the points from both samples tend to swarm together as a largely undifferentiated mass. One notable characteristic of all of the bivariate plots is that either the majority or all of the outlying points are from the San Francisco sample and thus match the observations made on the histograms. It is often difficult to identify outliers on the plots of two discrete variables because of the generally

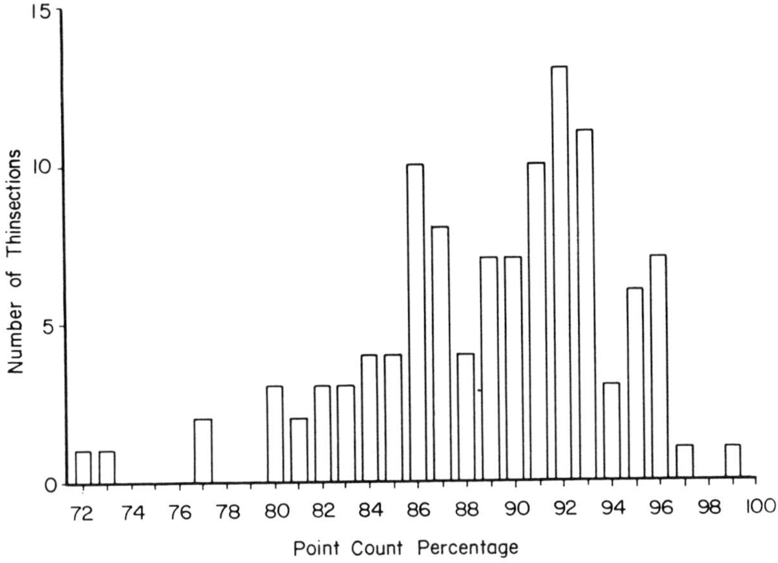

a. **Hopi Buttes sample.**

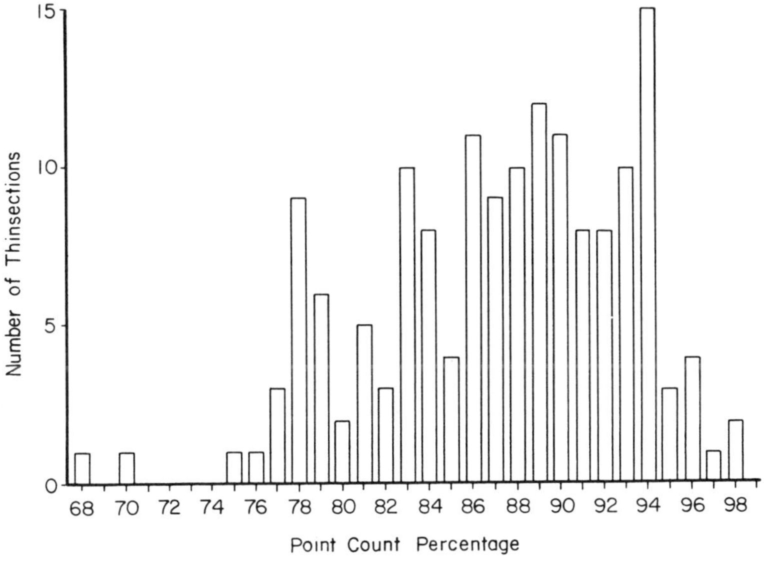

b. **San Francisco Peaks sample.**

Figure 9. Histograms of matrix percentages in the point count data.

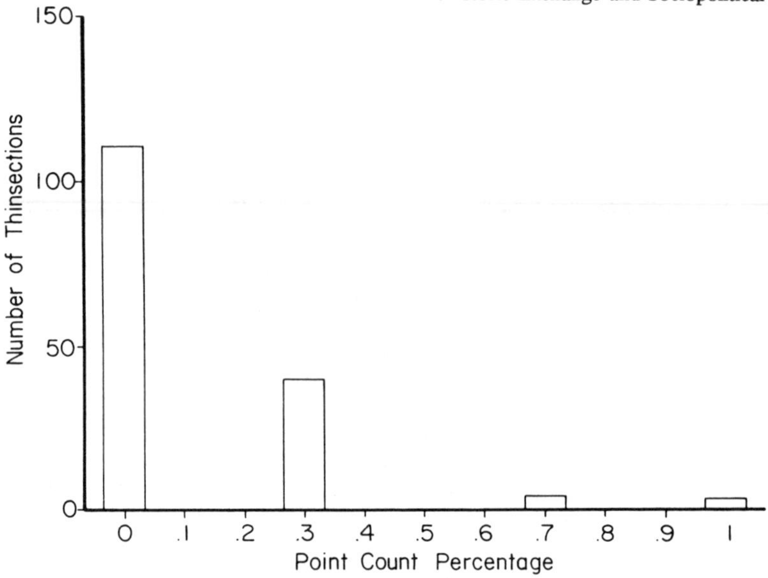

a. Hopi Buttes sample.

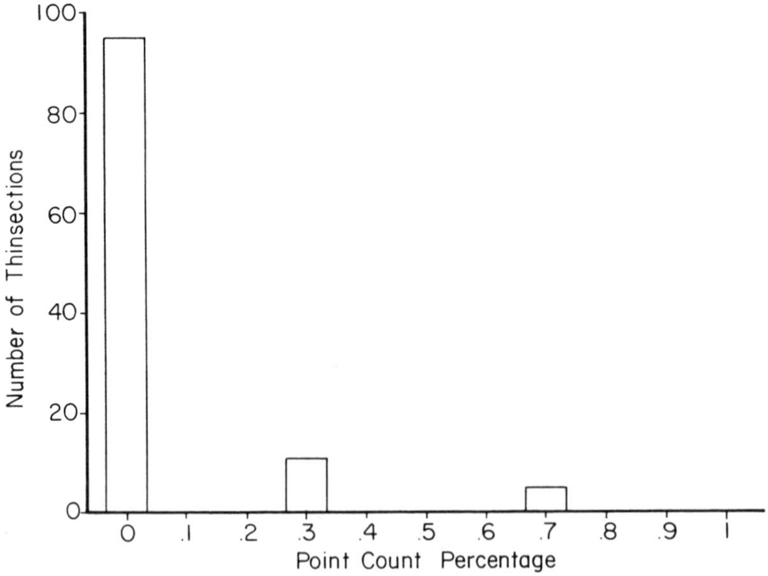

b. San Francisco Peaks sample.

Figure 10. Histograms of ferromagnesium percentages in the point count data.

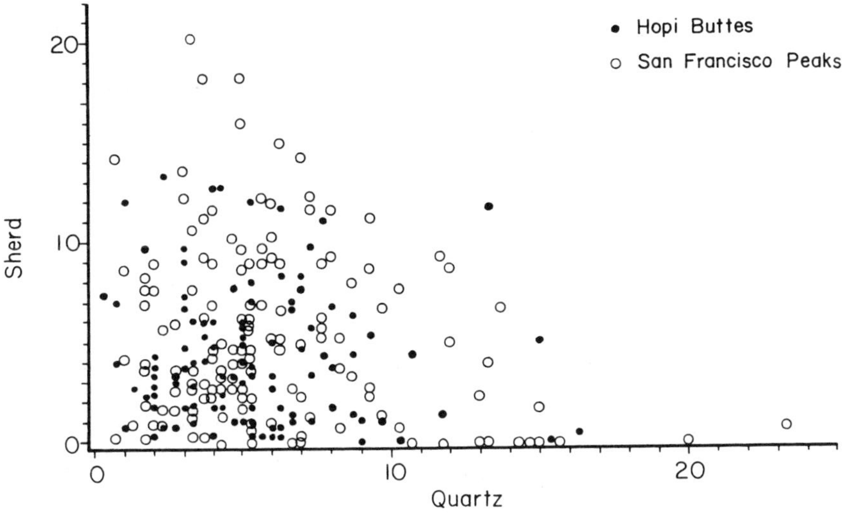

a. Quartz plotted against sherd temper.

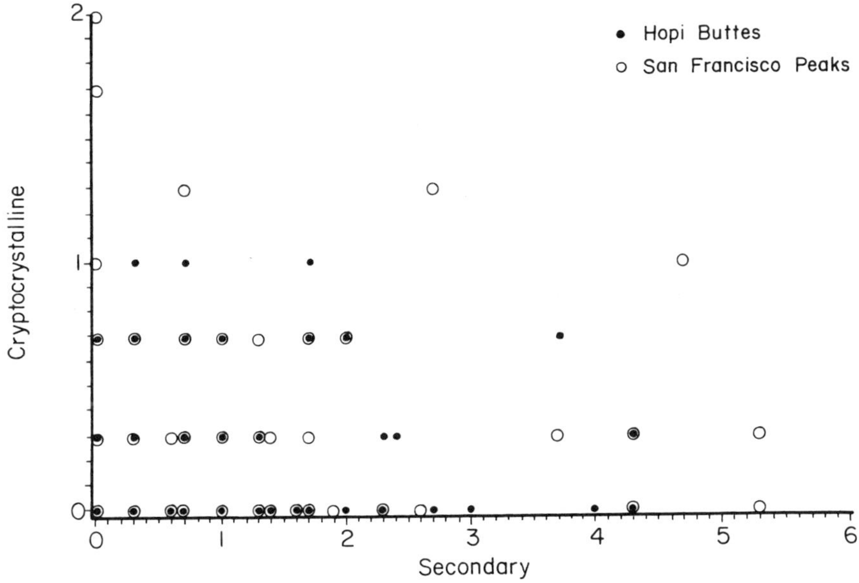

b. Secondary minerals plotted against cryptocrystalline quartz.

Figure 11. Bivariate plots of constituent percentages in the point count data.

scattered distribution of points. However, the extreme values on both axes on these types of bivariate plots are represented by San Francisco points in the great majority of cases.

To summarize, two general observations can be made from these descriptive procedures. First, the Hopi Buttes and San Francisco samples generally are quite similar to one another with respect to the parameters and shapes of the frequency distributions of the 11 types of constituents. This degree of similarity is to be expected if both samples originated from the same production source, as the qualitative assessment of the petrographic analysis has demonstrated. Second, the San Francisco sample generally exhibits a greater range of variability in the amounts of 10 out of the 11 types of constituents present in the thin sections. It has been argued that this characteristic is due mostly to its larger size.

Before reporting the results of the statistical analyses, it is necessary to discuss certain problems with the nature of the point count data which complicate both the use and interpretation of available two-sample tests. These data are decidedly non-normal, as can be seen by inspecting the histograms and bivariate plots illustrated in Figures 9 through 11. The interpretation of parametric tests becomes somewhat questional under these circumstances.

In addition, the data are not really continuous since the percentages in each mineral category are derived from the number of counts out of a total of 300. The percentages therefore vary in increments of 0.33% (i.e., one point count out of 300). As a result, such non-parametric rank-order tests as Mann-Whitney are plagued by an excessive number of ties which equivocate their results. Some categories possess more continuous distributions than others, as discussed above, which causes difficulties when attempting to evaluate all the variables as a set using multivariate techniques.

Finally, the 11 categories are not independent of one another. The correlation matrices calculated by BMDP3D show high correlations between many of the categories in both samples. As a result, tests on individual categories are not independent of one another.

It was felt that the best way to address the interpretive problems presented by the characteristics of the data was to use a variety of statistical tests. If most or all of these procedures yielded comparable results, which were also in line with observations made on the basis of the descriptive analyses discussed above, then it was felt that more confidence could be placed in the results of the statistical analysis.

The constituent categories were divided into two groups consisting of the more continuous categories on the one hand, and clearly discrete categories on the other. The continuous categories were subjected to a two-phase parametric statistical analysis. A multivariate approach, using both MANOVA and Hotelling's t^2, was pursued first since these variables possess high inter-correlations. In the event that a significant difference was found between the two samples with respect to the suite of continuous categories, univariate statistical tests (ANOVA and t-tests) would be used to determine which categories in particular were contributing to the difference. The discrete categories were subjected to chi-square analysis. It was felt that their distributions represented such extreme violations of the operating assumptions of both univariate and multivariate parametric techniques that the results of such tests would be affected adversely.

The results of the multivariate analyses are summarized in Table 6. A MANOVA was used to compare the two samples with respect to the means of the continuous categories using the PROC GLM procedure in the SAS statistical package. As Table 6 shows, it detected significant differences ($p \leq .05$) between the Hopi Buttes and San Francisco samples using several multivariate statistics (SAS Institute 1985:12; see also Pillai 1960). The multivariate t-test, Hotelling's t^2, (Dixon 1985:98) was performed on the four continuous categories using BMDP3D. It also detected a significant difference ($p \leq .05$) between the two samples.

Table 6. Results of Multivariate Statistical Analyses on the Five Continuous Categories from the Hopi Buttes and San Francisco Petrographic Samples.

MANOVA					
Wilks' Lambda	Pillai's Trace	Hotelling-Lawley Trace	Roy's Maximum Root	F(5,263)	P Value
0.9558	0.0442	0.0463	0.0463	2.43	0.0353

Hotelling's t^2	F(5,263)	P Value
12.3497	2.4329	0.0354

Univariate statistical analyses were undertaken on the continuous variables in order to determine why the multivariate tests had rejected the null hypothesis of equal means for the two area samples. Following the Bonferroni method (Nemenyi et al. 1977:518), the significance level of the univariate t-tests on the continuous categories were reduced to about .01 in order to maintain an approximate overall probability of .05. The results of the univariate tests are summarized in Table 7. Both the t-tests and ANOVA isolated significant differences at the appropriate level in the means of the clay matrix category. None of the other four categories proved to have significant differences in means at the .01 level. The discrete category percentages were converted into presence/absence data (zeros being recoded as "absent" and values greater than zero being recoded as "present"). This was deemed justifiable because of the overall small relative frequencies and the small ranges of non-zero values for all six of the discrete categories. The recoded data were used in a series of chi-square tests conducted by BMDP4F.

The p values on the individual discrete category tests would need to be reduced to 0.5/6, according to the Bonferroni method, in order to maintain an overall significance level of .05. However, this procedure results in an excessively small probability. Since the Bonferroni method is regarded as a conservative estimation of individual error probability, the more reasonable level of .01 was employed once again. It must be kept in mind, however, that it is extremely difficult to assess the effects of the inter-correlations between the categories on the overall p value. The chi-square tests show that the Hopi Buttes sample has significantly lower proportions of thin sections with ferromagnesium than the San Francisco sample. However, the qualitative evaluation has shown that the type of ferromagnesium present is constant across the entire petrographic sample. Therefore, this difference does not indicate more than one source for LCWW.

To summarize the statistical comparisons of the Hopi Buttes and San Francisco samples, their results are consistent with one another, at least with respect to the continuous variables. Both multivariate tests showed significant differences between the two samples

Table 7. Results of Univariate Statistical Comparisons of the Eleven Constituent Categories from the Hopi Buttes and San Francisco Petrographic Samples.

Category	Chi-Square	P Value	t-Test[a]	P Value	ANOVA F(1,267)	P Value
Clay Matrix	--	--	*2.55*	*0.01*	*6.49*	*0.01*
Quartz	--	--	-1.47	0.14	2.15	0.14
Sherd Temper	--	--	-2.12	0.03	4.51	0.03
Untwinned Feldspar	--	--	-1.65	0.10	2.71	0.10
Secondary/ Other	--	--	1.33	0.18	1.77	0.18
Albite Twinned Feldspar	0.060	0.8070	--	--	--	--
Cross Twinned Feldspar	2.872	0.0901	--	--	--	--
Volcanic Rock	0.858	0.3542	--	--	--	--
Ferro-magnesium	*8.546*	*0.0035*	--	--	--	--
Opaques	4.954	0.0260	--	--	--	--
Crypto. Quartz	0.156	0.6925	--	--	--	--

Note: Singificant statistics ($p \leq .01$) appear in *italics*.
[a] Pooled variances were used due to unequal variances between the area samples.

with respect to the five continuous categories. These results presumably reflect the significant differences in the proportions of the clay matrix which was isolated by the ANOVA and univariate t-tests. In addition, the sherd category showed a significant difference in means of the two samples in the univariate t-tests and ANOVA at the .02 and .03 levels respectively. Although these significance levels are too large according to the Bonferroni method, differences in the sherd temper means probably contributed to the results of the multivariate tests.

The results of any one of the tests on the continuous categories could be called into question because of the problems discussed above. However, the fact that they agree with one another supports the conclusion that they are detecting statistically significant differences between the mineralogical contents of the two petrographic samples. Unfortunately, the results of the chi-square tests cannot be compared to those of another univariate two-sample test because the frequency distributions of these data do not lend themselves well to other types of statistical analysis.

Despite the consistency of the results, some caution must be exercised against an overly mechanical approach to the interpretation of all of the comparative statistical tests. An important interpretive issue which must be considered is the amount of difference between the means of all 11 constituent categories in the Hopi Buttes and San Francisco samples as compared to the range of measurement error which is inherent in the point counting methodology. In other words, are the differences between the means of the constituent categories greater or lesser than the range of variability in the frequencies that would be derived by point counting the same thin section over several times? In turn, do the results of the statistics reflect meaningful differences between the LCWW found in the two areas, or are they the product of random measurement error?

Table 8 compares the differences in the means for all 11 constituent categories for the samples from the two areas to the appropriate measurement error. The error value was calculated using Van Der Plas' and Tobi's (1965:87) measure of standard deviation which takes into account the total number of point counts made per specimen and the actual proportion of the constituent in a thin section:

$$\sigma = \sqrt{\frac{p(100\text{-}p)}{n}}$$

where: p = the actual concentration of a mineral in percent by volume
n = the total number of points counted

In this case, the greater of the means from the two samples was used as the actual proportion of each constituent category in order to calculate the smallest possible measurement error.

These figures show that all the differences between the sample means are less than the corresponding measurement error, even when the smaller measurement error is used as a point of comparison. As a result, the differences between the Hopi Buttes and San Francisco samples could be due simply to measurement error, rather than to real differences in the raw material deposits used to manufacture the vessels from which the sample sherds originated. In this light, the statistically significant differences between the proportions of constituents in the two samples do not appear to be due to variability in the mineralogical makeup of the raw material deposits from which the ceramics were manufactured.

Table 8. Area Sample Means, Differences Between the Sample Means and Error Measurements for the Eleven Constituent Categories.

Category	Hopi Buttes Mean	San Fran. Mean	Diff. in Means	Measurement Error
Clay Matrix	88.6662	86.9146	1.7516	1.8761
Quartz	5.3216	5.9436	0.6220	1.3604
Sherd Temper	4.2360	5.2576	1.0216	1.2876
Untwinned Feldspar	0.5513	0.7766	0.2253	0.5047
Secondary/ Other	0.8441	0.6867	0.1574	0.5269
Albite Twinned Feldspar	0.0937	0.1114	0.0177	0.1914
Cross Twinned Feldspar	0.0387	0.0759	0.0372	0.1527
Volcanic Rock	0.1288	0.1203	0.0085	0.1999
Ferro-magnesium	0.0613	0.1127	0.0514	0.1914
Opaques	0.0486	0.0816	0.0330	0.1632
Crypto-crystalline Quartz	0.1856	0.2158	0.0302	0.2643

Note: The measurement error was calculated using Van Der Plas' and Tobi's (1965:87) measure of standard deviation for point count data.

However, it is possible that the relatively small differences in constituent mean proportions as compared to the associated error measurements are a result of the way in which the samples were divided. The San Francisco sample actually contains LCWW sherds from two groups of settlements which are geographically separated from one another: the Winona Village group located in the southeast portion of the San Francisco Peaks area, and the Juniper Terrace group situated in the northern portion of this area. The Hopi Buttes sample, on the other hand, is composed of LCWW sherds from a single group of settlements associated with the Plaza site. Greater differences in the mean proportions between these three settlement groups may have been obscured by combining the two San Francisco groups into a single sample. The greater ranges of values and standard deviations for most of the 11 constituent categories in the San Francisco sample noted earlier support this hypothesis.

Table 9 lists the differences between constituent means for the three possible pairs of settlement groups and the corresponding measurement error for each of the eleven constituent categories. Again, the largest of the three settlement group means was used in Van Der Plas' and Tobi's (1965) formula to provide the smallest possible margin of error. As the table shows, some of the differences between the constituent means are greater than they were in the case of the two area-wide samples, while other differences have been reduced. Interestingly, however, none of differences in means for the Plaza Site/Juniper Terrace comparison exceed their measurement errors. In contrast, both the Plaza Site/Winona and Winona/Juniper Terrace comparisons have differences in the clay matrix

Table 9. Differences Between the Settlement Group Sample Means and Error Measurements for the Eleven Constituents Categories.

Category	Plaza/ Winona	Plaza/ Juniper	Winona/ Juniper	Measurement Error
Clay Matrix	*2.6655*	0.5415	*2.1240*	1.8761
Quartz	0.8595	0.3078	0.5517	1.3902
Sherd Temper	*1.9573*	0.2169	*2.1742*	1.3913
Untwinned Feldspar	0.0943	0.3987	0.3044	0.5601
Secondary/ Other	0.2419	0.0456	0.1963	0.5269
Albite Twinned Feldspar	0.0096	0.0284	0.0188	0.1999
Cross Twinned Feldspar	0.0369	0.0378	0.0009	0.1527
Volcanic Rock	0.0168	0.0420	0.0588	0.2159
Ferro-magnesium	0.0498	0.0534	0.0036	0.1914
Opaques	0.0192	0.0514	0.0322	0.1825
Crypto-crystalline Quartz	0.0023	0.0732	0.0755	0.2883

Note: The measurement error was calculated using Van Der Plas' and Tobi's (1965:87) measure of standard deviation for point count data. The largest of the three settlement cluster means was used as the actual proportion of the constituent to calculate each error value. Mean differences greater than the corresponding measurement error appear in *italics*.

and sherd temper means which are greater than the corresponding measurement error figures.

The same set of multivariate and univariate statistical tests were used to compare the relative frequencies of the 11 constituent categories from the three settlement groups. The MANOVA once again revealed a statistically significant overall difference in the continuous category means. Pair-wise comparisons using Hotelling's t^2 showed significant differences between the Plaza Site and Winona settlement groups as well as the Juniper Terrace and Winona settlement groups. However, no significant difference was found between the Juniper Terrace and Plaza Site settlement groups. (Refer to Table 10.)

The results of the chi-square and ANOVA tests are comparable to the same tests performed on the two aerial samples, as can be seen in Table 11. The univariate t-tests showed significant differences in the clay matrix and sherd temper categories between the same settlement group pairs which had been isolated as being significantly different by Hotelling's t^2 (as shown in Table 12). However, the Winona and Juniper Terrace sherd temper categories were found to be significant at only the .02 level which is not sufficient to meet the criterion of the Bonferroni method. Nevertheless, these results clearly parallel the observations made concerning the relationship between the differences in constituent means and their corresponding measurement errors.

Two observations can be made from the results of the statistical analyses of the settlement group samples. First, the Plaza Site and Juniper Terrace samples seem to be more like one another than either one is to the Winona sample. Second, the statistically significant differences between settlement groups are in categories which are directly

Table 10. Results of Multivariate Statistical Analyses on the Five Continuous Categories from the Three Settlement Groups.

MANOVA

Wilks' Lambda	F(10,524)	P Value	Pillai's Trace	F(10,526)	P Value
0.8809	3.43	0.0002	0.1214	3.40	0.0003

Hotelling-Lawley Trace	F(10,522)	P Value	Roy's Max. Root	F(5,263)	P Value
0.1326	3.46	0.0002	0.181	5.69	Upper Bound

PAIR-WISE COMPARISONS

Plaza/Winona Hotelling's t^2	F(5,195)	P Value
24.1628	4.7354	0.0004

Plaza/Juniper Hotelling's t^2	F(5,173)	P Value
5.5790	1.0906	0.3674

Winona/Juniper Hotelling's t^2	F(5,152)	P Value
18.6107	3.6267	0.0040

Table 11. Results of Chi-Square and ANOVA Comparisons of the Constituent Categories by Settlement Group.

Category	Square	P Value	Chi- F(2,266)	ANOVA P Value
Clay Matrix	--	--	*6.19*	*0.0023*
Quartz	--	--	1.58	0.2085
Sherd Temper	--	--	*8.68*	*0.0002*
Untwinned Feldspar	--	--	2.84	0.0599
Secondary/ Other	--	--	1.71	0.1828
Albite Twinned Feldspar	0.1710	0.9180	--	--
Cross Twinned Feldspar	3.3330	0.1889	--	--
Volcanic Rock	2.3650	0.3065	--	--
Ferro-magnesium	*8.6310*	*0.0134*	--	--
Opaques	6.5440	0.0379	--	--
Crypto-crystalline Quartz	2.8700	0.2382	--	--

Note: Significant statistics ($p \leq .01$) appear in *italics*.

Table 12. Results of T-Tests on Pairwise Comparisons of the Five Continuous Categories by Settlement Group.

Category	Plaza/ Winona t-Test[a]	P Value	Plaza/ Juniper t-Test[a]	P Value	Winona/ Juniper t-Test[a]	P Value
Clay Matrix	*3.42*	*0.0008*	0.67	0.5046	-2.29	0.0232
Quartz	-1.79	0.0755	-0.62	0.5356	0.93	0.3530
Sherd Temper	*-3.40*	*0.0008*	0.44	0.6569	*3.29*	*0.0012*
Untwinned Feldspar	-0.77	0.4398	-2.15	0.0327	-1.52	0.1305
Secondary/ Other	1.86	0.0649	0.31	0.7590	-1.24	0.2163

Note: Significant statistics ($p \leq .01$) appear in *italics*.
[a] Pooled variances were used due to unequal variances between the area samples.

influenced by techniques of clay preparation, namely clay matrix and sherd temper. It is suggested that both of these observations indicate a closer exchange tie between the Plaza Site and Juniper Terrace settlement groups. Winona Village and other settlements in the southeastern portion of the San Francisco Peaks area may have been obtaining their LCWW vessels from a production locus geographically removed form the Plaza Site settlements.

Alternatively, the differences between the settlement group samples may reflect temporal change in clay preparation methods. Some portions of Winona Village may have been occupied slightly earlier than the Plaza Site and Juniper Terrace settlement groups (refer to Appendix A). If the latter two are closer in age than either is to the Winona settlement group, then it is conceivable that the greater compositional similarity of their LCWW assemblages is due to the fact that the vessels stem from the same production technology. The Winona settlement group vessels may have been manufactured under a slightly earlier set of strictures. Comparisons of mineralogical to stylistic variability, which are presented in Chapter VII, indicate that the differences between the settlement groups' samples are due to changes in production technology through time.

The third possibility, namely that a vessel's mineralogical composition is a function of its slated use, was tested by comparing statistically the mineralogical compositions of bowls versus jars. Unfortunately, a more detailed classification of vessel form was not possible using the sherd data. No significant difference was found between bowls and jars by the multivariate or univariate tests on the continuous categories. The chi-square tests isolated only one significant difference between bowls and jars with respect to the discrete categories. Bowls were found to have significantly more secondary/other minerals than jars. However, these minerals seem to have been formed by postdepositional processes, for the most part, and thus are not related to the geologic source of bowl constituents.

It appears, therefore, that the differences in the clay matrix and sherd temper proportions between the Plaza Site and Juniper Terrace samples on the one hand and the Winona sample on the other are not due to compositional differences between bowls and jars. It is possible that the bowl/jar division is too gross to pick up differences in the constituents of different types of vessels. However, given the present evidence, there is no reason to suspect that vessel function predetermined clay preparation procedures.

To summarize, two major conclusions can be drawn from the results of the statistical analysis. First, the constituent category frequencies from the Hopi Buttes and San Francisco samples are statistically similar enough to conclude that LCWW found in both areas originated from the same production source. The mean frequencies for both areas fall within the range of the measurement error associated with the point counting methodology. Second, the Juniper Terrace settlement group is more similar to the Plaza site settlement group than it is to the Winona group, or than the latter is to the Plaza site group. The statistically significant differences in frequencies also fall outside the associated measurement errors. They occur primarily in constituent categories related to production technology, namely clay matrix and sherd temper, and do not pertain to sourcing diagnostics. Nor do the technological differences appear to be related to vessel function. Stylistic evidence to be discussed in Chapter VII indicate that the variability is temporal. The x-ray diffraction to be discussed in the following section was undertaken in order to further pin down the geographic limits of LCWW's production source.

X-ray Diffraction of Clays

X-ray diffraction is a complementary sourcing technique to petrographic analysis when it is used specifically to determine the mineralogical composition of the clay matrix, rather than the non-plastic inclusions in the ceramic. This goal is accomplished by segregating and aligning the clay particles on a glass slide before analysis, as described below in the methodology section. In the present study, x-ray diffraction provided a qualitative analysis of the mineral constituents of the clay in LCWW sherds. It also was used to compare LCWW sherds to raw and fired samples of clay deposits from the Hopi Buttes area where this ware was produced, as demonstrated by the petrographic analysis. The aim of such comparisons was to determine from which geologic deposit the LCWW clay was derived.

Methodology

The mineralogical compositions of clay samples were analyzed via x-ray powder diffraction. The samples can be divided into four types: raw clays collected from deposits in the Hopi Buttes, the same raw clays after having been fired at 850°C, selected LCWW sherds from the petrographic sample and an unfired sherd identified as LCWW on the basis of its mineralogy. Guidelines set forth by Brown and Brindly (1980) and Starkey et al. (1984) were followed during sample preparation.

Natural clays are highly plastic, fine-grained sediments. They are composed primarily of clay minerals but also contain smaller amounts of quartz, feldspar and other types of impurities. In order to better identify the clay mineral fraction of the samples, it was necessary to remove coarse non-clay minerals such as quartz and feldspar. The sherds had to be crushed in a ball mill prior to being disaggregated. Each sample was disaggregated by placing it in a beaker of deionized water and subjecting it to magnetic stirring followed by ultrasonic agitation. A small amount of sodium hexametaphosphate was added to the disaggregated solution in order to prevent the clay particles from agglomerating. Most of the coarse non-clay minerals were separated out of the solution by means of centrifugation.

The coarse fraction of the sample was then discarded and the remaining solution was centrifuged until the clay particles could be brought down out of suspension.

Most clay minerals have a platey structure and therefore can be made to take up what is referred to as a preferred orientation. Such an orientation is achieved when all the clay particles are aligned so that their long axes lie parallel to the surface of the slide. After the final centrifugation, a small quantity of the clay solution was smeared onto a glass petrographic slide. The platey clay particles thus took up a preferred orientation as the water evaporated, resulting in a thin clay film on the slide (cf. Gibbs 1965). The glass slide was placed directly into the x-ray diffractometer.

X-ray diffraction is based on the fact that each mineral has a unique crystalline structure made up of a three-dimensional lattice whose angle, orientation and spacing are distinct. As a result, each crystalline structure will diffract x-ray beams in a distinct pattern. If a mineral is rotated in the path of an x-ray beam of a given wavelength, it will reflect the beam at a specific angle θ. The geometry of the x-ray reflection is such that the x-ray beam must rotate through 2θ in order for a reflection to occur at θ. The x-ray diffractometer produces a strip chart with a pattern of peaks of different heights at certain values of 2θ. Both the strip chart and the x-ray beam move at constant speeds so that a given distance on the strip chart represents a given angle of 2θ (Dana 1959:146). Each value of θ can be used to calculate the spacing between the crystal lattice planes, which is referred to as the d-spacing, using the Bragg equation (Brown and Brindley 1980:319):

$$n\lambda = 2d \sin \theta$$

where: n = 1,2,3. . . (the order of reflection from successive lattice planes)
λ = the wavelength of the radiation
d = the distance between the successive lattice planes
θ = half the angle of rotation of the x-ray beam, at which reflection occurs.

The d-spacings and their characteristic intensities have been determined experimentally for most minerals. The d-spacings and associated intensity values derived from these studies are presented in tabular form in the Powder Diffraction File (PDF) which is published by the Joint Committee on Powder Diffraction Standards. The measured intensities are directly related to the concentration of a particular mineral in a sample which is composed of several minerals. As a result, it is possible to estimate relative abundances of the different minerals in such a sample by comparing the intensities of their d-spacings. The relative intensity of each d-spacing can be determined by the height of the peak at the corresponding 2θ value on the diffractogram.

Dr. Ann Yeats of the Chemistry Department at Arizona State University conducted the analyses using a Rigaku D-Max-II-B x-ray diffractometer with monochromatic copper radiation. The specific parameters used and the method for calibrating the machine are discussed in detail in Schaller (1987).

An additional sample preparation procedure was necessary for those samples found to contain montmorillonite and chlorite during initial x-ray diffraction analyses. The glycolation technique (Brunton 1955) was used on these samples because chlorite and montmorillonite have certain lattice planes which exhibit identical d-spacings. An oriented x-ray sample was placed in a sealed vessel above a bath of ethylene glycol which had been heated to 60°. After exposure to the glycol vapor for several hours, the d-spacing of the montmorillonite plane would expand, allowing it to be distinguished from the chlorite plane.

Clay Mineralogy

The crystalline structure of clay is largely destroyed or altered during the firing process, making the characterization of the clay mineralogy in ceramics via x-ray diffraction a difficult undertaking. However, such structural changes have been documented through the experimental firing of samples of known composition (Starkey et al. 1984). It is therefore possible to work backward from the fired specimen and reconstruct, at least in part, the mineralogy of the unfired clay. Alterations are dependent upon firing temperature, atmosphere and duration as well as the mineralogy of the original clay. Since LCWW is relatively uniform in color and hardness, the firing technology employed in its manufacture was probably uniform as well. Thus, it was assumed that the effects of firing could be held constant when evaluating the diffraction peaks for the fired LCWW samples.

Eight clay samples from outcrops within the Hopi Buttes area which could have served as raw material sources for LCWW paste were collected in the field. Samples were collected from outcrops which were located within reasonable walking distance of the Hopi Buttes sites included in the core site sample. In some cases, clays were collected from more distant outcrops in order to obtain samples from all the clay-bearing formations in the Hopi Buttes area, preferably from more than one locus within each formation.

Collections were made on the Navajo Reservation with the permission of the Bureau of Indian Affairs (Permit Number NAO ARPA-86-002) and the Navajo Tribe (Permit

Number 1986-4). Clay samples were collected from the Wingate Sandstone Formation, the Chinle Formation and the Lower Member of the Bidahochi Formation. A sample from the Moenkopi Formation in the San Francisco Peaks area also was obtained from the Museum of Northern Arizona. (Refer to Figure 12 for the collection loci). All the samples were x-ray diffracted in their raw state after undergoing processing as described above. The same samples were subsequently fired at 850°C and re-x-rayed in order to provide a direct comparison with the fired LCWW sherds.

The samples are listed, along with the formation from which they were derived and their mineral content, in Table 13. The clay mineral composition of the Moenkopi Formation, the Chinle Formation and the Lower Member of the Bidahochi Formation are quite distinct from one another (see Figure 13). As a result, it is possible to identify from which formation a clay sample was derived, even if its provenience is not known.

An unfired sherd was obtained from NA 10,757 which is probably the remains of a LCWW vessel in the process of manufacture. The sherd lacks the thick white slip and organic paint associated with this ware. However, it possesses the characteristic grey sherd temper. Part of the sherd was made into a petrographic thin section and examined microscopically. The thin section revealed a mineralogy and matrix texture which are typical of the LCWW sherds in the petrographic sample. Alfred E. Dittert (personal communication 1987) also examined the unfired sherd and agreed that it was probably slated to become LCWW. Therefore, for the purposes of the present study, this sherd has been classified as LCWW. The clay portion of the unfired sherd, as revealed by x-ray diffraction, consists of approximately equal amounts of montmorillonite and illite with a

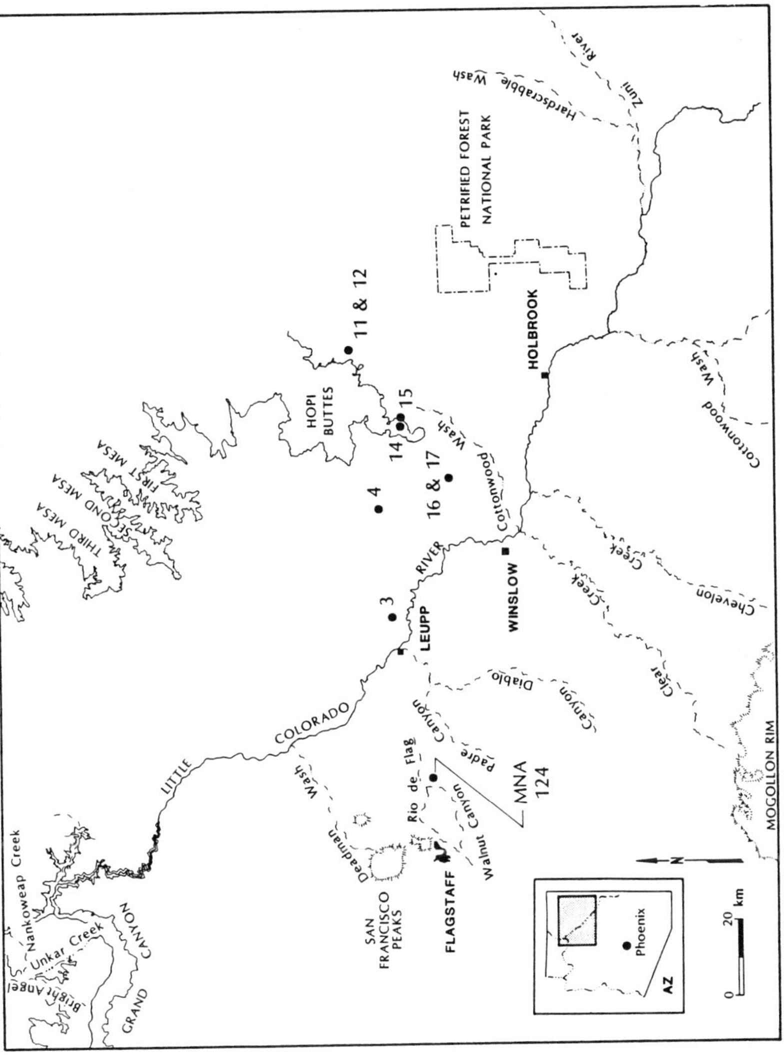

Figure 12. Location of collection points for clay samples analyzed by x-ray diffraction.

Table 13. Geologic Origin and Mineralogical Content of the Raw Clay Samples.

Sample Number	Geologic Unit	14Å	10Å	7Å
3	Shinarump Mem., Chinle Form.	26	16	58
4	Rock Point Mem., Wingate Sand.	60	36	4
11	Lower Mem., Bidahochi Form.	59	29	12
12	Lower Mem., Bidahochi Form.	46	34	20
14	Lower Mem., Bidahochi Form.	66	30	4
15	Lower Mem., Bidahochi Form.	45	45	10
16	Petrified Forest Mem., Chinle	100	0	0
17	Petrified Forest Mem., Chinle	86	14	0
MNA 124	Moenkopi Formation	24	50	26

Notes: Angstroms are the unit of measure for the d-spacing. Peak intensity values given are peak height multiplied by 100 and divided by (7Å+10Å+14Å). Thus, the given 7Å value is: (7Å)(100)/(7Å+10Å+14Å).

The 14Å peak corresponds to the [001] value of montmorillonite. The 10Å peak corresponds to the [001] value of illite. The 7Å peak corresponds to the [001] value of kaolinite.

The peak heights corresponding to the different clay minerals in a particular sample are not strictly comparable on a one-to-one basis for the purposes of determining the absolute concentration of each clay species (Starkey et al. 1984).

lesser abundance of kaolinite. On the basis of this analysis, Schaller (1987:26) concludes that "the unfired LCWW? sample may be unequivocally correlated with the Lower Member of the Bidahochi Formation." The striking similarity between the unfired sherd and Lower Member diffractograms is evident in Figure 14. Notably, an outcrop of the Bidahochi Formation exists less than 3km from NA 10,757. The unfired LCWW sherd is also the same buff color as the Bidahochi Formation in the immediate area of the site.

Five LCWW sherds from sites in the Hopi Buttes and San Francisco sites were selected from the petrographic sample. X-ray diffraction was performed on the whole sherds and was repeated after the sherds had been powdered and oriented. Both methods produced

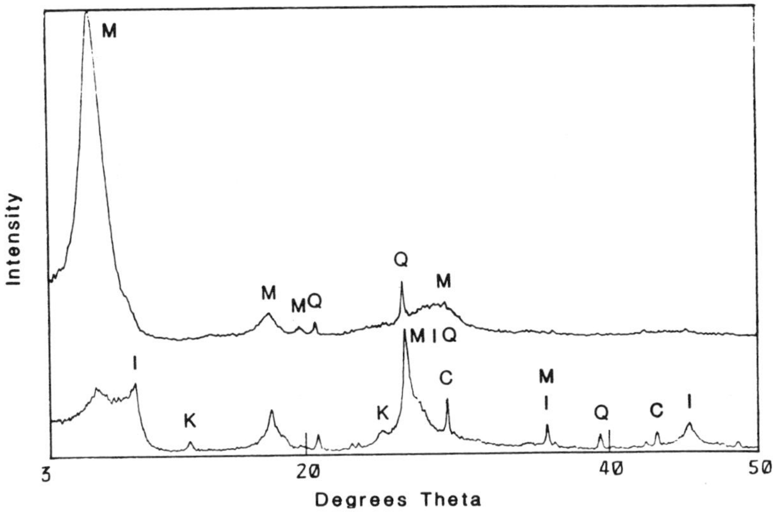

a. Petrified Forest Member, Chinle Formation (top) and Lower Member, Bidahochi Formation (bottom).

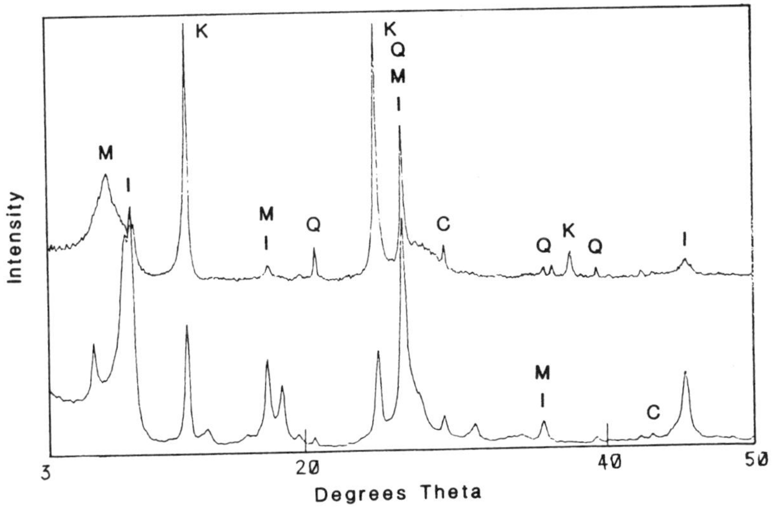

b. Shinarump Member, Chinle Formation (top) and the Moenkopi Formation (bottom).

Figure 13. X-ray diffractograms for raw clay samples. C: calcite; I: illite; K: kaolinite; M: montmorillonite; Q: quartz.

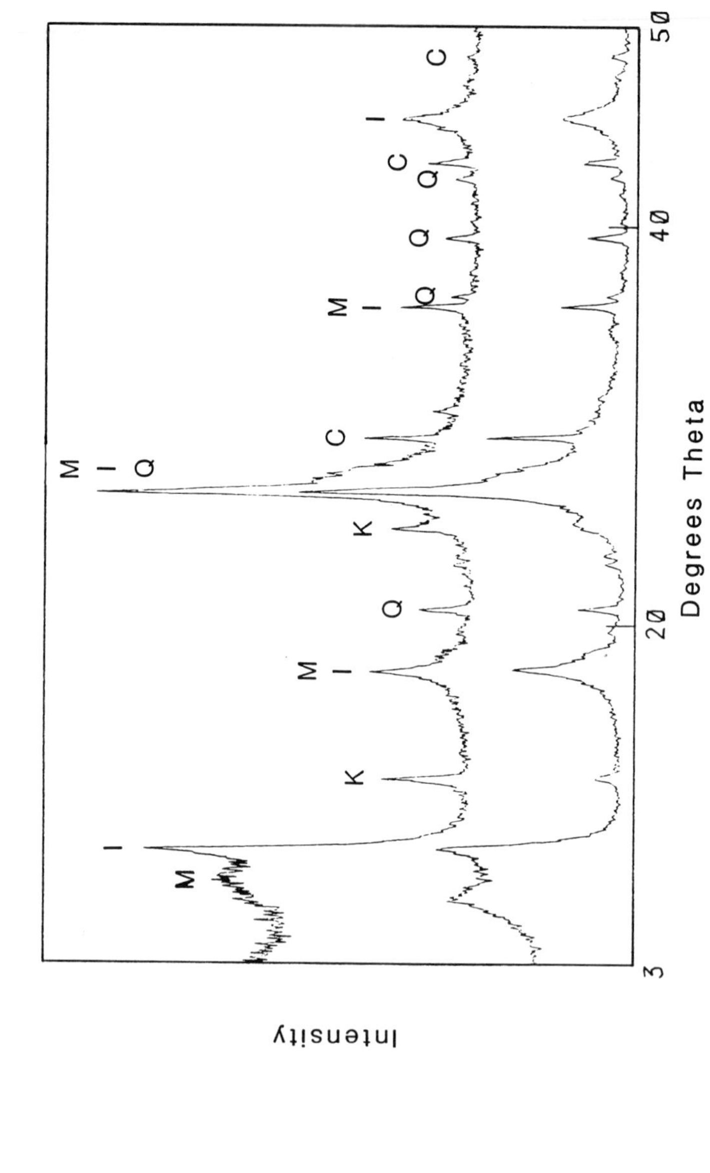

Figure 14. X-ray diffractograms for the unfired LCWW sherd (top) and a raw clay sample from the Lower Member of the Bidahochi Formation (bottom). C: calcite; I: illite; K: kaolinite; M: montmorillonite; Q: quartz.

relatively strong peaks for the non-clay minerals. However, the diminished clay peaks resulting from the firing of the sherds were better defined once the sherds had been processed.

The x-ray diffraction revealed similar clay mineralogies for all five specimens. A very attenuated peak corresponding to one of the illite and montmorillonite peaks is all that remains of the crystalline structure of the raw clay. The kaolinite peaks are absent altogether. This is to be expected since the crystalline structure of kaolinite is largely destroyed at 500 to 550°C (Brown and Brindley 1980:Table 5.8). Such alterations match the expected results of firing a clay which is a mixture of montmorillonite, illite and kaolinite (Starkey et al. 1984). Feldspar and pyroxene probably were formed during the firing process since they are absent from the raw clay and unfired sherd diffractograms. In addition, the feldspar and pyroxene peaks are higher than the quartz peaks in the diffractograms of the powdered sherds as compared to those obtained for the whole sherds. This observation suggests that the feldspar and pyroxene originated in the clay matrix rather than in the sand-sized temper fraction of the paste.

A portion of the unfired LCWW sherd had been set aside before the initial x-ray diffraction. It was fired to 900°C and x-ray diffracted. (Examination of the completed LCWW sherd diffractograms showed alterations in the mineralogy of the clay which suggested firing at this temperature.) Subsequently, the sherd was powdered, oriented and re-x-rayed. After firing, the diffractogram of the originally unfired LCWW sherd displayed shifts in the position and decreasing amplitudes of peaks corresponding to montmorillonite and illite. Kaolinite peaks were completely removed as a result of firing. Again, feldspar and pyroxene appear only after firing and appear to be within the clay matrix.

Significantly, the diffractogram of this powdered sample closely resembles those of the five LCWW sherds from completed vessels. These results strongly suggest that the original clay mineralogy of the five LCWW sherds was very similar to the unfired sherd. By extension, it is highly probable that the five LCWW sherds also contain clay derived from the Lower Member of the Bidahochi Formation. Figure 15 shows the diffractograms for the originally unfired LCWW sherd after firing, a LCWW sherd from a completed vessel and a fired Lower Member clay sample. The similarities in the peak patterns are readily apparent.

In summary, the results of the x-ray diffraction analysis of the clay samples and sherds point to the Bidahochi Formation as the clay source for LCWW. This conclusion is predicated on the fact that the unfired sherd is LCWW and that the clay used to produce this ware was derived from a single geologic formation. The similarities between the x-ray patterns of the fired Lower Member and sherd samples, together with the textural and mineralogical uniformity of LCWW, make this conclusion a reasonable one. In addition, the Bidahochi Formation would have been a good choice for two reasons. First, it is the highest grade clay for pottery manufacture in the Hopi Buttes area. Second, it would have been readily available to the prehistoric occupants of this area.

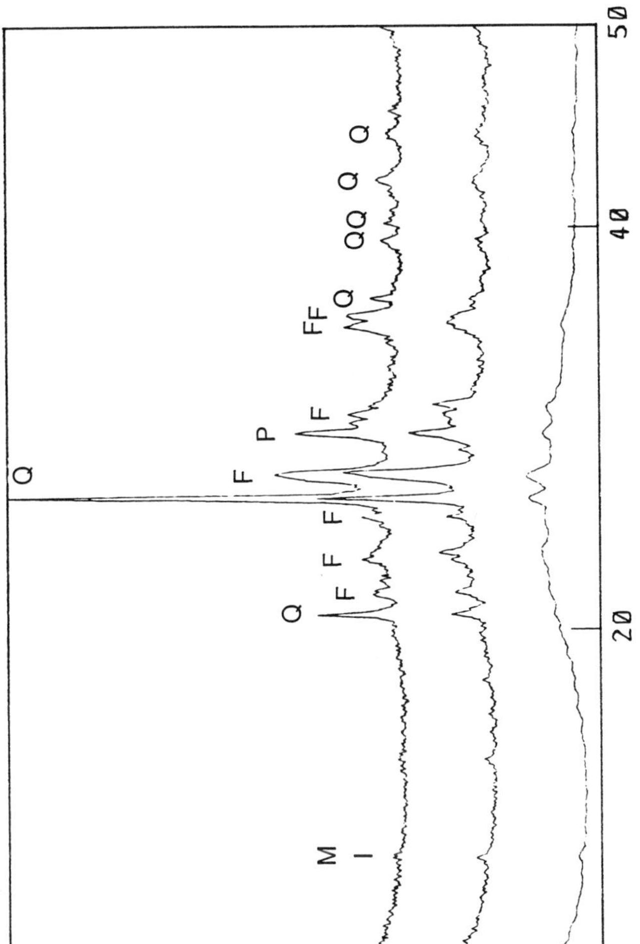

Figure 15. X-ray diffractograms for the unfired sherd after firing (top), a complete LCWW sherd (middle) and a fired sample from the Lower Member of the Bidahochi Formation (bottom). F: feldspar; I: illite; M: montmorillonite; P: pyroxene; Q: quartz.

Microprobe Analysis

One of the most distinctive characteristics of LCWW petrology is the abundance of augite in its sand-sized inclusions. Both the San Francisco and Hopi Buttes volcanic fields contain augite-bearing rocks. However, the volcanic rocks from these areas differ in their chemical composition. The San Francisco volcanics range between alkali-olivine basalts and rhyodacites. In contrast, the Hopi Buttes volcanics are alkalic lamprophyres. By extension, it is possible that the augite inclusions in these volcanics are also chemically distinct, particularly since augite can vary significantly in its chemical composition. Augite crystals within LCWW sherds as well as volcanic rocks from the San Francisco and Hopi Buttes volcanic fields were subjected to electron microprobe analysis in order to compare their chemical compositions.

Methodology

Chemical analysis employing the electron microprobe is based on the fact that x-rays are released when the electrons within an atom change the position of their orbits. Such transitions can be initiated, and x-rays can be generated, by bombarding the specimen with electrons having sufficient kinetic energy. The wavelengths of the emitted x-rays are dependent upon the atomic number of the bombarded atom, thus allowing for the identification of the chemical elements present in the sample. The intensities of each wavelength are compared to intensities from standard samples of known composition.

However, the intensity is not directly proportional to the concentration of the chemical element in the sample. Matrix corrections are used to convert the ratio of the standard intensities into actual concentrations. These corrections are dependent upon various factors such as the absorption of emitted x-rays, background radiation and the loss of x-ray intensity caused by the backscattering of incident electrons (Reed 1975). Iterative computer operations are employed in order to apply the matrix corrections and determine the true concentrations of an element in the sample. The accuracy of the quantitative analysis is usually ±1% (Mulvey 1983). The use of electron optics on the microprobe allows for the electron bombardment of an area that is less than 1μ in diameter. Therefore, it is possible to analyze individual mineral grains within sherds.

Alternative methods are available for measuring the wavelengths and intensities of the emitted x-rays in the electron microprobe. These methods are discussed in Schaller (1987). The present analysis employed wavelength dispersive spectroscopy on the JEOL JXA-8600 microprobe in the Department of Chemistry at Arizona State University. The abundance of ten oxides (Na_2O, MgO, Al_2O_3, SiO_2, K_2O, CaO, TiO_2, Cr_2O_3, MnO and FeO) were measured in augite crystals within LCWW sherds. These chemical elements were chosen since they (excluding chromium) are commonly the most abundant elements in silicate minerals. Chromium is an abundant trace element found in pyroxenes.

Uncovered thin sections were polished to a smoothness of 0.05μ since a smooth surface is necessary for microprobe analysis. A thin layer of vacuum evaporated carbon was placed on the surface of each sample in order to remove the incident electrical charge created by the electron beam, thus grounding the sample.

Chemical Composition of the Augite

Twenty six augite crystals from nine LCWW sherds from both the San Francisco Peaks area (7432.12, 10803.10, 10779.7, 10779.19) and the Hopi Buttes (9183.2, 7806.2, 10757.15, 10757.13, 10757.2) were analyzed by this method. In addition, 16 augite crystals in five San Francisco rocks and six augites from three Hopi Buttes rocks were analyzed.

Marked differences were found between the San Francisco and Hopi Buttes augites in terms of titanium and sodium contents. A plot of TiO_2 against Na_2O is shown in Figure 16. The Hopi Buttes and San Francisco augites cluster separately, overlapping with one another in only one case, which seems to represent an anomalous San Francisco sample. None of the San Francisco or LCWW augites overlap with one another with respect to their titanium or sodium contents. One LCWW sherd has an unusually low content of titanium (0.47%) for reasons that are not clear and appears as an outlier in the plot. The titanium/sodium content of the Hopi Buttes and LCWW samples overlap with the exception of the one anomalous LCWW augite and three Hopi Buttes augites which are extremely high in titanium (3.05%, 4.53% and 5.31%). Despite the anomalies, the LCWW augites more closely resemble the Hopi Buttes augites in terms of their chemical composition.

It is therefore possible to conclude that the augite crystals incorporated within LCWW paste originated in Hopi Buttes volcanic rocks. It would be beneficial to perform additional microprobe analysis on augite crystals derived from the Hopi Buttes volcanic field in order to obtain a better measurement of the range of their chemical composition. These data would help to substantiate the match between the titanium/sodium content of Hopi Buttes and LCWW augites.

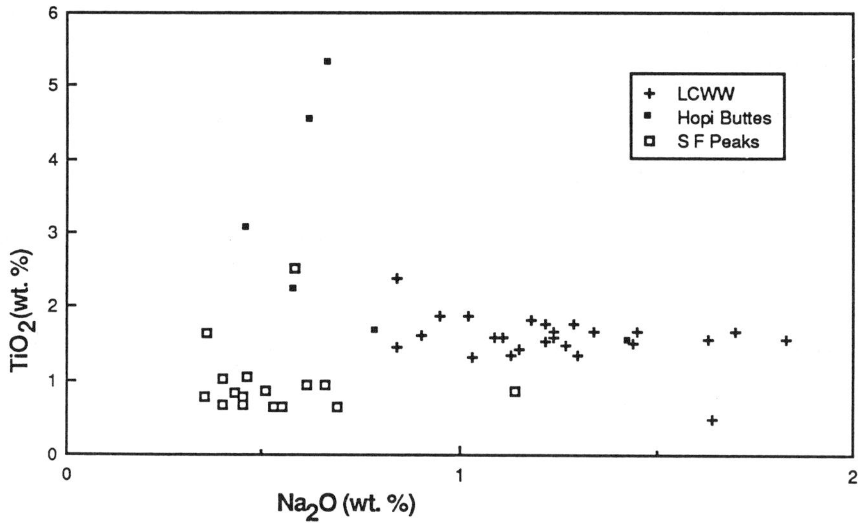

Figure 16. Plot of the TiO_2 and Na_2O contents of augites from Hopi Buttes volcanic rock, San Francisco volcanic rock and LCWW sherds.

Conclusion

The sourcing study has provided strong evidence that LCWW vessels found both in the Hopi Buttes and San Francisco Peaks area were manufactured in the Hopi Buttes. The results of a petrographic analysis on sherds from the Chevelon area (S. Plog 1980a) and descriptions of inclusions in sherds from the Grand Canyon (Schwartz et al. 1980) indicate that LCWW vessels found in other areas also were produced in the Hopi Buttes. Putting all these data together, it is possible to conclude that LCWW was produced in a single, geographically restricted area. Its presence in areas outside the Hopi Buttes is therefore a product of exchange activity rather than widespread production. The extensive geographic distribution of this ware by the twelfth century runs counter to the assertion by Hantman and Plog (1982) that exchange networks were shrinking throughout the plateau Southwest between ca. A.D. 900 and 1100.

The sourcing study has shown that the Lower Member of the Bidahochi Formation provided the clay for this ware, while the sand-sized inclusions in the paste such as quartz, augite crystals and basaltic rock fragments were derived from the lava flows in the Hopi Buttes area. The Lower Member of the Bidahochi Formation is lacustrine in origin. As a result, it is relatively uniform in its mineralogical composition from one outcrop to the next. Samples of this formation collected from widely dispersed locations are nearly identical in terms of their clay mineralogy. This lack of variation makes it extremely difficult to identify specific outcrops from which clay was mined for the manufacture of LCWW.

It is equally difficult to pin down precisely where the makers of this ware were extracting sand for temper. In all likelihood, they were obtaining sand out of the local washes. The minerals present in these sands have eroded from the lava flows and have been transported several kilometers from their original source, being mixed in with sand-sized particles from other lava flows in the process. This intermixture of eroded materials from lava flows throughout the Hopi Buttes area makes different sand deposits indistinguishable from the standpoint of the scope and methodologies of the present study.

Extremely detailed petrographic and chemical analyses of a large sample of sherds and sand samples from different loci within the Hopi Buttes would be necessary in order to determine more precisely which sand deposits were being used for LCWW production.

Even such fine-grained analyses might not prove successful if the drainage patterns in the Hopi Buttes area have changed substantially since the thirteenth century.

However, given the present data, it is possible to delineate a source area in the northeastern portion of the "pure" LCWW area designated by Gumerman and Skinner (1968) where clays from the Lower Member of the Bidahochi Formation are available (refer to Figure 17). It is not clear at this time whether LCWW was the product of only one or several communities within this area. However, the raw materials were available throughout this area and could not have been controlled easily by any one community. The lack of archaeological visibility of ceramic production areas suggests widespread household production at relatively low volumes per production unit, as opposed to high volume centralized production. Although it has not been possible to determine which communities or settlement clusters within the Hopi Buttes were producing LCWW, the source area has been substantially reduced from the general area of "pure" LCWW sites, as shown in Figure 17.

It must be noted that one component of this ware has not been investigated in this sourcing study: the distinctive thick white to light grey slip which was applied to both surfaces of bowls and jar exteriors. This slip is probably mostly kaolinite. Several of the clay-bearing formations in the Hopi Buttes area contain kaolinite in varying amounts, such as the Shinarump Member of the Chinle Formation and the Mancos Shale Formation. Samples of the slip would have to be scraped off LCWW sherds and x-ray diffracted in order to determine which formation it was derived from. However, since kaolinite is widely available within the Hopi Buttes, it is doubtful if information concerning the source of the

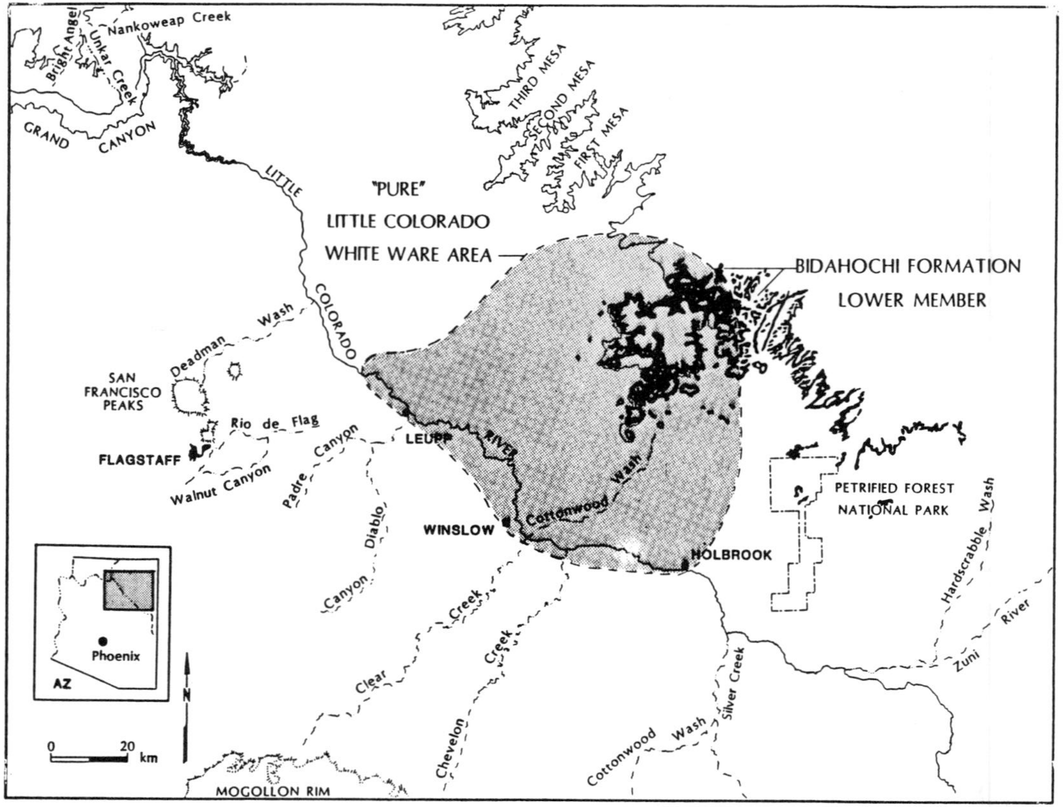

Figure 17. Location of the postulated LCWW production area, as indicated by the co-occurrence of the "pure" LCWW sites and the Lower Member of the Bidahochi Formation.

slip would alter the conclusions of this study concerning the source area of LCWW, or the unrestricted access of communities within the source area to the raw materials.

As a consequence of the sourcing study, exchange contexts for this ware can be distinguished from production contexts and its movement across space can be measured. The following chapter will examine the geographic distribution of LCWW. The goal of the distributional study will be to determine the structure and function of its exchange system.

CHAPTER VII

THE STRUCTURE OF LITTLE COLORADO WHITE WARE EXCHANGE

It is now possible to examine the long-distance transport of LCWW, having delineated its source area. This chapter will present the results of a distance decay study, the major purpose of which is to determine the basic structure of LCWW exchange at the inter-community level. Two techniques of Exploratory Data Analysis, resistant line-fitting and smoothing, are used to model the rate of fall-off in the exchange of LCWW with increasing distance from its source. The resulting mathematical and graphical representations of fall-off are used, in conjunction with contextual information, to characterize the nature of LCWW exchange and to hypothesize about the function of this ware within a regional interaction sphere. Finally, the implications of the structure and function of LCWW exchange on the developmental model are discussed.

Distance Decay Analysis

Distance decay analysis is a methodology adapted from models of human interaction employed in economic geography (e.g., Claeson 1968; Haynes 1974). It is used to reconstruct different types of exchange systems by examining the spatial distribution of exchange goods. It thus utilizes the end product of exchange transactions in order to determine the nature of the processes which controlled the movement of goods between settlements (Renfrew 1975).

Distance decay or fall-off studies are based on what Renfrew (1977) has called the law of monotonic decrement. This law states that, given a commodity which is produced in a geographically restricted area, the frequency of occurrence decreases at a constant rate with increasing distance from the source, other things being equal. Fall-off studies are therefore based on the principle that human beings minimize energy expenditure: the greater the distance across which exchange goods are transported, the greater the energy which is required and thus the fewer the goods which will be exchanged.

The fall-off of exchange with increasing distance is represented by plotting some measure of the intensity of exchange (usually the frequency of the exchange good in question) against distance from the production source. Linear regression analysis is then used to express mathematically the rate of distance decay.

As Hodder (1974:172) has pointed out, the relationship between exchange and distance can be described by a curve having the general form:

$$I = a - bD^{\alpha}$$

where:
- I = interaction (e.g., inter-community exchange)
- a = the amount of interaction, irrespective of distance
- b = the rate of decrease in interaction with increasing distance
- D = distance from the source
- α = an exponent of distance.

This curve can be converted into a straight line by transforming interaction and/or distance into logarithms, and by varying the value of α (Hodder 1974; Hodder and Orton 1976). Several linear models have been proposed, based on the types of transformations which are necessary in order to linearize the fall-off curve. Empirical studies have shown each of these models describes a different type of regional exchange.

There are three basic types of fall-off models. The simplest form is a linear model in which neither I nor D are transformed, and in which α is equal to 1. Renfrew et al. (1968) hypothesize that the linear model is appropriate for "supply zone" exchange where access to the commodity is directly from the source. In contrast, Hudson (1978) concludes that the exchange of obsidian, turquoise, shell, copper bells and macaws throughout various parts of the Southwest between A.D. 1000 and 1400 can best be described by the linear model. However, this author does not use individual site distance and frequency measurements in her analysis. Instead, Hudson measures the distance from the source of each type of exchange good to the center of every Arizona quadrat with sites containing that good. Hudson uses the percentage of sites which contain the exchange good within each quadrant as the frequency variable. This practice of lumping distance and frequency measurements probably has resulted in a distance decay curve with a significantly different shape than a site-by-site set of measurements would yield. Therefore, it is doubtful that the movement of these exchange goods to individual settlements across the Southwest would be characterized by a linear fall-off pattern.

The second type of fall-off model is a single-log or log-normal case in which only I is transformed into logarithmic form:

$$\log I = a - bD^{\alpha}$$

Different versions of the single-log model can be produced by varying the value of α. Altering the value of α affects the shape of the curve of the untransformed data and also varies the slope of the linear function for log I and log D. Hodder and Orton (1976:101) list three variants of the log-normal model: the normal or Gaussian ($\alpha = 2$), the exponential

(α = 1) and the square root exponential (α = 0.5). The Gaussian variant has been associated with exchange systems which resemble random walk patterns. Hogg (1971) was the first to apply this model to archaeological data. He demonstrated that the movement of late Iron Age Dobunnic coins from their source in Bagendon closely fits a random walk pattern (Hodder and Orton 1976:114). However, Hodder and Orton (1976) have been able to generate other types of models using random generation procedures, as discussed below.

The exponential version has been attributed to down-the-line exchange in which exchange goods are transported between neighboring communities, eventually traveling great distances from their sources through a long series of transactions (Renfrew 1975, 1977). Renfrew et al. (1968) found that Neolithic obsidian exchange in the Zagros and Levant regions of the Near East could be expressed linearly by the exponential fall-off model. Hodder and Orton (1976:113) attribute α values between 0.1 and 0.6 to goods of low value produced in small-scale operations, such as Romano-British tiles and coarse Savernake pottery, which are not exchanged over long distances.

The third type of model takes on a double-log form in which both I and D are transformed into logarithms (Hodder and Orton 1976):

$$\log I = a - b \log D^{\alpha}$$

This type of model is also referred to as a power function (Findlow and Bolognese 1982). Again, the shape of the curve can be altered by varying the value of α.

The Pareto model is a particular type of double-log model in which α has a value of 1 (Hodder 1974:172-173). Renfrew (1977) claims that there is no clear link between power models and a particular type of interaction, citing the fact that geographers have not been able to fit their data to such a function. However, Findlow and Bolognese (1982:72-73) suggest that a power function model "can be used to model prehistoric exchange systems in which an area of direct-access, supply-zone procurement is joined to areas with down-the-line, directional exchange by a steep falloff zone." Wright (1970) used a Pareto model to examine Near Eastern obsidian exchange from the Lake Van source between 7500 and 5500 B.C. Hodder and Orton (1976:101) also mention a "log-normal" version of the double-log model which has an α value of 2. However, this type of function has not been applied to archaeological data as yet.

Five out of the six fall-off models discussed above will be compared to the LCWW data: the linear, the Pareto, the Gaussian, the exponential and the square root exponential. These models have been selected because they have been used in conjunction with archaeological data with some measure of success and because there is some evidence to suggest that they reflect specific types of exchange systems. Once the best-fit regression function has been found, the processes and circumstances responsible for the spatial distribution of exchange goods can be elucidated by examining the slope of the regressed distance decay function and its statistical outliers.

The amount of energy input, and hence the volume of exchange activity, can vary with such factors as the nature of the terrain to be traversed, the volume of the demand at the destination, the amount of output at the source and the type of exchange good (Hodder and Orton 1976; Renfrew 1977; Hodder 1982). All of these factors, in turn, affect the rate of fall-off between the source and the destination(s). Violations of the law of monotonic decrement are often the result.

A major problem for interpreting regressed distance decay functions is due to equifinality: the same spatial distribution of goods potentially can be the result of more than one set of initial conditions and exchange processes. For example, linear fall-off models assume a uniform distribution of population throughout the exchange sphere. However, if population density falls off with increasing distance from the source, it can result in a distance-decay function which resembles the down-the-line model (Renfrew 1977). Hodder and Orton (1976:127-134) have conducted random walk simulations in which the distances and directions of movement from a single source point are chosen at random. They found that a down-the-line type of fall-off curve could be generated repeatedly, even when step length and/or number were varied.

Meaningful choices between alternative models can only be made if independent data are brought to bear on the interpretive process. Different mechanisms of exchange may be distinguishable if the archaeological context of the exchange goods (e.g., within settlements, burials, storage facilities or caches) is considered. Certain formal attributes of the goods may vary as their value augments with increasing distance from the source (Hodder 1982; Hodder and Lane 1982). Or one might expect an increase in curation and/or recycling of exchange goods at greater distances. Such variation could signal changes in the type of exchange mechanism by which the goods were transported, changes which would in turn affect the shape of the fall-off curve.

In addition, the settlement pattern within the exchange sphere should be taken into account since fall-off rates can be affected by changing population densities and the distribution of settlements (Renfrew 1977; Hodder 1978). The function of exchange can also be better determined by examining the types of settlements in which the goods tend to concentrate. In short, a contextual framework is necessary in order to enhance what would otherwise be a rather simplistic "dots-on-maps" approach (Hodder and Lane 1982). As a result, both intra-site artifact contexts and settlement patterns are used to reconstruct the structure and function of LCWW exchange.

The Variables

The two primary variables considered herein are: 1) how far LCWW vessels traveled to reach their various exchange contexts (distance from the source) and 2) relative volume of LCWW exchange activity at each locus, expressed as the percentage of LCWW sherds of the total decorated ceramic assemblage for each site.

A datum was selected in approximately the middle of the LCWW source area delineated by the compositional analyses discussed in the previous chapter. However, it must be born in mind that the datum is merely an arbitrary reference point used to measure distances from the source since the necessary materials for the production of LCWW were available throughout the source area.

The extended site sample (see Table 3) was plotted on USGS 1:250,000 topographic maps and distances from the datum to each site were measured with an opisometer. Likely routes were traced, taking into consideration the limitations of travel on foot as well as the constraints of topography and the need for a relatively dependable water supply.

Of course, several possible routes usually can be traced between two points. The one chosen by the prehistoric travelers would depend on such factors as the location of friendly or hostile settlements along the way and whether or not other procurement tasks were embedded in the export of LCWW. These factors cannot be controlled for at present, given the limited understanding of the dynamics of intercommunity interaction or the structure of prehistoric procurement systems within the Little Colorado River drainage. However, it was felt that attempting to reconstruct transport routes would provide a more direct approximation of exchange behavior than using straight line distances, or complex multivariate procedures to estimate transport costs (see Findlow and Bolognese 1982).

Intensity of exchange was measured by calculating the percentage of LCWW sherds in the decorated ceramic assemblage of each site in the extended sample. It is assumed that the proportions of sherds recovered from the archaeological record are representative of the proportions of corresponding whole vessels which once existed in the ceramic assemblages of the living communities. Refer to Table 14 for the frequency and distance measurements for the 40 sites in the extended sample.

The percentage was calculated from the decorated assemblage, as opposed to the entire ceramic assemblage, because of differential biases which have been imposed on the plain and decorated ceramics by judgmental collection procedures. Such procedures tend to favor the retrieval of decorated wares due to their value as temporal diagnostics. Percentages of LCWW sherds from judgmentally collected assemblages would thus be inflated in comparison to percentages from statistically representative samples if the whole assemblage were used in the calculations.

The relationship between distance from the source and the percentage of LCWW within a decorated assemblage was examined via exploratory data analysis. The basic

Table 14. Percentage of LCWW and Distance Measurements for the Extended Site Sample.

Site	Percentage	Distance
NA 10,757	99.13	15.00
NA 9165	51.43	21.00
NA 9183	88.71	23.75
NA 9182	32.43	25.00
Plaza Site	96.73	28.75
NA 9192	21.43	29.00
NA 7806	26.48	33.00
NA 12.574	25.51	76.50
NA 7817	15.63	100.00
Agate House	37.94	100.50
DoBell Site	2.78	102.50
NA 7818	59.18	103.25
Grand Falls	10.00	104.50
Tse Tlani	71.53	107.25
Hibbard Pueblo	44.21	109.75
Rincon Pueblo	29.44	112.75
Turkey Tank	38.30	117.00
CS 731	8.00	119.25
Winona Village	9.79	120.00
CS 690	37.00	122.00
CS 43	12.00	125.50
CS 900	9.00	128.25
NA 10,803	26.40	129.00
NA 103	28.00	130.25
AZ I:10:30	20.00	131.50
Crack-in-Rock	22.67	136.25
NA 17,271B	10.34	136.50
NA 17,282	5.63	138.75
Juniper Terrace	12.69	139.00
NA 680	4.01	139.50
Metate House	10.00	141.75
AZ Q:7:9	3.09	157.93
AZ Q:7:14	2.63	162.70
AZ Q:3:63	5.0	169.10
AZ Q:7:26	3.27	175.75
AZ Q:3:8	19.05	182.40
AZ Q:4:50	5.56	194.50
Unkar Delta	9.74	258.50
Nankoweap	19.26	282.00
Bright Angel	15.96	282.00

theory behind this analytical approach will be discussed below, along with the specific techniques used in the distance decay study and their results.

Exploratory Data Analysis

Exploratory data analysis (EDA) was developed as an alternative approach by researchers who had become disillusioned with the more traditional hypothesis testing mode in statistics (Tukey 1977; Hartwig and Dearing 1979; Leinhardt and Wasserman 1979; Velleman and Hoaglin 1981). As its name implies, EDA focuses on allowing the patterning in the data to reveal itself, rather than attempting to define the data in terms of preconceived models or statistical summaries. From the perspective of EDA, hypothesis testing is limited in its ability to reveal patterns because of its heavy reliance on statistical summaries, which may obscure other characteristics of the data, and its use of only two alternative hypotheses (i.e., either the data fits the model being tested or it does not) (Hartwig and Dearing 1979; Clark 1982).

EDA is founded on the notion that data are composed of two components, the smooth and the rough:

$$\text{data} = \text{smooth} + \text{rough}$$

Both components can reveal important information and contribute to a better understanding of the data. The smooth is the underlying patterning or structure in the data. The rough is what is left behind once the smooth has been extracted from the data: the residuals or deviations from the patterning. The primary task of EDA is to extract as much smooth out of the data as possible through an iterative process until the remaining rough is patternless.

One of the unique features of EDA is that the rough is viewed as a significant component of the data which must be dealt with in its own right. Only by examining the rough will one be able to determine if all the smooth has been extracted by asking, "is the rough rough enough?" (Hartwig and Dearing 1979:11). It is often the case that a single view or representation of the data will not extract all the smooth out of the data. In essence, there will still be some smooth left in the rough.

More smooth can be extracted by re-expressing the data using different transformations (e.g., squares, square roots or logarithms). Generally, the more re-expression which is employed, the more smooth will be extracted from the data. The only restriction is that the particular transformations used bear some meaningful relationship to the original data.

The rough should not be set aside even once all the smooth has been extracted from it. Completely unstructured rough can suggest alternative hypotheses or guide the search for explanatory models by highlighting aspects of the data that do not become part of the smooth even after successive re-expressions.

As an inductive approach to data analysis, EDA makes no prior assumptions about the basic characteristics of the data, such as the shape of its distribution, its dispersion or central tendencies. EDA techniques are designed to be resistant against the disproportionate effects of outliers, unlike such parametric techniques as linear regression (Hartwig and Dearing 1979; Clark 1982). One reason for its greater resistance to outliers is its use of medians instead of means as summary points (Velleman and Hoaglin 1981; Clark 1982).

EDA also employs visual representations of the data through various graphical techniques which allow the investigator to observe the effects of the various transformations employed during the process of pattern extraction. It is thus possible to monitor the behavior of outliers and their relationship to the smooth (Hartwig and Dearing 1979).

There is currently some disagreement as to whether or not EDA can be used in a hypothesis testing mode analogous to more traditional confirmatory procedures such as t-tests and linear regression. It has been suggested that such a mode is inappropriate to EDA because patterns are generated from the data themselves and it would therefore be meaningless to test the validity of the patterns using the same data (Hartwig and Dearing 1979). However, exploratory techniques can be used to suggest which hypotheses might provide more meaningful explanations than others. As Hartwig and Dearing (1979:11) suggest,

> the data are explored to discover the smooth, and models generated from the data can then be compared to models specified by the theory. The more similar they are, the more the data confirm the theory.

In summary, EDA represents an alternative approach to standard confirmatory procedures in which data are measured against preconceived patterns. It combines a healthy skepticism of apparent structure in the data with an openness toward unanticipated patterning. In the proper context, it can be used to evaluate the relative merits of alternative models as explanations for the observed patterning, particularly in the case of models which do not stipulate clearly the relationships between variables.

EDA is an appropriate form of analysis for the distance decay study because it is resistant to outlying cases and highlights them in displays of the rough. As a result, such potential problems as incompatible excavation procedures, miscalculations of distances from the source or local changes in the overall interaction pattern can be assessed.

Two techniques of EDA were employed in the distance decay study. First, resistant line-fitting was used to summarize the overall effect of distance on LCWW exchange. It was used in a hypothesis testing mode in the sense that alternative distance decay models were compared in order to determine which one, if any, provides the closest fit to the data. Second, smoothing was used to display departures away from the general distance decay trend. This procedure aided in the identification of particular sites or areas which might have been participating more or less intensively in the exchange system of LCWW. Both techniques and their results will be described in greater detail in the following two sections.

Resistant Line-Fitting

Resistant line-fitting is analogous to linear regression. It summarizes the relationship between two variables with a linear function. The slope and intercept of the line are calculated by using what are called summary points of the bivariate data. The data set is first divided into three portions, each containing approximately one third of the cases. Cases with low, middle and high x-values fall within each of the three portions respectively. Median values are calculated for the x-values and y-values within each portion separately, ignoring the case-by-case pairing of the x-y data. Using medians to define the summary points makes the linear function resistant to anomalous x- of y-values in the data set.

The slope is calculated by dividing the change in y by the change in x between the right and left summary points:

$$b = \frac{y_R - y_L}{x_R - x_L}$$

where: b = the slope
(x_R, y_R) = the right summary point
(x_L, y_L) = the left summary point

All three summary points are used to calculate intercept estimates which are then averaged. Thus,

$$1/3\ (a_L + a_M + a_R) = 1/3\ [(y_L + y_M + y_R) - b(x_L + x_M + x_R)]$$

where: a_L = the left intercept estimate
a_M = the middle intercept estimate
a_R = the right intercept estimate.

Once a line has been fitted to the data, the residuals are found:

$$r = y_i - (a + bx_i).$$

The residuals can be used to evaluate the fit of the data to the linear model, as is the case with linear regression. However, in keeping with the EDA objective of extracting all the smooth out of the data, the residuals are examined as data points themselves:

$$(x,r_i) = [x_i y_i - (a + bx_i)]$$

where: r_i = the residual.

The summary points for the residual plot are calculated. If the residual slope is not close to zero, it is added to the original slope and a new set of residuals is calculated. This process is repeated until the residual slope is close to zero, at which point it is assumed that little or no patterning is left in the residuals. However, it is advisable to examine a plot of the residuals to determine if they swarm in a relatively cohesive mass, or if some of them cluster separately. Such visual inspection can help isolate persistent outliers which do not follow the general linear trend in the data.

A second technique for evaluating the fit of the linear function involves determining whether or not the relationship between x and y is indeed linear. The three summary points are used to calculate a left and right half-slope:

$$b_L = \frac{y_M - y_L}{x_M - x_L} \quad \text{and} \quad b_R = \frac{y_R - y_M}{x_R - x_M}$$

where: b_L = the left half-slope
b_R = the right half-slope.

The half-slope ratio (b_R/b_L) is used as a measure of linearity. If the ratio is negative, the two halves of the data trend in different directions, indicating a parabolic relationship between x and y. If the half-slopes are equal, and thus the relationship between x and y is indeed linear, the half-slope ratio is one. If the ratio is a positive value close to one, the relationship between x and y can often be made more linear by transforming one or both variables. Repeated transformations can be applied, summary points and half-slope ratios being calculated for each successive transformation. This process is repeated until a half-slope ratio close to one is achieved (Velleman and Hoaglin 1981).

The Results

The plot of the untransformed variables, frequency of LCWW and distance from the source (Table 14), for the 40 sites in the extended sample was resistant line-fitted, yielding a half-slope ratio of 4.792. This ratio indicates that the relationship between the untransformed variables is not linear, as shown in Figure 18. Frequency and distance were transformed in accordance with the four other distance decay models shown in Table 15. None of these models were found to be satisfactory linear expressions of the effects of increasing distance from the source on the intensity of LCWW exchange, as reflected in their half-slope ratios.

In fact, the models involving logarithmic transformations had higher positive half-slope ratios than the linear model, indicating that such transformations were actually producing a more curvilinear relationship. The linearizing transformations are therefore in the direction of exponential powers, not logarithms or square roots.

As a result, several combinations of exponential transformations were tried by raising one or both variables to powers between two and three. The results of these transformations are also listed in Table 15. A half-slope ratio closest to one was achieved with squared frequencies and distance values raised to the 2.5 power. However, the data are so altered at this point that the resistant line becomes almost horizontal with a slope of -0.01, as illustrated in Figure 19.

The results of the resistant line-fitting indicate that the intensity of LCWW exchange does not fall off consistently with increasing distance from the source. The almost horizontal slope of the resistant line indicates that distance in and of itself does not have a strong frictional effect on exchange activity. Clearly, some other factor or combination of factors is affecting LCWW frequencies found in the various trade contexts represented

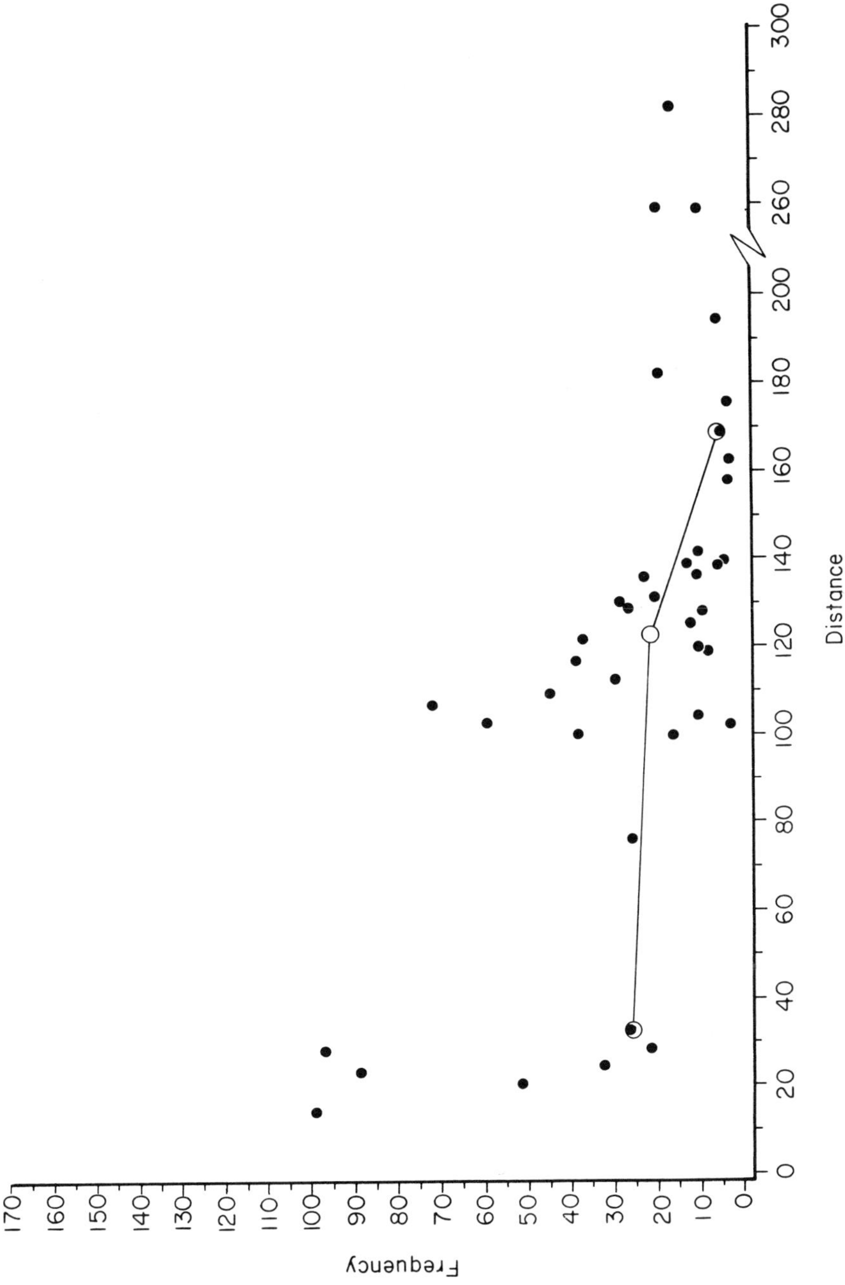

Figure 18. Plot of LCWW frequencies against distance with summary points and half slope lines.

Table 15. Effects of Various Transformations on the Half-Slope Ratio.

Model	Frequency Tran.[a]	Distance Tran.[b]	Half-Slope Ratio
Linear	----	----	4.792
Exponential	log I	----	10.429
Square Root Exponential	log I	$D^{0.5}$	14.914
Gaussian	log I	D^2	5.585
Pareto	log I	log D	22.054
----	----	D^2	2.566
----	I^2	D^2	1.378
----	I^2	$D^{2.25}$	1.198
----	*I^2*	*$D^{2.5}$*	*1.048*
----	I^2	D^3	0.814
----	$I^{2.25}$	D^2	1.203

Note: Best fit transformations are shown in *italics*.
[a] Frequency Transformation
[b] Distance Transformation

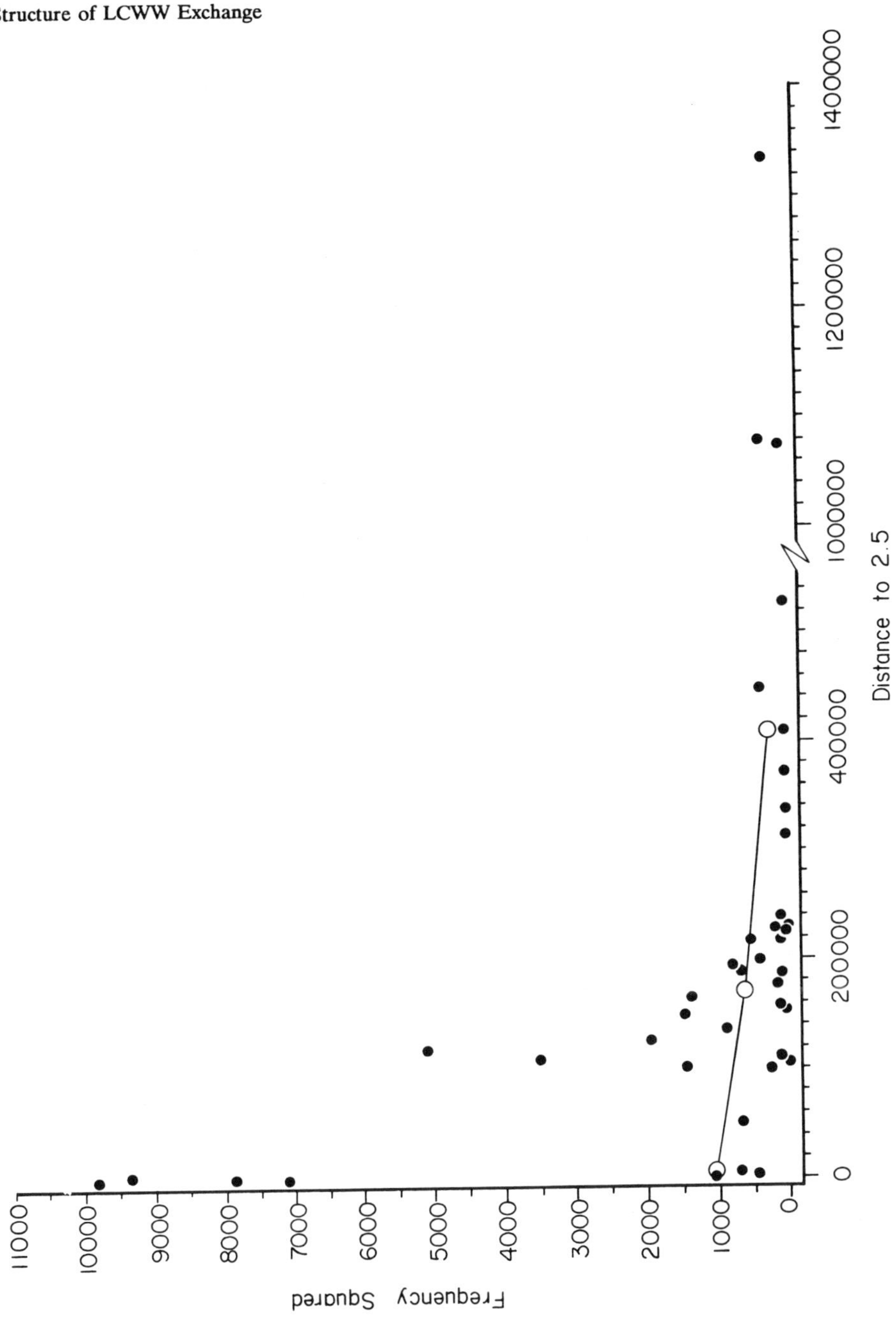

Figure 19. Plot of the best fit transformations of LCWW frequencies against distance with resistant line.

in the extended site sample. Examining the residuals of the resistant line can be an effective means of determining what these factors might be.

Certain patterning remained in the residuals throughout the various transformations which were applied to the data. Therefore, some aspect of the smooth remained behind when the relationship between frequency and distance had been extracted. The residuals for the best fit transformations are listed in Table 16.

There is some variability in the frequencies of LCWW sherds at the Hopi Buttes sites, even though they all fall within what Gumerman and Skinner (1968:185) have referred to as the "pure" LCWW area. The residuals of four Hopi Buttes sites are high outliers, while three of the sites have negative residuals. Three out of the four sites with positive outlier residuals and two out of the three sites with negative residuals were excavated by Gumerman (1969), which would preclude the variability being due to differences in sampling procedures or classification criteria between separate excavation projects.

Two sites with negative residuals, NA 9182 and NA 9192, had earlier Pueblo I components. The ceramics from these earlier components were not used in calculating the LCWW percentages. However, subsequent inspection of the ceramic tables for these sites revealed that some mixing of the components had occurred and that earlier Tusayan White Wares had intruded into the later occupations, thus reducing the relative frequencies of LCWW in the later decorated assemblages. Nevertheless, the percentage of LCWW in the decorated assemblage of these sites remains below 50% even with the earlier white wares being factored out of the calculations.

Table 16. Residuals for the Best Fit Resistant Line.

Site	Residual
NA 10,757	8740.32
NA 9165	6021.58
NA 9183	6788.26
NA 9182	-28.45
Plaza Site	8280.17
NA 9192	-617.00
NA 7806	-370.24
NA 12,574	-295.57
NA 7817	-566.11
Agate House	632.53
DoBell Site	-784.95
NA 7818	2715.04
NA 1292	-678.01
Tse Tlani	4359.38
Hibbard Pueblo	1217.03
Rincon Pueblo	153.73
Turkey Tank	790.33
CS 731	-592.45
Winona Village	-553.77
CS 690	737.91
CS 43 -453.55	
CS 900	-489.19
NA 10,803	134.39
NA 103	234.27
AZ I:10:30	-136.70
Crack-in-Rock	28.45
NA 17,271B	-375.79
NA 17,282	-425.72
Juniper Terrace	-293.54
NA 680	-432.77
Metate House	-322.74
AZ Q:7:9	-206.52
AZ Q:7:14	-141.75
AZ Q:3:63	-28.47
AZ Q:7:26	62.04
AZ Q:3:8	525.19
AZ Q:4:50	411.13
Unkar Delta	1997.55
Nankoweap	2288.12
Bright Angel	2884.35

These sites do not appear to be any less permanent settlements than other sites in the area such as NA 9183. There is no apparent reason why some sites in the area should have much lower frequencies of LCWW than others, given their close proximity to one another and the raw materials used to produce this ware. It is possible that not all of these sites were producing LCWW, despite their access to the necessary materials. Alternatively, functional differences between sites may exist which are not reflected in the excavation data.

The ceramic data reported for NA 7806, which also has a relatively low LCWW frequency, are questionable due to the fact that the most abundant decorated white ware listed by Olson (1963:57) is Dogoszhi Black-on-white. I saw no Dogoszhi Black-on-white during my inspection of the ceramic collections from this site at the Museum of Northern Arizona. Instead, I encountered relatively large amounts of Padre Black-on-white which is the LCWW equivalent to Dogoszhi Black-on-white. Padre Black-on-white is not listed in the published ceramic table. It is impossible to say at this point if there was no Dogoszhi Black-on-white at NA 7806, and if Olson was confusing Dogoszhi for Padre Black-on-white, since the ceramic collection for this site is no longer intact. The relatively low frequency of LCWW at NA 7806 site must remain suspect, however.

The residuals from the San Francisco sites showed some surprising characteristics. Winona Village and Juniper Terrace, which had been classified as possible distribution centers, both displayed negative residuals. Two explanations are possible. First, these sites may not have been distribution centers for LCWW. Smaller settlements in the area may have obtained their vessels directly. Second, Winona Village and Juniper Terrace may have been distribution centers which did not hold stockpiles of LCWW vessels for extended periods of time. As soon as the tradeware came into these centers, it may have been dispersed throughout various surrounding communities where it was used and subsequently entered the archeological record. If this were the case, the residents of these centers did not have preferential access to LCWW relative to other communities, despite their central role in its distribution.

LCWW frequencies from the ballcourts associated with Winona Village (NA 2132) and Juniper Terrace (NA 804), as well as a kiva within Juniper Terrace (NA 1814F) range between 32% and 85.71%. These figures are significantly higher than the frequencies from the domestic structures. The sherd samples collected from NA 804 and NA 1814F are very small (i.e., 25 sherds or less). The potential for bias in such limited samples is quite high, particularly given the judgmental collection procedures in practice at the time that Winona Village and Juniper Terrace were excavated. However, there were 41 decorated sherds found on the floor of NA 2132, 67% of which were LCWW.

Although the evidence is somewhat questionable, it is difficult to dismiss totally the greater frequencies of LCWW within these specialized structures. It would appear as if these structures might have been loci for LCWW exchange, although the centers themselves probably were not used to stockpile this ware for subsequent distribution and did not control its distribution. It is possible that members of surrounding communities were bringing their vessels to such facilities to exchange with each other. Alternatively, these structures may have been used for activities which required greater quantities of LCWW vessels than necessary for activities conducted in domestic structures.

LCWW vessels were found in association with two cremations (23 and 24) and one burial (13) at Winona Village, which contained a Walnut Black-on-white jar, two Walnut Black-on-white pitchers and a Holbrook Black-on-white jar respectively, according to site records on file at the Museum of Northern Arizona. The burial data from Juniper Terrace has been rendered virtually uninterpretable due to contradictory and incomplete records. The most that can be said is that three burials out of the six which were excavated contained LCWW vessels. Burial 1, found in the wooden pithouse (NA 1814C) was associated with at least one, and possibly as many as three, LCWW vessels. Two out of the four burials in the kiva (NA 1814F) had LCWW vessels with them, but it is not clear which burials they were or how many vessels each contained. There were a total of three LCWW vessels found with the burials in the kiva. In summary, certain cremations and/or burials at these two centers contained LCWW vessels while others did not. However, the vessels are not found in unusually large concentrations which might indicate that certain individuals were controlling access to this ware. Nor are they associated with other burial goods or methods of internment which would be expected if these individuals held a higher status within their communities than individuals who were not interred with LCWW vessels.

The San Francisco sites with the highest positive residuals are Tse Tlani, NA 7818 and Hibbard Pueblo, all of which are located on the eastern fringes of the San Francisco Peaks area. Their ceramic assemblages are also characteristic of the later Padre (A.D. 1100-1130) or Elden (A.D. 1130-1210) focus settlements. Therefore, the greater participation of these communities in the exchange of LCWW could be a product of their location or their period of occupation, and not their position within a settlement hierarchy.

The San Francisco sites were plotted separately and resistant line-fitted (Figure 20) in order to examine more closely the effects of distance on LCWW exchange within this area. The half-slope ratio for the linear model was 1.015, which was the closest ratio to one out of the five models used in the distance decay study. These results suggest that LCWW exchange within the San Francisco area was affected by distance from the source.

The linearity of the distance decay function also suggests that exchange was operating much like it would within the supply zone, with all settlements having fairly direct access to this ware (cf. Renfrew et al. 1968). Such a situation would exist if individuals from the Hopi Buttes were traveling directly to settlements in the San Francisco area to exchange LCWW vessels, or vice versa. The pattern of LCWW distribution within the San Francisco area is therefore indicative of close and probably frequent interaction with the inhabitants of the Hopi Buttes. Exchange ties were strongest with communities in the south and east portions of the San Francisco area and attenuated further to the north and west.

Significantly, distance seems to be a more important determinant of the intensity of exchange than time with regards to the San Francisco sites in the extended sample. Although these sites have ceramic assemblages ranging between the Angell-Winona and Elden foci (ca. A.D. 1066 to 1210), the residuals for the extended sample resistant line (Table 16) show no patterning which might suggest changes in exchange activity through time: neither the earlier nor the later sites fall consistently on one side of the line or the other.

It can be concluded that the variability in LCWW frequencies within the distance decay analysis are not caused by temporal differences. The earlier Angell-Winona focus

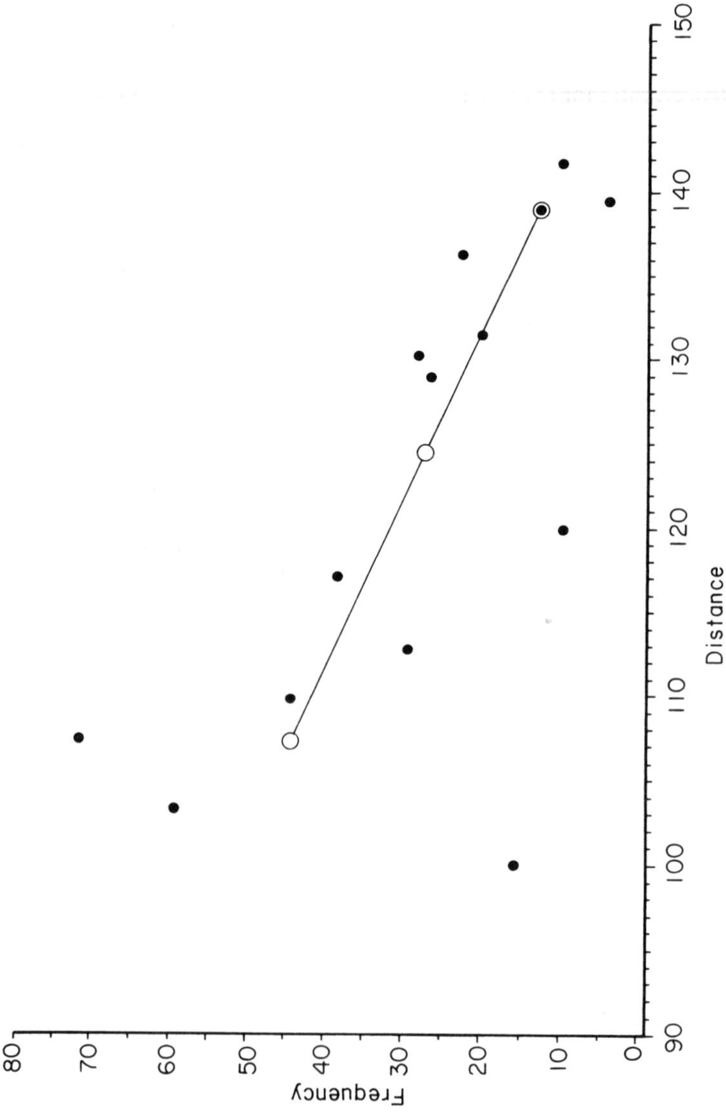

Figure 20. Plot of San Francisco site LCWW frequencies against distance with resistant line.

sites are concentrated at shorter distances from the source and possess greater frequencies of LCWW than later sites further away, contrary to expectations if time were the major determining factor. Therefore, the pattern of monotonic decrement in LCWW frequencies within the San Francisco Peaks sample can be attributed primarily to distance from the source, rather than changes in exchange activity through time.

Despite the present results, it has been stated by some archaeologists that tradewares from the east, such as LCWW and Cibola White Ware, increase in frequency after the beginning of the Elden focus (A.D. 1130), replacing Tusayan White Ware from the north (Fish et al. 1980; Pilles 1987). In view of this claim, it is possible that the site sample used in this study does not reflect temporal shifts in exchange relationships which actually occurred. I compared LCWW percentages for San Francisco sites pre- and post-A.D. 1130 in the extended sample and sites reported in *The Sinagua* (Colton 1946) in order to determine if an increase through time in eastern ceramic wares was measurable. Generally, there is a great deal of variability in frequencies for both periods. However, a t-test comparing the earlier and later sites with respect to their LCWW percentages was significant ($p \leq 0.01$). Therefore, if the ceramic dating of the sites is correct, LCWW frequencies do tend to increase after ca. A.D. 1130.

However, Downum (1984) found that sites both pre- and post-dating ca. A.D. 1130 showed a concentration of LCWW in the southeastern portion of the San Francisco Peaks with decreasing frequencies to the north and west. This pattern persisted through time, even though more LCWW was reaching the northern Peaks area around Wupatki after A.D. 1130 than had been exchanged into this area during the earlier period.

In summary, the various analyses conducted on the San Francisco Peaks settlements, have shown that distance was an important factor in determining the intensity of LCWW exchange for the two centuries that it operated in this area. Distance remained a significant factor in the twelfth century, at which time there was an increase in the volume of LCWW vessels being imported into the area.

Both the Petrified Forest and Chevelon areas exhibit variability in the percentages of LCWW present at sites which are relatively close to one another. In the case of the Petrified Forest sites, this variability does not correspond to differences in the occupation periods of the sites, as ceramically defined. Nor does it appear to be due to differences in site type between Agate House and the DoBell site. The former site does not possess any specialized community structures which might have operated as loci of exchange.

In the case of the Chevelon sites, however, there is some indication that time may be a factor in the variability of LCWW frequencies. CS 690 has the greatest percentage of LCWW out of the four sites in the extended sample. It also has the earliest outside tree-ring date of A.D. 1198. The Chevelon sites with even earlier dates also have greater frequencies of LCWW sherds.

S. Plog (1980a:32-34) has stated that the Chevelon area experienced a predominance of three different decorated white wares during distinct periods of time. Tusayan White Ware was the earliest, followed by LCWW post A.D. 1100, which was subsequently replaced by Cibola White Ware some time during the thirteenth century. The temporal shifts in Chevelon white ware assemblages may be due to the fact that this area was located at the intersection of three exchange spheres whose spatial distributions shifted relative to one another through time.

The three Grand Canyon proveniences (Unkar Delta, Nankoweap and Bright Angel) have large positive residuals. Therefore, they might have had a more direct access to LCWW than their great distances from the source would suggest. It is possible that the frictional effects of down-the-line type of exchange were not in operation and that vessels were transported to the Grand Canyon without changing many hands.

In summary, the variability in LCWW frequencies between sites which are relatively close together is not totally clear. It does not appear to correspond to differences in site type within the Hopi Buttes or Petrified Forest areas. There is some evidence to suggest, however, that such variability is at least partially due to temporal differences in the Hopi Buttes, San Francisco Peaks and Chevelon areas.

Nevertheless, the resistant line-fitting has demonstrated clearly that the relationship between the frequency of LCWW sherds and distance from the source is not strictly linear. The residuals show that certain areas, such as the San Francisco Peaks and the eastern Grand Canyon, might have been interacting relatively intensively with the Hopi Buttes, thus minimizing the frictional effects of distance. Other areas, such as Snowflake, were more peripheral to the LCWW exchange sphere even though their distances from the source are not any greater than the areas which did participate more extensively in this system.

The smoothing technique was employed in order to further study the fluctuations in exchange intensity throughout the extended site sample. Once these results have been described, factors which might have caused these perturbations will be presented.

Smoothing

Smoothing is analogous to time series analysis. This technique is used to summarize the patterning in bivariate data sequences, or data sets in which the x-values are relatively evenly spaced. The main function of the x-values in data sequences is to provide an ordering of the y-values in temporal, spatial or some other type of increment. To be most effective, smoothing should be performed on data sequences with relatively evenly spaced increments, although some deviation is allowable (Velleman and Hoaglin 1982). The sites in the extended sample were chosen to provide as even a spacing between the distance measurements as was possible.

Smoothing proceeds by summarizing consecutive, overlapping segments of the data sequence. Medians and averages are most commonly used as data smoothers. Running median smoothers usually proceed in overlapping segments of three or five data values. Each y-value is replaced with the median of itself and either two or four adjacent values in the sequence. Even-length running medians can also be employed. However, it is necessary to calculate the median in the gap between the two middle values in this case. A running median of four therefore shifts the data sequence over half an increment along the x axis. It is necessary to employ a running median of two in order to recenter the data sequence over the original y increments. Thus, as illustrated by Velleman and Hoaglin (1982:164),

	y_5	y_6	y_7	y_8	y_9	
becomes	$z_{4.5}$	$z_{5.5}$	$z_{6.5}$	$z_{7.5}$	$z_{8.5}$	$z_{9.5}$
and is centered	z_5	z_6	z_7	z_8	z_9	

Another type of smoothing operation is a running weighted average called hanning. Each data value is replaced by the average of itself and the data values on either side of it. The data values in each smoothing segment are multiplied by weights. For example, within a segment composed of three data values, y_i could be replaced by:

$$z_i = 1/4y_{i-1} + 1/2y_i + 1/4y_{i+1}$$

where: z_i = the smoothed counterpart of y_i.

Any combination of weights can be used as long as they sum to one within each smoothing segment.

The rough, or the residuals of the smoothing process, must also be checked for additional patterning. The rough sequence is therefore smoothed as well and any patterning extracted from it is added to the smoothed sequence of y-values. This process is referred to as twicing if the same smoother is used in smoothing the original data sequence and the residuals.

The most effective way to smooth a data sequence is by using a compound smoother which incorporates several passes over the data with a combination of different types of running median and averaging operations. The particular combinations of smoothers and the order in which they are carried out is designed to complement their various strengths and weaknesses. The objective is to achieve a smoothed pattern which is resistant to anomalous y-values, but which is not so smooth as to be a poor representation of the original data sequence. The smoothers which are more sensitive to outliers keep the smooth from getting too smooth, while the more resistant smoothers diminish the effects of anomalous values.

The compound smoother employed in the distance decay analysis is referred to as 4235H, twice. First, a running median of four is centered by a running median of two. Running medians from segments of three and five are then employed. Once the outliers have been smoothed by these more resistant passes over the data sequence, a hanning procedure is employed. Finally, the residuals are smoothed using the same sequence of smoothers (twicing) and the result is added to the smooth of the y-values (Velleman and Hoaglin 1981).

The Results

The smoothed frequencies and the rough are listed in Table 17. Figure 21 shows the smoothed frequencies plotted against distance. The plot has been divided into seven sections, labeled A through G, corresponding to the peaks and troughs in the smoothed data.

The peaks represent areas where LCWW exchange is relatively intense. Section A is the peak of the Hopi Buttes supply zone. Section C delineates a peak in the smoothed frequencies created by the southern and eastern San Francisco Peaks settlements who possessed high residuals in the resistant line-fitting, as discussed above. Thus both EDA analyses indicate that the settlements in the southeastern portion of the San Francisco Peaks area were interacting fairly intensively with the Hopi Buttes communities. The two Petrified Forest sites also occur in this peak, but they are at its lowest portion close to the 100 km mark. The peak in section E also is composed primarily of San Francisco sites.

Table 17. Smoothed and Rough Frequency Values for the Extended Site Sample.

Site	Smooth	Rough
NA 10,757	77.9945	21.1355
NA 9165	73.4358	-22.0058
NA 9183	69.4052	19.3048
NA 9182	60.6966	-28.2666
Plaza Site	44.4675	52.2625
NA 9192	29.7310	-8.3010
NA 7806	23.8436	2.6364
NA 12,574	23.0955	2.4145
NA 7817	23.1033	-7.4733
Agate House	23.3479	14.5921
DoBell Site	24.8489	-22.0689
NA 7818	30.8287	28.3513
NA 1292	39.2237	-29.2237
Tse Tlani	42.9034	28.6266
Hibbard Pueblo	42.5340	1.6759
Rincon Pueblo	37.3503	-7.9103
Turkey Tank	26.7734	11.5266
CS 731	18.6036	-10.6036
Winona Village	15.1062	-5.3162
CS 690	14.0243	22.9757
CS 43	15.3334	-3.3334
CS 900	18.7523	-9.7523
NA 10,803	21.6948	4.7052
NA 103	22.5195	5.4805
AZ I:10:30	21.4934	-1.4934
Crack-in-Rock	18.0057	4.6643
NA 17,271B	13.2106	-2.8706
NA 17,282	9.5164	-3.8864
Juniper Terrace	7.5914	5.0986
NA 680	6.3919	-2.3819
Metate House	4.8537	5.1463
AZ Q:7:9	3.5806	-0.4906
AZ Q:7:14	3.2106	-0.5806
AZ Q:3:63	3.4325	1.5675
AZ Q:7:26	4.2793	-1.0093
AZ Q:3:8	6.4465	12.6035
AZ Q:4:50	9.7783	-4.2183
Unkar Delta	12.8082	-3.0682
Nankoweap	14.8219	4.4381
Bright Angel	15.9600	0.0000

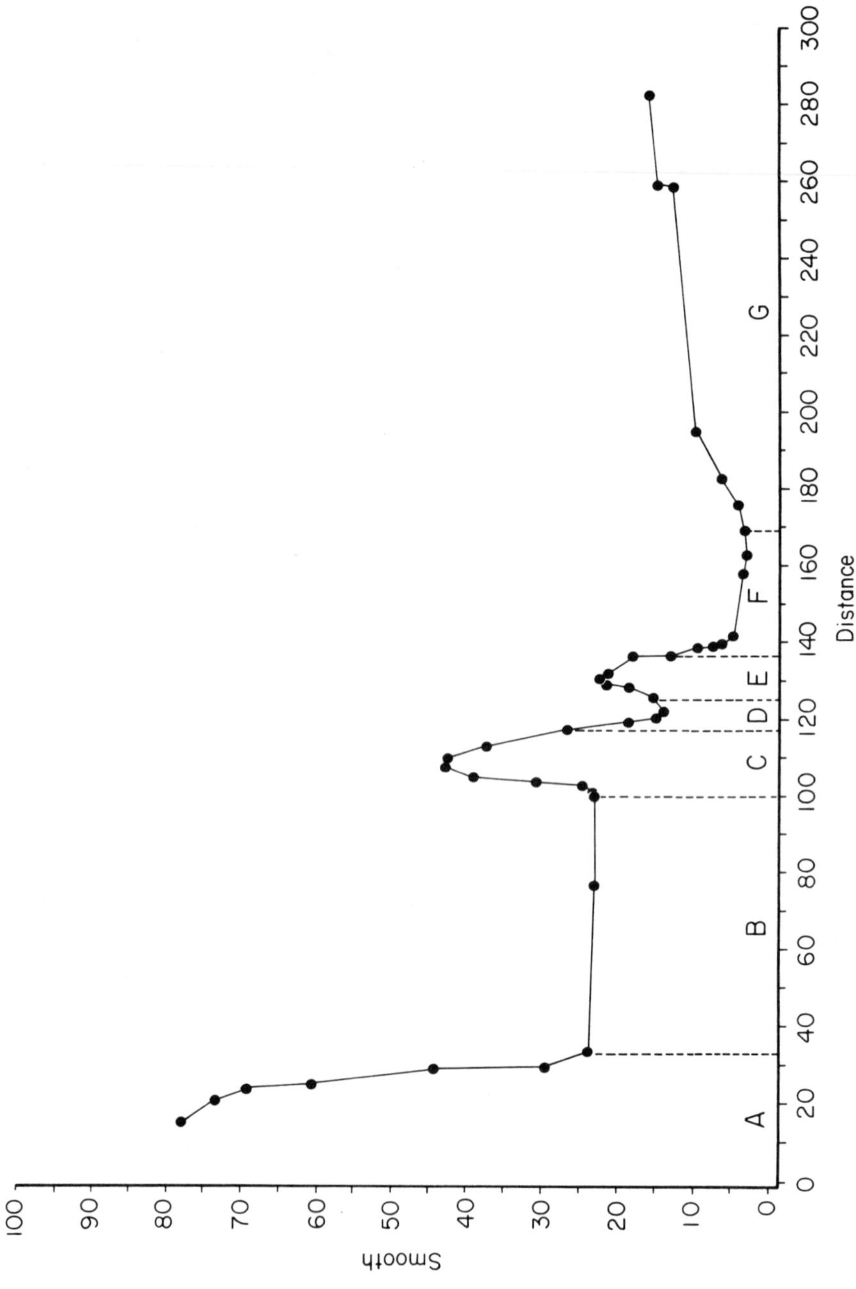

Figure 21. Plot of the smoothed freqencies against distance.

Section G incorporates both the majority of the Beeson survey sites and the Grand Canyon sites. It is surprising that both extremities of the exchange system should display an increase in exchange activity, given their great distances from the source. However, they possess two characteristics in common with the other peak areas in the smoothed data. First, all of the areas which participated intensively in LCWW exchange are characterized by contrasts in topography and vegetation zones. Second, they incorporate border zones between different cultural groups. The co-occurrence of environmental and cultural boundaries in areas of relatively intensive LCWW exchange suggest that this ware may have been functioning in the context of a risk-minimizing interaction system.

Braun and Plog (1982; see also S. Plog 1980a) have hypothesized that, at least by A.D. 1100, population growth and the year-round colonization of areas which were previously used by several populations on a seasonal basis effectively eliminated one of the major behavioral adaptations designed to mitigate against periodic shortages in subsistence resources. Individual social groups' exploitation ranges were reduced in size. Groups were no longer free to move between several different environmental zones to exploit alternative resources or plant their crops in various locations as a safeguard against environmental variability (cf. Ford 1972b). Instead, they could gain access to resources in environmental zones outside their home bases only by trading with other groups which now occupied those zones.

White (1974) uses a similar model to explain the existence of cooperative relationships between various ethnographic cultures along an east-west axis from southern California, across the Great Basin into the Southwest. He argues that such east-west interactions cross-cut environmental zones and were designed to reduce subsistence stress by moving diverse types of resources between groups (White 1974:120).

Given the spatial variability in the plateau southwestern paleoenvironment discussed in Chapter III, it is reasonable to suggest that tensions would exist between social groups inhabiting different environmental zones, especially during periods when the resource differential between zones was particularly marked. The tension would be amplified in areas where the "haves" and the "have-nots" possessed separate cultural or ethnic identities. In such cases, there would be few or no kinship ties with which to initiate exchange transactions. No social sanctions against raiding or stealing would have existed across cultural boundaries. However, as Ford (1972a) has pointed out, raiding is an inefficient means of obtaining resources. It invites future hostilities which may come at an inopportune time when surpluses are not available.

Some type of formalized mechanism would have to be maintained between cultural groups in order to minimize tensions and facilitate the peaceful exchange of resources across environmental zones during times of subsistence stress. Such a mechanism might take the form of marriage agreements or trading partnerships which would create the necessary social ties for harmonious and relatively risk-free interaction. It is hypothesized herein that LCWW could have circulated within such a system of intergroup interaction, its value being converted into subsistence goods when necessary.

A few brief descriptions of the peak areas will serve to illustrate their environmental and cultural diversity. There can be no doubt that the eastern portion of the Grand Canyon exhibits some of the most dramatic contrasts in topography and environmental zones in the plateau Southwest. This area is also at the intersection of what have been designated traditionally as two different cultural units: the Kayenta Anasazi and Cohonina. Both groups occupied the South Rim of the Grand Canyon at least as far west as Pasture Wash. The Kayenta also occupied deltas and pockets of land in the inner gorge east of Kanab Canyon, as well as parts of the North Rim above this section of the Colorado River (Janet Balsom, personal communication 1987).

The latter group practiced agriculture and located their settlements in areas with arable land. They constructed various water and soil control devices such as check dams and terraces both in the inner gorge and along the rims of the canyon (Schwartz et al. 1980; Jones 1983). Cohonina subsistence is less well understood because few sites have been excavated and no flotation samples have ever been taken from Cohonina sites. The limited evidence suggests a reliance on both hunting and gathering and agriculture. However, the prevalence of projectile points at Cohonina sites indicates a "considerable reliance upon hunting" (Cartledge 1987:5) which may have been greater than among the Kayenta. If this were the case, the Cohonina could have exchanged periodic surpluses of meat with the Kayenta. In addition, certain Cohonina groups probably controlled the supply of Government Mountain and Mount Floyd obsidian which were located well within Cohonina territory (Cartledge 1987). Both types of obsidian are found on Kayenta sites. It seems likely that the Kayenta exchanged for this raw material with the Cohonina, or that the Cohonina controlled Kayenta access to the obsidian.

One could view the entire region from the Hopi Buttes to the San Francisco Peaks as one macro area containing both contrasting environmental zones and cultural boundaries.

The San Francisco Peaks area ranges from open desert along the Little Colorado River, to pinyon and juniper forests which give way to ponderosa pine, douglas fir and spruce forests in the higher elevations. It also contrasts sharply with the open arid plateau to the east of the Little Colorado River. The Anasazi/Sinagua border roughly coincides with the border between the San Francisco volcanic field and the open plateau (Colton 1968). These environmental and cultural lines of demarcation might explain why the San Francisco distance decay pattern exhibits a linearity which has been linked to supply zone exchange. In essence, the Hopi Buttes and San Francisco Peaks were tied together into a single area of intensive LCWW exchange activity. Such a situation would stand to reason, particularly if the area between the Hopi Buttes and the San Francisco Peaks was devoid of settlements.

The drainage of the upper Little Colorado River where Beeson (1966) conducted his survey is characterized by a change in elevation and increasing topographic relief as one moves northeast. The Little Colorado River, Carrizo Creek and the lower Zuni River flow through open country marked by sand dunes covered with pinyon and juniper trees, interspersed with basalt mesas. The upper Zuni River, Jaramillo Wash and upper Hardscrabble Wash flow through uplands cut by steep canyons and are interspersed with mesas and hills. To the far northeast along the Arizona/New Mexico border, there is an abrupt increase in elevation. The area is dissected by steep-walled canyons and Ponderosa pine trees grow in the higher elevations (Beeson 1966:21-28).

Pueblo II and III sites are distributed between these two zones of open country along Platt Wash and the Little Colorado River on the one hand, and the dissected uplands on the other (Beeson 1966:Figures 9-23). Beeson (1966:256) has delineated borders for the

Adamana and Mogollon based on the ceramic assemblages of sites in his survey area, as shown in Figure 22. LCWW is concentrated in the area between these two borders in the drainages of the Zuni River and Hardscrabble Wash. Beeson (1966:254) hypothesizes that the Adamana occupation predates the Mogollon and Anasazi based on Wendorf's (1953) conclusion that Adamana Brown is earlier than Lino Grey. If this interpretation is correct, then only the Mogollon/Anasazi border zone needs to be considered.

Beeson (1966:259) points out that any clearly definable border between the Anasazi and Mogollon in the upper Little Colorado River valley disappears during the Pueblo I period and does not reappear until Pueblo IV times. He states,

> The traded pottery suggests an established trade relationship between the two groups. . . The abundance of pottery of Anasazi tradition on Mogollon sites, and vice versa, strongly suggests trade rather than trophies (Beeson 1966:258).

Had the Beeson survey sites been unique in their possession of high smooth values, their frequencies would have been called into question because of the fact that these sites were not excavated, unlike the other sites in the extended sample. However, the Beeson data fit the patterning of the other peak areas with respect to their geographic and cultural contexts, making the relatively high frequencies of LCWW recorded for this area more credible.

It should be noted that the topographic and vegetational differences also exist within the Chevelon area. There is a steady climb in altitude towards the Mogollon Rim and the upper portions of Chevelon Canyon and Potato Wash are characterized by relatively high relief (about 1000 to 3000 ft). The southern portion of this area is dissected by parallel ridges running north and south, some of which are separated by deep canyons (F. Plog

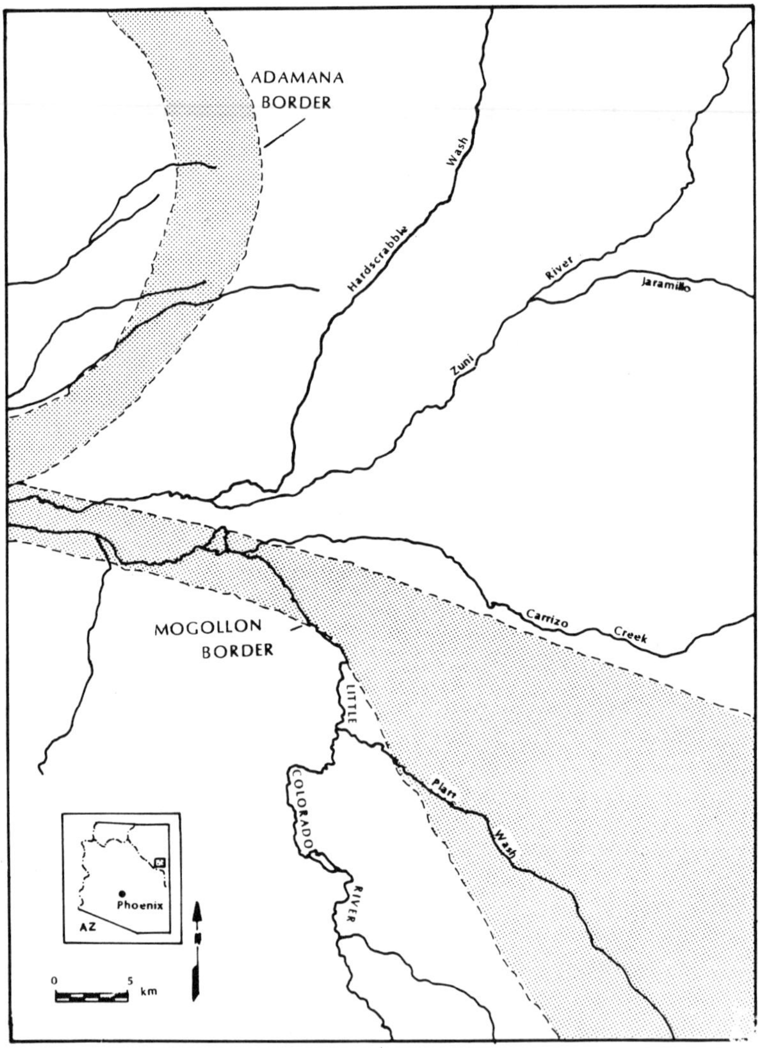

Figure 22. Location of the Mogollon and Adamana borders designated by Beeson (1966:Figure 37).

1981:10). In addition, this area represents a border zone between the Anasazi and Mogollon. Both of these characteristics would qualify the Chevelon area as a locus of relatively intense LCWW interaction. Its positioning within a trough in the smoothed data sequence is primarily a product of the late occupation dates of the Chevelon sites within the extended sample. Examination of S. Plog's (1980a) Table 3.3 reveals that the earlier dated sites possessed higher frequencies of LCWW which are comparable to those of sites in the San Francisco Peaks area. In addition, a study of the spatial distribution of LCWW within the Apache-Sitgreaves National Forest has shown that the Chevelon sites are within the area of high to moderate density for this ware (F. Plog 1981:Map 18).

To summarize, it is possible that LCWW was tied into a formalized mechanism of interaction given its concentration along the borders of different cultural "provinces" (F. Plog 1983) and environmental zones. In addition to maintaining cooperative intergroup relationships, this ware might have been used for "banking" (Braun and Plog 1980) surplus goods and creating inter-community obligations which could be called upon in future times of shortage. Significantly, the LCWW exchange system was developing between ca. A.D. 1050 and 1150, a period which Dean et al. (1985) have characterized as optimal for subsistence exchange because of the high spatial variability in climate on the Colorado Plateau.

Exchange as a "spatial averaging mechanism" (Braun and Plog 1982:514) for subsistence risk also might have motivated the Hopi Buttes communities to export LCWW. Cross-cultural studies have demonstrated that areas which are marginal for agriculture often supplement their subsistence base by producing ceramics for export. Agriculturally poor areas in Peru (Arnold 1975), Guatemala (Arnold 1978:330-331), the Jutland region of Europe, and villages in northwestern Spain and northern Portugal (Peacock 1981:189) have engaged in the household manufacture of ceramics for export at different points in time.

Gumerman and Skinner (1968:186-187) describe the marginal nature of the middle Little Colorado River drainage which includes the Hopi Buttes area:

> . . . [T]he central Little Colorado drainage system comprises an ecosystem distinguishable from the surrounding higher and, consequently, wetter regions. . . The only permanent stream is the Little Colorado River, and even it is occasionally dry for several weeks at a time. . . Only on the higher elevations can thin stands of juniper and an occasional pinyon be found. Ground cover is sparse and mainly bunch grass.
>
> The high terrain surrounding the Painted Desert acts as a barrier to the movement of low-level moist air, and, consequently, the precipitation averages little more than 8 in. a year along the Little Colorado. Much of this rainfall is lost because of the intensity of the storms and the sparseness of the ground cover. . . The prevailing south-southwest wind, which often causes considerable damage to young crops, was apparently of similar direction and severity prehistorically, as indicated by fossil dunes. . .

Given the risks of crop failure due to the lack of rain, damaging run-offs and desiccating winds, it would make sense for the inhabitants of the Hopi Buttes to maintain exchange ties with areas who had more optimal agricultural conditions due to their higher altitude and/or their proximity to drainages (such as the San Francisco Peaks and Chevelon area). In addition, no nonlocal goods or raw materials have been found in large enough quantities within the Hopi Buttes to qualify as counterparts in LCWW exchange transactions outside this area, suggesting that this ware could have been exchanged for perishable foodstuffs which have not survived in the archaeological record.

In direct contrast to the peaks, the troughs demarcate areas which were more peripheral in terms of the LCWW exchange sphere. Section B corresponds to the area between the Hopi Buttes and San Francisco Peaks. Very few sites are known from this area. It is not possible to determine at this time whether the trough is due to a real drop in population density between the Hopi Buttes and San Francisco Peaks, or if this apparent "no man's land" is an artifact of poor survey coverage. In addition, the trough in section B may have been artificially augmented by the break in the distance measurements within the extended site sample between ca. 70 and 100 km from the source.

It is possible that prehistoric communities did inhabit this area and that their remains are simply waiting discovery. It remains to be seen whether such sites, if they exist, will display high frequencies of LCWW. However, there is limited evidence to suggest that the trough might be due to a real drop in LCWW frequencies in this area. Bliss and Ezell (1956) surveyed a pipeline right-of-way which crossed the southern portion of the Navajo Reservation, in the process of which they passed through the Little Colorado River valley between the Hopi Buttes and San Francisco volcanic field. In summarizing the distribution of LCWW, they state:

> From the cinder cones [of the San Francisco volcanic field] west almost to Flagstaff, its occurrence is persistent but sporadic in quantity, sharing the painted classification with Tusayan White Ware in unpredictable percentages. In the area between Oraibi Wash and the cinder cones, Tusayan White Ware is the dominant decorated ware (Bliss and Ezell 1956:105).

Section D is another trough which incorporates the Chevelon sites and Winona Village. Again, Winona's low percentage of LCWW clearly stands out from other San Francisco communities. The Chevelon area's much lower LCWW exchange activity is probably at least partially due to the fact that three out of the four sites used in the distance decay analysis date to the twelfth century, at which time LCWW exchange in this area was attenuating. Inclusion of these Chevelon sites in the extended sample has caused an interruption in the general pattern of intense LCWW exchange in the San Francisco area, as reflected by the peaks in C and E. If these sites are removed from the analysis, the smoothed frequencies display a continuous peak between 100 and ca. 136 km which is not affected significantly by the single anomalous case of Winona.

Section F marks a trough containing the northern San Francisco sites (Juniper Terrace, NA 680 and Metate House), the Snowflake area sites and two of the Beeson survey sites in east-central Arizona. The occurrence of the northern San Francisco sites in the lowest trough of the smoothed frequencies clearly sets them apart from the intense LCWW exchange of the more southerly and easterly sites within this area. Again, this distinction appears to be caused primarily by distance from the LCWW production source. Similarly, it is clear that the Snowflake area was on the fringes of LCWW exchange. This conclusion is supported by the fact that LCWW appears in very low densities or is entirely absent from sites on the Apache-Sitgreaves National Forest in the area immediately to the south of Snowflake (F. Plog 1981:Map 18).

It is noteworthy that neither the Snowflake area nor the Petrified Forest (which is at the lowest portion of the peak in section C) were located near cultural borders between the eleventh and first half of the thirteenth centuries. The Petrified Forest area also lacks the contrasting vegetation types of the peak areas, since it is entirely within the plains/desert grassland zone.

Finally, it is necessary to examine the rough in order to conform to the basic principles of EDA. The plot of the rough against distance (Figure 23) shows a relatively

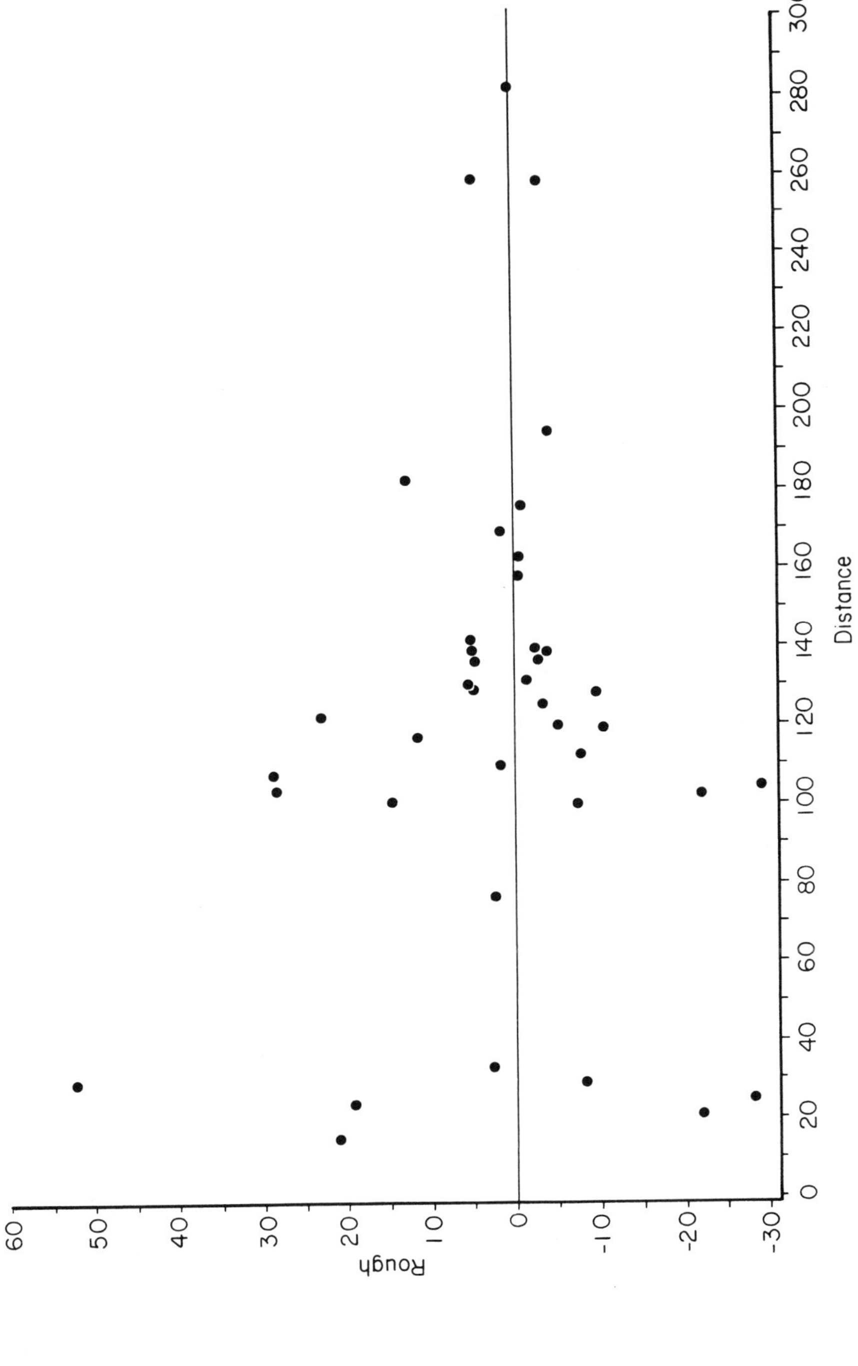

Figure 23. Plot of the rough against distance.

amorphous scatter of points, indicating that the patterning in the data has been extracted effectively. Many of the sites with large positive and negative residuals of the best-fit resistant line (e.g., NA 10,757, NA 9165, NA 9183, the Plaza Site and Tse Tlani) also exhibit large rough values, as is to be expected since both resistant line-fitting and smoothing are resistant to outliers.

There is a noticeably greater degree of variability in the rough values below approximately 130km than there is at greater distances. Similarly, the smoothed sequence (Figure 21) exhibits a reduction in the amplitude of its peaks and troughs at about 140km from the source. In addition, the plot of the untransformed frequency and distance values (Figure 18) has a steeper right half slope which begins at just over 120km. Putting all these characteristics of the plots together, it seems that distance becomes a more important determinant of the intensity of LCWW exchange somewhere between 120 and 140km from the source.

In conclusion, the smooth data has revealed a pattern of relatively intense LCWW exchange along environmental ecotones which also coincide with boundaries between different cultural groups. The eastern Grand Canyon, the southern and eastern portions of the San Francisco Peaks area and Beeson's survey area in east-central Arizona meet these two criteria and appear as peaks in the smoothed frequency pattern. These results agree with the patterning of the residuals in the resistant line-fitting. It is postulated that the Chevelon area was also a locus of fairly intensive LCWW exchange. It is argued that this area has shown up as a trough in the smooth data because the sites included in the extended site sample postdate the period of most intensive exchange activity with regards to this ware.

Therefore, the location of borders between different environmental zones and cultural groups seems to have been a stronger determinant of the intensity of LCWW exchange than distance from its source. The varying degrees of interaction intensity between the Hopi Buttes and other areas within the Little Colorado River drainage obviates the selection of a linear model to describe the overall structure of LCWW exchange.

Exchange between the Hopi Buttes, and areas to the south and east might have been conducted in a more down-the-line fashion than exchange with the San Francisco Peaks area. The Homolovi area might have acted as an intermediary in such down-the-line transactions since LCWW occurs there in frequencies which are comparable to areas of relatively intense LCWW exchange (Richard C. Lange, personal communication 1987; see also Table 18 below). The northern San Francisco Peaks area, the Snowflake area and the Petrified Forest were peripheral participants in the LCWW exchange sphere. The following section will consider other aspects of the archaeological record besides the frequency distribution of LCWW in order to shed more light on the nature of the exchange system and its function within the broader cultural context.

Other Contextual Factors

Hodder (1982) has argued for a contextual approach to the analysis of prehistoric exchange which takes into account the cultural milieu within which such economic transactions took place. Some factors, such as site type and intra-site contexts already have been considered. However, several other cultural and environmental factors, discussed in the distance decay section of this chapter, can affect the rate of fall-off within an exchange

Table 18. Pueblo II/Pueblo III Population Density Estimates for Five Areas Within the Little Colorado River Drainage.

Area	Rms/km^{2}[a]	LCWW Frequency
Nankoweap Canyon	26.35[b]	19.26
Petrified Forest	6.60[c]	20.36[f]
Purcell-Larson	1.94[d] (A.D. 1051-1125) 5.06[d] (A.D. 1126-1200)	34.75[f]
Snowflake	1.06[d] (A.D. 901-1100) 21.45[d] (A.D. 1101-1250)	7.99[f]
Homolovi area	1.5[e]	22.00[f]

[a] habitation sites only
[b] Janet Balsom, personal communication 1987
[c] A. Trinkle Jones, personal communication 1987
[d] Hantman 1983:Tables 15 and 17
[e] Richard C. Lange, personal communication 1987
[f] mean frequency

sphere. Each of these will be discussed in turn in order to determine what their effect on the intensity of LCWW exchange might have been.

An important factor to consider is the nature of the terrain across which LCWW was transported. As discussed above, there is a great deal of variability in topography throughout the Little Colorado River drainage. Elevation generally increases as one moves away from the channel of the river to the south toward the Mogollon Rim, the west toward the San Francisco Peaks, the east toward the Arizona/New Mexico border and the northwest toward the Grand Canyon. In short, the distance decay gradient should increase farther away from the river valley. However, all the concentrations of LCWW exchange isolated in the smoothed pattern occur in areas where the cost of transport in terms of energy expenditure was high. Clearly, the difficulties of travel were outweighed by the benefits gained from the exchange. A violation of the law of monotonic decrement is comprehensible if LCWW exchange were linked with the movement of subsistence goods across environmental zones created by high topographic relief.

Another factor which can influence the rate of distance decay is the type of good being exchanged. LCWW seems to have been very much a part of the daily lives of those who exchanged for it. There is no evidence that it was cached. Although it occurs in higher frequencies in community structures such as kivas and ballcourts, there is no evidence that sites possessing these structures were repositories for large numbers of LCWW vessels, or that the residents of these sites controlled the exchange of this ware.

LCWW is found primarily in domestic contexts such as the fill of pithouses and masonry rooms as well as trash middens. It is found in all types of sites within the exchange sphere, both large and small, with or without community structures. These facts suggest that this ware was not designated for specific religious functions such as inter-community ceremonials. It is possible that LCWW did operate within a socioeconomic ceremony such as the presentation of bride price or exchange between trading partners. However, once this ware entered the receiving household, it became part of the domestic inventory.

There is no association between high concentrations of LCWW and certain domestic structures or burials within settlements. Thus it does not appear to have been differentially distributed among the population or used as a status marker. Therefore, there would not have been a demand "pull" created by high-status factions which would have initiated directional exchange links within the LCWW sphere.

Given its primary function as a household item, the demand for LCWW throughout its various exchange destinations was probably sporadic and more or less evenly spread throughout the year. Each importing community's demand would follow its own cycle, irrespective of the demand of other communities. There would be no peak periods of demand that one would expect if LCWW were associated with a particular ceremonial season. Nor would there be coordinated demand cycles as in redistributive systems in which centers could effectively store up the demand of their satellite settlements until a certain volume of demand was achieved, at which point exchange would be initiated.

It is possible that periods of peak demand for this ware could be generated by widespread climatic factors which were simultaneously affecting several areas within the LCWW exchange system. For example, high spatial variability in growing conditions would result in uneven resource distributions, therefore creating a widespread demand on the part of many communities for such exchange goods as LCWW. However, such periods of demand would be relatively infrequent and unpredictable. As a result, there would be no consistent "pull" created by periods of high demand which would counteract the frictional effects of distance or institute directional exchange. As Stephen Plog (1980b:142-143) has pointed out,

> While thousands of imported vessels may be found in an area, this does not mean that thousands of vessels were traded within a short period of time. For example, assume that in a small area of 100 km^2 an average of one family occupied each square kilometer over a period of 100 years. If each family received just one vessel per year, then 10,000 trade vessels would be found in

> that area. . . I would suggest that exchange of one vessel per family per year easily could be accomplished through reciprocal exchange ties.

Given the potential date range of 200 years for sites within the extended sample, it stands to reason that the relatively high frequencies of LCWW found in areas such as the San Francisco Peaks and the Chevelon Creek drainage could be due to reciprocal exchange on a community-to-community basis (whether through direct access to the supply zone or down-the-line exchange).

In addition, there would be no need for a high volume of production at the source in specialized workshops. Enough vessels could be manufactured through household production to meet the needs of the exchange system. The amount of variability in the constituents of LCWW sherds indicates a lack of technological standardization that is characteristic of household production. No caches of raw clay or potting tools, concentrations of wasters or ceramic firing features characteristic of specialized workshops have been identified in the Hopi Buttes area. Therefore, high production output would not have been a factor in counteracting the frictional effects of distance associated with the transport of LCWW into areas of high topographic relief.

The last important factor to be considered in this section is changes in population density throughout the drainage of the Little Colorado River. The effects of population density on the volume of LCWW exchange are difficult to assess because of the spotty nature of the survey data which is now available for this region. The area between the Hopi Buttes and San Francisco Peaks is largely unexplored, for example. Surveys have been conducted recently near the Homolovi site group in the middle Little Colorado River valley

(Adams 1985) and the Petrified Forest National Monument (A. Trinkle Jones, personal communication 1987) which will shed more light on the nature of LCWW exchange in these areas.

It is possible that the troughs in the smoothed data may be at least partially due to incomplete coverage of these areas. However, there is some limited evidence to suggest that this patterning cannot be completely explained away by differences in archaeological reconnaissance, and that the intensity of LCWW exchange was not necessarily determined by population density. Population density figures and LCWW frequencies for five areas within the Little Colorado River drainage, for which such data are available, are listed in Table 18. It must be emphasized that most of these figures are only estimates since they are based on the preliminary results of survey data.

Nevertheless, these data demonstrate that LCWW frequencies do not parallel population density. The Purcell-Larson area, which contains the Chevelon sites, has a much lower population density than the Snowflake area, in which NA 17,271B and NA 17,282 are located, at least by A.D. 1100. However, the frequencies of LCWW sherds in the decorated assemblages of the Chevelon sites dating to this time period are higher than those of the Snowflake sites. Similarly, the Homolovi and Petrified Forest areas have comparable frequencies of LCWW even though the population density estimates indicate that the latter area was much more densely populated than the former area. Thus the boundaries of inter-community interaction networks can be seen as stronger determinants of exchange activity than the potential size of the market in any one area.

Conclusion

This chapter has examined the frequency distribution of LCWW throughout the Little Colorado River drainage. These distributional patterns have important implications for the developmental model. Expectations derived from the model concerning pre-thirteenth century exchange have not been fully met. In addition, the results of this study can offer insights for the interpretation of later exchange systems.

The distance decay study has shown that LCWW exchange does not follow a pattern of monotonic decrement with increasing distance from its source. Areas of relatively active exchange are located further from the source than areas which were less intensively involved in the exchange network, as suggested by the first expectation listed in Chapter IV. However, the contextual evidence does not reveal a redistributive or hierarchically organized production-distribution system, despite the directional nature of the exchange. Several of the areas within the exchange sphere, such as the Hopi Buttes, San Francisco Peaks and Snowflake, possessed bimodal settlement patterns, as discussed in Chapter III. In addition, the LCWW sphere incorporated sites which were probably exchange centers and which occupied the highest tier within their respective settlement systems. Yet these centers did not function as redistribution points for LCWW, nor were they receiving preferential access to this tradeware in relation to the smaller sites within their immediate environs, as postulated in the second expectation.

A primary case in point is Winona Village, which was linked to the Hohokam exchange sphere. Despite its participation in the exchange of such long-distance goods as marine shell, copper bells and argillite (Fish et al. 1980), Winona Village was not a center of LCWW exchange, as indicated by its negative resistant-line residual and its location in a trough of the smoothed frequency data. Nor does the Plaza Site exhibit extraordinarily high frequencies of LCWW within the source area, as would be expected if it were either a production center or a collection point for export.

The ballcourts and kiva associated with Winona Village and Juniper Terrace do show higher relative frequencies of LCWW than the domestic structures at these centers. However, it does not appear as if the residents of these centers controlled the access of this ware to surrounding communities. The specialized structures may have provided a place for other communities to exchange LCWW vessels. It is also possible that other types of activities requiring relatively large quantities of LCWW were being conducted in these specialized structures, exclusive of exchange.

Generally, LCWW occurs in small enough quantities to suggest that it was not an ubiquitous household item, thus supporting the third expectation. However, the intra-site contextual evidence does not indicate that access to this ware was controlled tightly by a select group, or that such access was status related, contrary to the fourth expectation.

This case study demonstrates that geographically restricted production and directionality in exchange can exist in the absence of centralized control. The results are consistent with the theory that regional exchange was initiated in the prehistoric plateau Southwest as an adaptive strategy for dealing with environmental variability and concomitant subsistence stress during a period when mobility was no longer a viable option. The distributional pattern of LCWW suggests that it was exchanged in order to maintain interaction between cultural groups occupying distinct environmental zones, or who controlled different natural resources. However, there is little evidence that LCWW developed into a "self-serving" political tool of decision-makers (Upham 1982:120).

It has been stated that systems like the one proposed for LCWW are inherently unstable and ineffective at minimizing risk. F. Plog (1984:219) argues that "weak alliances" and "'slight' tribalization" can spread risk from one group to another instead of minimizing it through inter-group exchange. However, Plog does not define clearly what he means by "weak" and "strong;" nor does he specify at what level of integration an interaction system reverts from a "weak" one which spreads problems instead of solving them, to a "strong" one which can buffer subsistence risk among its participants when necessary. Therefore, despite his argument, it has not been demonstrated that centralized leadership and prestige exchange are necessary components of an effective system of risk minimization among sedentary agriculturalists.

It is difficult to generalize beyond LCWW to other contemporaneous exchange goods. Their exchange systems could have been structured quite differently depending on their function, the cost of transport and the nature of the target populations, only to name a few factors. The exchange of such goods as copper bells and turquoise was probably more centralized and may have been controlled by exchange centers such as Chaco Canyon (Judd 1954; Mcguire 1980) and Winona Village (Fish et al. 1980). However, LCWW can serve as a starting point and basis of comparison, particularly for research of ceramic exchange predating A.D. 1200.

In addition, the present study has implications for the reconstruction of long-distance ceramic exchange in the later periods of southwestern prehistory. Upham (1982:128; 132-

133) has equated geographic concentrations of fourteenth century tradewares with the organizational centralization of production and exchange. However, as the LCWW case study has demonstrated, the directionality inherent in Upham's distance decay graphs for Jeddito Yellow Ware, Winslow Orange Ware, White Mountain Red Ware and Zuni Glaze Ware need not be the result of political alliances between elite leaders. LCWW's regional distributional patterns closely match the distributions of these later decorated wares, yet there is no evidence to suggest that it functioned as a prestige good. In addition, the Hopi Buttes production area is not characterized by a highly integrated, hierarchical settlement pattern which would indicate centralized political organization; nor is there evidence of specialized production of a ceramic ware which was exchanged over long distances.

Positive deviations from the law of monotonic decrement can be caused by various factors, alliance formation being only one of them, as discussed above. It is essential to examine independent contextual data in order to determine which factor(s) best explain the frequency distribution of a given commodity. It is not clear from Upham's data whether the peaks in his distance decay graphs are due to greater population densities (more vessels for more people) or preferential access by a select group (greater per capita consumption by a small elite). This issue can only be resolved by comparing population estimates for different settlement systems and examining intra-site distributions of the tradewares, as well as their occurrence in the burial populations of all nine settlement clusters.

It is also unclear what the structure of the exchange systems were within the settlement clusters since Upham uses only large sites in his analysis. There is no way of knowing whether the large settlements were indeed distribution centers, and whether the smaller communities only had indirect access to these commodities through such redistributive intermediaries. There is little doubt that fourteenth century ceramic exchange was highly directional. What still remains to be demonstrated, however, is the cause of that directionality. Intra-site contextual data and frequency distributions for lower order sites are needed in order to determine which interpretation is the most plausible.

One final aspect of the LCWW production-distribution system needs to be considered: the role of design style within this system. This issue must be examined from the standpoint of production as well as exchange. First, differences between the LCWW design styles with respect to their mineralogical composition would indicate that different loci within the Hopi Buttes production area were using distinctive styles to decorate their vessels. Second, changes in the design styles of LCWW vessels throughout different parts of the regional system might be due to the fact that there were separate exchange spheres within the larger regional system, or that the function of this commodity shifted at varying distances from the source (Hodder and Lane 1982). Alternatively, the differential geographic distribution of design styles might be a reflection of changes in the configuration of the exchange system through time. The role of design style within this production-distribution system will be addressed in the next chapter by examining the relationship between mineralogy, design style and vessel form, and by comparing the geographic distributions of the six LCWW design styles to one another.

CHAPTER VIII

STYLISTIC VARIABILITY IN LITTLE COLORADO WHITE WARE

Design style represents a second dimension of variability within LCWW, the analysis of which can contribute toward a greater understanding of the structure and function of this ware's production-distribution system. As Stephen Plog (1980a) has pointed out, stylistic variation can be influenced by a number of factors including temporal variation, functional variation, modes of production and exchange. However, it is not yet known how these factors interacted with one another to produce the ceramic design variability evident in the archaeological record of the plateau Southwest. The purpose of this chapter is to examine various potential causes of design style variability within LCWW.

The sourcing study has demonstrated that LCWW was produced within a geographically restricted and geologically homogeneous area in the northeastern sector of the Hopi Buttes. One would therefore expect to find different design styles on sherds with essentially the same mineralogical composition. However, the statistical analysis of the petrographic data revealed significant differences in the frequencies of matrix and sherd temper across the sherd sample. Such variation could have been caused by spatial or temporal variation in production technology within the source area. If the amount of matrix and sherd temper in LCWW varies across space, it is possible that different production loci manufactured vessels decorated with distinct styles in addition to using slightly different methods of paste preparation.

Variations in production technology and design styles could have been the result of cultural drift if different communities producing LCWW were relatively isolated from one another. As Binford (1963:92-94) has pointed out, random sampling error can be caused by slight biases in the transmission of cultural information from one generation to the next, or from parent community to a budding daughter community. In addition, as the heritage of design styles grows through time, the probability that potters will resurrect and reinterpret stylistic attributes from the past grows in turn.

If different production loci were producing stylistically distinct vessels, one would expect frequencies of matrix and sherd temper to covary with certain contemporaneous styles.

If production loci altered their paste preparation techniques through time, one would expect different matrix and sherd temper frequencies to covary with styles manufactured at different periods of time.

Alternatively, different production loci might have shared the same stylistic repertoire even though their production technologies were distinct. Such uniformity in style could have occurred if potters in the different producing communities interacted regularly with one another (Whallon 1968; Friedrich 1970; Hill 1970; Longacre 1970). If this were the case, one would expect the same design styles to appear on sherds with very different matrix and sherd temper frequencies.

From the perspective of exchange, the spatial distribution of the various contemporaneous styles relative to one another must be examined in order to determine whether or not they were slated for different exchange spheres. Style might have signalled function if different styles, whether produced in one or more loci, were transported to the same communities. The issue of functional variability can be pursued by examining the relationship between vessel form and style.

Alternatively, different styles might have operated within separate exchange networks, regardless of who was producing them. If this were the case, one would expect styles to exhibit distinct geographic distributions. In this context, design styles might reflect inter-community political and economic cooperation rather than vessel function. Design style could have operated as a dynamic medium of communication which signalled cooperation between settlement systems (Wobst 1977; S. Plog 1980a; Hantman and Plog 1982).

Again, it is necessary to consider the temporal dimension in stylistic variability. The co-occurrence of different styles in the same areas may indicate continuous occupation and extended exchange relationships across two or more stylistic periods. In the same manner, distinct geographic distributions for different styles might be the result of shifting populations and/or changes in exchange relationships through time.

Several interpretations have been offered above for the relationship of LCWW style to mineralogy and the distribution of styles across space. The selection of the most appropriate interpretation(s) will depend to a large degree on the definition of stylistic variability and whether it is attributed to temporal, functional or spatial factors. The following section will discuss the evidence for the classification and dating of LCWW styles. Subsequently, three aspects of style will be considered in this chapter: the relationship of stylistic to mineralogical variability within this ware, the geographic distribution of different LCWW styles and vessel forms, and the relationship of style to vessel form.

The Classification and Dating of Styles

Colton's (1955) description of LCWW is still the most comprehensive and widely used typology of this ware. He subdivided LCWW into six types based on various design attributes and the presence or absence of corrugated exteriors. Table 19 summarizes Colton's principal stylistic criteria for the six types. His typology is inconsistent in terms of the amount of stylistic variability within each type. According to his definitions, Holbrook and Chevelon Black-on-white are composed of two styles (Black Mesa and Sosi), while Walnut Black-on-white is composed of three styles (Sosi, Walnut and Tularosa). St. Joseph, Padre and Leupp Black-on-white each consist of a single style. In addition, the types overlap stylistically since Holbrook, Chevelon and Walnut Black-on-white have Sosi style varieties, and since the Black Mesa style can appear on either Holbrook or Chevelon Black-on-white. Therefore, Colton's typology of LCWW runs contrary to the definition of a type as a stylistically distinct and internally uniform classificatory unit (Colton and Hargrave 1937:2).

I propose an alternative means of classifying LCWW which is based strictly on design style (refer to Appendix C for a detailed description of this system). Table 20 shows the correspondence between Colton's typology and the different design styles which appear on LCWW sherds and vessels. I do not consider Chevelon Black-on-white to be a valid classificatory unit because it is defined solely on the basis of a corrugated exterior surface. In addition, I have seen exterior corrugation on LCWW sherds bearing Sosi, Black Mesa and Flagstaff designs. One of the whole LCWW bowls at the Museum of Northern Arizona has a Leupp style design and a corrugated exterior. I have eliminated St. Joseph Black-on-

Table 19. Stylistic Criteria for LCWW Types in Colton's (1955) Classification System.

Type	Stylistic Criteria
St. Joseph	narrow lines; triangles with pendent dots
Holbrook A	wide lines over 5mm in width; triangles with pendent dots
Holbrook B	wide lines over 5mm in width; absence of pendent dots
Padre	hatched rectangular and triangular panels; some cross-hatching; occasional solid triangles and stepped elements combined with hatched elements
Chevelon	same as Holbrook (A and B?) but with corrugated exteriors on bowls
Walnut A	barbs and serations; lines under 0.5cm in width
Walnut B	interlocking triangular scrolls
Walnut C	contrasting hatched and solid elements
Leupp	over 50% of surface painted, creating a negative design; sawtoothed lines; interlocking scrolls; mosquito barring and other elements similar to Kayenta and Tusayan Black-on-white

white since it is only represented by a single type sherd (Colton 1955) which I could not locate in the type collections at the Museum of Northern Arizona. Nor did I encounter any St. Joseph Black-on-white during my examination of thousands of LCWW sherds.

Holbrook Black-on-white has been subdivided into a Black Mesa and a Sosi style which correspond with Colton's A and B varieties respectively. My design analysis revealed that Walnut is actually composed of a Flagstaff and Walnut style, as was indicated to me by Peter Pilles (personal communication 1984) at the outset of my research. I only

Table 20. Correspondence Between Colton's (1955) Typology and the Proposed Stylistic Categories.

Colton's Type	Style
St. Joseph	None
Holbrook A	Black Mesa
Holbrook B	Sosi
Padre	Padre
Chevelon	None
Walnut A	Flagstaff
Walnut B	Walnut
Walnut C	None
Leupp	Leupp

encountered two sherds which might be classified as Tularosa style (Colton's Walnut Variety C) although the solid elements were narrower than the hatched elements. [According to Carlson (1970), solid and hatched elements should be the same size in Tularosa style designs.] In fact, these sherds strongly resembled some of Colton's (1955) illustrations of Padre Black-on-white type sherds. Colton (1955) describes the Walnut Black-on-white, Variety A style as having "barbs and serations," which are diagnostic characteristics of the Flagstaff style. Walnut Variety B, Padre and Leupp represent distinctive enough styles to retain them as separate stylistic units.

The inconsistencies in Colton's (1955) classification of LCWW with regards to style are due to a concern with this ware as a temporal diagnostic. The use of LCWW as a time marker has predominated the classification of this ware to the present day. This application of LCWW to chronology building is particularly evident in the Holbrook/Walnut Black-on-white dichotomy. Not surprisingly, these two types are also the most diverse stylistically.

Colton (1939) first used Holbrook and Walnut Black-on-white to define and date the Holbrook and MacDonald Foci of what he termed the Winslow Branch of the Anasazi. Gumerman and Skinner (1968) later employed the same foci, which they called phases, in their Hopi Buttes chronology. However, they used revised dates derived from Colton (1955) and Breternitz (1966).

Colton (1946) later used a series of ceramic groups in his synthesis of Sinagua prehistory in order to provide a dating system for sites in the San Francisco Peaks area. He defined a ceramic group as "an assemblage of contemporary, usually painted, pottery types recognized at a site of short occupation" (Colton 1946:18). Colton listed Holbrook Black-on-white as a diagnostic for Group 6, while Walnut Black-on-white appeared in the definitions of Groups 7 through 9. He referred to Holbrook and Walnut as "the two types in this ware [LCWW] most useful for dating" (Colton 1946:22). Colton proposed dates for various types, based on their co-occurrence with one another and associated tree-ring dates from Sinagua sites. He dated Holbrook Black-on-white between A.D. 1050 and 1125, while he assigned Walnut Black-on-white to the period between A.D. 1120 and 1275 (Colton 1946:253). His dates for Group 6 on the one hand, and Groups 7 through 9 on the other, roughly correspond to these dates. Implicit in Colton's dating scheme, therefore, is the assumption that each ceramic type was produced throughout the period represented by its associated ceramic group.

In his more recent synthesis of Sinagua prehistory, Wilson (1969:Table 20) presented a revised system of ceramic groups. Holbrook Black-on-white is listed as a diagnostic of Group IV (A.D. 1067-1130) and Walnut Black-on-white is shown as a predominant type of Groups V (A.D. 1130-1210) and VI (A.D. 1210-1300). If one uses the same assumption concerning the correspondence between the dates of ceramic groups and types, Wilson's dates for the two LCWW types do not contradict Colton's dates, despite the revisions in ceramic groups.

The discrete date ranges associated with Holbrook and Walnut, and the ceramic groups in Colton's and Wilson's dating systems are misleading, however. Such systems are categorical and break up temporal continual into discrete, internally homogeneous (from the perspective of ceramic assemblages) blocks of time. If one examines the date ranges assigned to LCWW types by Breternitz (1966), it is apparent that there is a significant amount of overlap, as shown in Table 21.

Breternitz' dates suffer from two major problems which probably have contributed to the overlapping, relatively wide date ranges for ceramic types. First, his distinction between "indigenous" and "trade" contexts is not valid since they are not based on compositional analyses of the ceramic types. Second, the contextual associations between the tree-ring samples and the ceramic types are not clear. This problem is particularly acute because Breternitz used tree-ring dates from many large, complex sites (Hantman 1983). In addition to these methodological problems, the dendrochronological data base has been growing in

Table 21. Breternitz' (1966) Dates for LCWW Types.

Type	Indigenous	Best Indigenous	Trade	Best Trade
St. Joseph		no dates given		
Chevelon		no dates given		
Holbrook	701-1279	1075-1130	1023-1061	--
Walnut	914-1390	1085-1250	957-1275	1050-1200
Padre	1086-1279	1100-1200	957-1275	1075?
Leupp	1086-1279	--	--	--

the twenty years since Breternitz published his synthesis. Therefore, Breternitz' ceramic dates are probably in need of revision.

Even if these problems were eliminated, however, it is likely that the overlap between dates would remain at least to some degree, assuming that changes in design styles (upon which ceramic types are based) were not abrupt and underwent periods of transition from one style to the next. There is some evidence to support this assumption, at least in the case of LCWW. Gumerman and Skinner (1968) state that Holbrook Black-on-white is still present in the early part of the MacDonald Phase. They also note that both types are present at the Plaza Site, though in different contexts. The relatively thin layer of trash accumulation at this site, coupled with the fact that it was built as a single unit, suggest a short period of occupation. Therefore, the co-occurrence of these two types at the Plaza Site cannot be attributed to a two-phase occupation.

Approximately 1% of the 2400 sherds in my design analysis sample possessed the characteristics of two styles. Walnut and Leupp co-occurred on sherds the most frequently. Other combinations encountered were Flagstaff and Walnut, and Walnut and Padre. The latter two were relatively rare, however. I also examined the whole LCWW vessel collection at the Museum of Northern Arizona and noted several cases in which two design styles co-occurred on a single vessel, usually in separate fields. For example, one jar, which is illustrated in Gumerman (1969:Figure 17a), has a Padre design around the body and a Walnut design around the neck and shoulder. Walnut motifs occasionally occur on bowls and jars with Padre or Leupp motifs. Black Mesa style ticks also can be found on triangles within Sosi or Flagstaff style designs.

Slightly less than half of the sherds in the design sample were not classifiable into one of the six styles. I often had difficulty in distinguishing between Sosi and Flagstaff on the one hand, and Flagstaff and Walnut on the other, when I was classifying sherds. (Problematic sherds were classified according to combination or transitional stylistic categories.) It is highly probable that Colton and other southwestern ceramicists have experienced the same difficulties. As a consequence, it is easy to understand why Colton defined both Holbrook B and Walnut A as Sosi style. The widespread practice of reporting Walnut Black-on-white without specifying the variety is also a product of these classificatory problems.

I maintain that the combination of styles on single vessels and the sometimes ambiguous distinctions between style categories are due at least in part to the fact that the process of stylistic change occurred along a continuum in which periods of transition from one style to the next are difficult to demarcate. These classificatory problems are not, in my view, solely an artifact of the classification system itself. Seen from this perspective, it is not surprising that there is a significant amount of temporal overlap between the different types and styles of LCWW, over and above the problems with contextual relationships between dendrochronological samples and ceramics artifacts.

However, it is necessary to break up the continuum artificially into more or less discrete classificatory blocks in order to analyze the process of change. This division can be done in one of two ways. First, one can view each style as a temporally distinct unit. Second, one can attempt to break up the continuum into sections which group strongly overlapping styles and distinguish between styles with a greater degree of temporal separation.

Each approach will have different consequences on any comparisons that are made between the styles. The first alternative is based on an artificial separation which tends to stretch out the continuum and over-emphasize the differences between styles. The second alternative has the opposite effect: it creates a false dichotomy which tends to underestimate the separation between the styles. In addition, it puts more weight on the opposite ends of the continuum which are likely to show the most marked differences.

In reviewing the available "best indigenous" dates for the LCWW types, the strongly overlapping relationships between the date ranges allow for only an early/late dichotomy between the types. The Walnut and Padre dates completely overlap. One can assume that the overlap between Walnut and Leupp would be comparable since Padre and Leupp share the same "indigenous" dates. Fully 82% of the Holbrook Black-on-white "indigenous" production period overlaps with that of Walnut Black-on-white. However, viewed from another perspective, only 27% of Walnut's date range overlaps with Holbrook, suggesting that the bulk of its production period postdates that of the latter type.

In the San Francisco Peaks area, Walnut Black-on-white is rare or absent in contexts at Winona Village which have been tree-ring dated between the mid 1070s and 1140s. Holbrook Black-on-white, on the other hand, is present in the same contexts in relatively large quantities. Walnut Black-on-white has been reported from Wupatki, Two Kivas and Metate House, which have been tree-ring dated between the 1170 and the early 1200s. Holbrook Black-on-white is rare or absent in these later contexts. The only datable context for Leupp Black-on-white in this area is at Two Kivas Pueblo, which would place it sometime in the early thirteenth century (Chris E. Downum, personal communication 1987).

In reviewing the evidence, one could argue that the best (although far from ideal) boundary for an early/late dichotomy lies between Holbrook Black-on-white on the one hand and Walnut, Padre and Leupp Black-on-white on the other. Translating this contrast into stylistic terms, Sosi and Black Mesa would be classified as "early" and Flagstaff, Walnut, Padre and Leupp would be classified as "late." Both the dichotomous and style-by-style approaches will be used in comparing the six LCWW styles to each other.

Production Organization: Mineralogical and Stylistic Variability

The first task was to determine whether or not the six styles proved to be homogeneous in terms of their basic mineralogy. Similar statistical analyses were carried out on the petrographic data as those described in Chapter V. In this case, however, style was used as the grouping variable for the 269 sherds in the petrographic sample instead of area or settlement group.

The presence/absence of the six discrete constituents (albite twinned feldspar, cross-twinned feldspar, volcanic rock, ferromagnesium, opaques and cryptocrystalline quartz) were compared across style using Goodman and Kruskal's tau. This statistic is a proportional-reduction-in-error measurement. That is, it expresses the reduction in error of predicting the value of one variable based on knowing the value of another independent variable (Goodman and Kruskal 1972; Reynolds 1977). Goodman and Kruskal's tau was used because it is less susceptible than the chi-square test to the asymmetric table dimensions and uneven marginal distributions inherent in these data (cf. Reynolds 1977:32).

The tau statistics are listed in Table 22. (This statistic was calculated using both the raw counts and presence/absence percentages by style in order to reduce the effects of unequal margin totals. The tau scores showed only a negligible improvement when percentages were used. As a result, the statistics calculated with the raw counts are presented here.) It is evident from these results that all six styles are markedly homogeneous with respect to the majority of the constituents which are diagnostic in terms of sourcing. This outcome is to be expected, given that all LCWW styles were produced within a geologically uniform region.

MANOVA and Hotelling's t^2 tests were run on the five continuous constituents (matrix, quartz, sherd temper, untwinned feldspar and secondary minerals). The results are summarized in Table 23. All the MANOVA test criteria show significant differences ($p \leq .05$)

Table 22. Tau Statistics for the Presence/Absence of the Discrete Constituent Categories by Style.

Category	Tau (Style)[a]	Tau (Category)[b]
Albite Twinned Feldspar	0.002	0.010
Cross Twinned Feldspar	0.003	0.015
Volcanic Rock	0.002	0.010
Ferro-magnesium	0.001	0.004
Opaques	0.004	0.019
Crypto-crystalline Quartz	0.002	0.008

Note: The tau statistic equals 0 if the variables are statistically independent and 1 under complete association (Reynolds 1977:44).
[a] style as the dependent variable
[b] category as the dependent variable

in the continuous constituents across style. In addition, the Hotelling's t^2 tests revealed significant differences between Black Mesa and Flagstaff, Black Mesa and Padre, Sosi and Flagstaff, Sosi and Padre, Flagstaff and Leupp and Padre and Leupp.

Each continuous category was compared across all six styles by ANOVA, and across all pairs of styles using univariate t-tests. The ANOVA results are shown in Table 24. They revealed significant differences ($p \leq 0.01$) in matrix and quartz means. The results of the

Table 23. Results of the Multivariate Statistical Analyses on the Five Continuous Categories by Style.

MANOVA

Wilks' Lambda	F(25,963.64)	P Value	Pillai's Trace	F(25,1315)	P Value
0.8032	2.34	0.0002	0.2105	2.31	0.0003

Hotelling-Lawley Trace	F(25,1287)	P Value	Roy's Max. Root	F(5,263)	P Value
0.2285	2.35	0.0002	0.1281	6.74	Upper Bound

PAIR-WISE COMPARISONS

Black Mesa/ Flagstaff Hotelling's t^2	F(5,120)	P Value
22.3165	4.3193	0.0012

Black Mesa/ Padre Hotelling's t^2	F(5,85)	P Value
25.5134	4.8733	0.0006

Table 23. Results of the Multivariate Statistical Analyses on the Five Continuous Categories by Style (Continued).

PAIR-WISE COMPARISONS (Continued)

Sosi/ Flagstaff

Hotelling's t^2	F(5,113)	P Value
12.4728	2.4093	0.0408

Sosi/ Padre

Hotelling's t^2	F(5,78)	P Value
27.2598	5.1860	0.0004

Flagstaff/ Leupp

Hotelling's t^2	F(5,71)	P Value
16.2028	3.0677	0.0145

Padre/ Leupp

Hotelling's t^2	F(5,36)	P Value
15.1491	2.7268	0.0345

Note: Only significant ($p \leq .05$) Hotelling's t^2 Pair-wise Comparisons are shown.

Table 24. ANOVA Results for the Continuous Categories by Style.

Category	ANOVA F(5,263)	P Value
Matrix	4.74	*0.0004*
Quartz	4.23	*0.0010*
Sherd Temper	1.87	0.1004
Untwinned Feldspar	2.54	0.0291
Secondary/ Other	1.96	0.0851

Note: Significant statistics ($p \leq .01$) appear in *italics*.

t-tests concurred with the ANOVA. Several of the pair-wise comparisons between styles revealed significant differences in matrix and/or quartz, as shown in Tables 25 and 26. In addition, Leupp appears to have significantly more secondary minerals than Sosi, Flagstaff, Walnut and Padre (see Table 27).

The differences between the matrix, quartz and secondary means of the style pairs with significant t statistics were compared to the corresponding point-count measurement errors calculated using Van der Plas' and Tobi's (1965) formula. (Again, the largest mean for each pair-wise comparison was used in the calculations in order to be consistent with the measurements reported in Chapter VI.) All the differences in means were greater than the measurement error, suggesting that they represent real variability in matrix, quartz and secondary mineral frequencies across style.

Table 25. P Values for T-Tests of Matrix Percentages Across Style.

	Black Mesa (85.42)	Sosi (86.89)	Flag. (89.51)	Walnut (87.84)	Padre (89.80)	Leupp (87.21)
Black Mesa (85.42)	--	0.1613	*0.0001*	0.0313	*0.0005*	0.2928
Sosi (86.89)	--	--	*0.0093*	0.3974	*0.0171*	0.8458
Flagstaff (89.51)	--	--	--	0.1150	0.7968	0.1489
Walnut (87.84)	--	--	--	--	0.1154	0.7184
Padre (89.80)	--	--	--	--	--	0.1047

Note: Pooled variances were used due to unequal variances between style samples. Style means are indicated in parentheses. Significant values ($\leq$.01) are indicated in *italics*.

As discussed in Chapter VI, the majority of quartz grains in LCWW was either added deliberately as temper or was incorporated into the paste as a by-product of the crushed sherd temper (which is itself tempered with quartz). Therefore, the variability in quartz as well as matrix frequencies across style can be attributed to differences in production technology, as was the case with the matrix and sherd temper variability between settlement groups discussed in Chapter VI. Secondary minerals appear to be a product of post-depositional alterations in the mineralogy of the sherds and therefore do not pertain to the structure of the prehistoric production-distribution system.

Two questions arise as a result of the comparison of stylistic and mineralogical variability. First, do the mineralogical differences between styles somehow map onto the

Table 26. P Values for T-Tests of Quartz Percentages Across Style.

	Black Mesa (7.15)	Sosi (5.68)	Flag. (5.02)	Walnut (5.66)	Padre (4.09)	Leupp (5.40)
Black Mesa (7.15)	--	0.0320	*0.0017*	0.0491	*0.0005*	0.1317
Sosi (5.68)	--	--	0.2623	0.9823	*0.0188*	0.7561
Flagstaff (5.02)	--	--	--	0.3167	0.1724	0.6731
Walnut (5.66)	--	--	--	--	0.0311	0.7844
Padre (4.09)	--	--	--	--	--	0.0837

Note: Pooled variances were used due to unequal variances between the style samples. Style means are indicated in parentheses. Significant values ($p \leq .01$) are indicated in *italics*.

stylistic and mineralogical variability between settlement groups and, if so, why is quartz more variable across style than sherd temper?

Table 25 shows that both Black Mesa and Sosi have a significantly lower mean matrix frequency than Flagstaff and Padre. An examination of the distribution of the six LCWW styles across settlement groups within the petrographic sample (Table 28 below) reveals that the Winona group has higher relative frequencies of Black Mesa and Sosi, while the two other settlement groups have higher percentages of Flagstaff and Walnut. The Plaza group also has more Padre than it does Black Mesa or Sosi.

The style frequencies in the petrographic sample cannot be viewed as representative of the actual stylistic variability inherent in the three settlement groups. The goal of the

Table 27. P Values for T-Tests of Secondary Mineral Percentages Across Style.

	Black Mesa (0.78)	Sosi (0.62)	Flag. (0.70)	Walnut (0.71)	Padre (0.79)	Leupp (1.48)
Black Mesa (0.78)	--	0.4206	0.6326	0.7524	0.9508	0.0646
Sosi (0.62)	--	--	0.5845	0.5988	0.3707	*0.0082*
Flagstaff (0.70)	--	--	--	0.9120	0.5012	*0.0024*
Walnut (0.71)	--	--	--	--	0.6668	*0.0187*
Padre (0.79)	--	--	--	--	--	0.0430

Note: Pooled variances were used due to unequal variances between the style samples. Style means are indicated in parentheses. Significant values ($p \leq .01$) are indicated in *italics*.

sample selection was to collect as equal a number of sherds representing the different styles as possible. However, this goal was not entirely met and the frequencies show that the differences in matrix content of LCWW sherds from the three settlement groups do correspond to the variability in matrix across style.

T-tests also were run on the continuous petrographic data using the two contrasting categories of "early" (Black Mesa and Sosi) versus "late" (Flagstaff, Walnut, Padre and Leupp) styles. These tests showed a significant difference in sherd temper frequencies, as well as matrix and quartz grains, between the two categories. The results demonstrate that the change in sherd temper from one style to the next is more subtle and therefore does not

Table 28. Frequencies of the Six LCWW Styles Across Settlement Groups.

Style	Plaza	Winona	Juniper Terr.
Black Mesa	15.3	45.6	7.4
Sosi	14.4	30.0	19.1
Flagstaff	21.6	16.7	35.3
Walnut	23.4	5.6	20.6
Padre	18.9	1.1	8.8
Leupp	6.3	1.1	8.8
Total	100.0	100.0	100.0

show up until the styles are lumped into two contrasting groups. The early/late dichotomy emphasizes the two extremes of the continuum along which sherd temper frequencies vary, thus highlighting the differences between styles. This dichotomy also parallels the stylistic differences between the settlement groups, as demonstrated in the fact that they also possess significant differences in sherd temper frequencies.

Finally, the amount of sherd temper present in a vessel might also be a function of vessel form since the Winona and Juniper group sherds in the petrographic sample are more heavily weighted toward bowls, while the Hopi Buttes sherds are almost evenly divided between bowls and jars. However, t-tests revealed no significant differences in sherd temper frequencies between bowls and jars. The differences in the bowl:jar ratios of the different settlement groups and styles will be discussed in greater detail below.

In conclusion, the data suggest that variability in matrix, quartz grains and sherd temper is at least partially a function of change in production technology through time. The statistics in Tables 25 and 26 show that, in general, Black Mesa sherds have significantly less matrix and more quartz grains than Flagstaff or Padre sherds. Sosi sherds generally have significantly less matrix than Flagstaff sherds, while they have less matrix and more quartz grains than Padre sherds. In addition, the early styles have significantly more sherd temper than the later styles. These differences could be the result of a broad trend toward using less quartz and sherd temper through time. An x-ray diffraction analysis of 44 LCWW sherds from the Purcell-Larson area, in which the Chevelon sites are located, detected a similar trend with respect to quartz inclusions. Sherds from earlier sites tended to have more quartz than sherds from later sites (F. Plog 1981:84). Again, it is not clear why quartz does not vary significantly across the three settlement groups in the present study as does the matrix, given that they both vary through time and that the assemblages from the settlement groups have different percentages of earlier and later styles.

The statistical comparisons of mineralogical and stylistic variability have demonstrated that all the LCWW styles share the same basic mineralogy with respect to sourcing diagnostics. In addition, all six styles occur throughout the Hopi Buttes. However, it is difficult to establish whether or not the styles were the products of different production loci within the source area, given the present scale of analysis. Their ubiquitous distribution within the Hopi Buttes might be the product of inter-community exchange, instead of production throughout the entire source area. More fine-grained chemical analyses would be needed in order to pick up minute differences between clay and temper deposits within the source area. In addition, design element and structural analyses would have to be conducted on whole designs in order to determine if local variants exist which could be the products of different manufacturing loci. Such analyses are beyond the scope of the present research.

It remains to be seen if the six styles were slated for different exchange spheres, or if they were functionally distinct within their exchange contexts. The following section will compare the spatial distribution of the different styles and their relationships to vessel form in order to address these issues.

The Structure of Exchange: Geographic Distributions and Functional Variation

The process of tracing the geographic distribution of the six styles is made difficult because of the conventional practice of classifying LCWW according to Colton's (1955) typological categories. These types, as discussed above, incorporate more than one style. Holbrook Black-on-white is not always separated into its two varieties (A and B) in published reports and ceramic tally sheets. Colton's (1955) variety designations for Walnut Black-on-white are never used.

As a result, it is often impossible to distinguish between the distributions of Black Mesa and Sosi styles on the one hand, and Flagstaff and Walnut styles on the other. These difficulties are compounded by the problem of distinguishing between the various styles based on fragmentary designs found on sherds. The Sosi/Flagstaff distinction is particularly important in this regard since it will determine whether a sherd is classified as Holbrook or

Walnut Black-on-white. In addition, Leupp Black-on-white was not a recognized type until Colton (1955) published his description (Wilson 1969:459). Therefore, this type does not appear in the ceramic counts in *The Sinagua* (Colton 1946) and other early reports and site records. It probably was lumped in with Walnut Black-on-white.

Because of these limitations, any attempt to reconstruct the geographic extent of the six styles relative to one another will be limited in its degree of detail, barring a comprehensive examination of sherd collections from throughout the Colorado Plateaus, which time does not permit for the present study. It is assumed that the discrepancies between sherd counts caused by inconsistencies in classification can be overcome by taking a broad scale perspective and by comparing different analyses done on LCWW sherds from the same areas.

The spatial extent of each style will be examined in turn using data from published reports, unpublished documentation, my own examination of collections from various parts of the Little Colorado River drainage and observations communicated to me by other researchers. I was able to assign the designs on 1242 out of the 2400 sherds in my design sample to one of the six LCWW styles. These data, together with my examination of sherds from Beeson's (1969) survey and various sites in the Verde Valley, form the basis of my direct observations concerning the geographic distribution of the styles. The relationship between vessel form and style also will be examined in order to determine if styles operating within the same areas were functionally distinct. Finally, implications of the results concerning the structure of LCWW exchange, functional differences between styles and temporal shifts in the exchange system through time will be discussed.

Geographic Distributions

Black Mesa and Sosi style sherds are often lumped under the general rubric of Holbrook Black-on-white, making it difficult to delineate distinct geographic distributions. However, where the distinction is made between Black Mesa (Holbrook A) and Sosi (Holbrook B), they do seem to co-occur consistently. Both styles are present in the San Francisco Peaks area (e.g., Pilles 1969; Ward 1969; Tagg and Layhe 1985), Walnut Canyon (Michael Bremmer, personal communication, 1985), the Chevelon area, the Hopi Buttes (Keller 1979; Trott and McPherson 1984), the Homolovi area (Richard C. Lange, personal communication 1987) and the Petrified Forest area (A. Trinkle Jones, personal communication, 1987). Exceptions to this pattern of co-occurrence are the upper Verde Valley (Caywood and Spicer 1935; Stebbins et al. 1981) and Prescott area (Ward 1975) where only Sosi style sherds have been reported to date. A Sosi style LCWW sherd is also illustrated in a report on Montezuma's Castle (Jackson and Van Valkenburgh 1954:Figure 10), although it is classified as Walnut Black-on-white.

Hantman (1983) states that both Black Mesa and Sosi styles occur throughout the Apache-Sitgreaves National Forest. He does not specify on which ware(s) these styles are found. However, the 25 Sosi style sherds from this area, which were analyzed petrographically, contain sherd temper, volcanic rock fragments, ferromagnesium and opaques. There is little doubt, based on their composition, that these sherds are LCWW. The presence or absence of Black Mesa style LCWW in the Apache-Sitgreaves National Forest outside the Chevelon area remains equivocal. Beeson (1969) reports Holbrook Black-on-white as the predominant type of LCWW within his survey area, but he does not specify which style(s) are present. I have examined sherds from his surface collections housed at the Arizona State Museum and found that both styles of Holbrook are present, although Sosi is more numerous than Black Mesa.

I have reviewed the limited quantitative data that are available for the types and styles of LCWW in an attempt to summarize their frequency distributions across space. I defined a core area for each style (or type when stylistic information was lacking) somewhat arbitrarily, based on its relatively high frequencies within the decorated assemblage of sites within that area. I separated the core area from loci which were more peripherally involved in the exchange of the style or type in question by noting where significant drops occurred in the frequencies.

Both the Sosi and Black Mesa styles parallel one another with respect to their frequency distributions across space in the areas where they co-occur. They generally have higher frequencies in certain areas and lower frequencies in others, although Black Mesa frequencies are consistently lower than those for Sosi. The core area for Black Mesa (see Figure 24), where its mean frequency exceeds 3% of the total decorated assemblage per site, encompasses the San Francisco Peaks area, the Hopi Buttes the Homolovi area and the Chevelon area. In other locations for which data are available (e.g., the Zuni River drainage, the Arizona/Utah border, the Prescott area and the upper Verde Valley) Black Mesa style sherds comprise less than 1% of the total decorated assemblage or they are absent altogether.

Sosi style LCWW has a broader core (defined as the area where its mean frequency is at least 13% of the total decorated assemblage per site), as shown in Figure 25. It

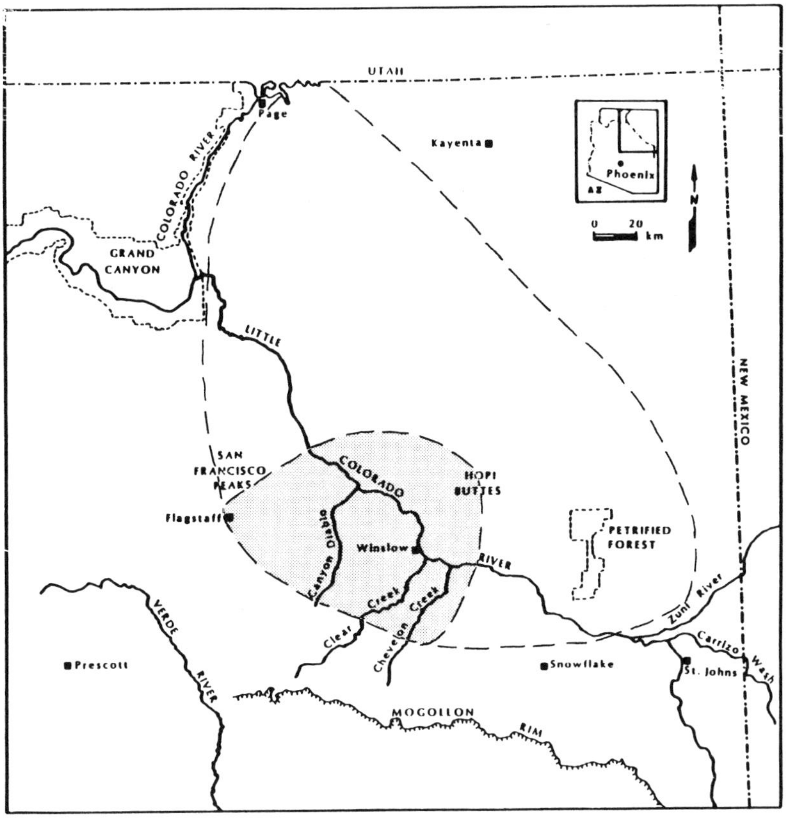

Figure 24. Postulated geographic distribution of Black Mesa style LCWW. Core area is shaded.

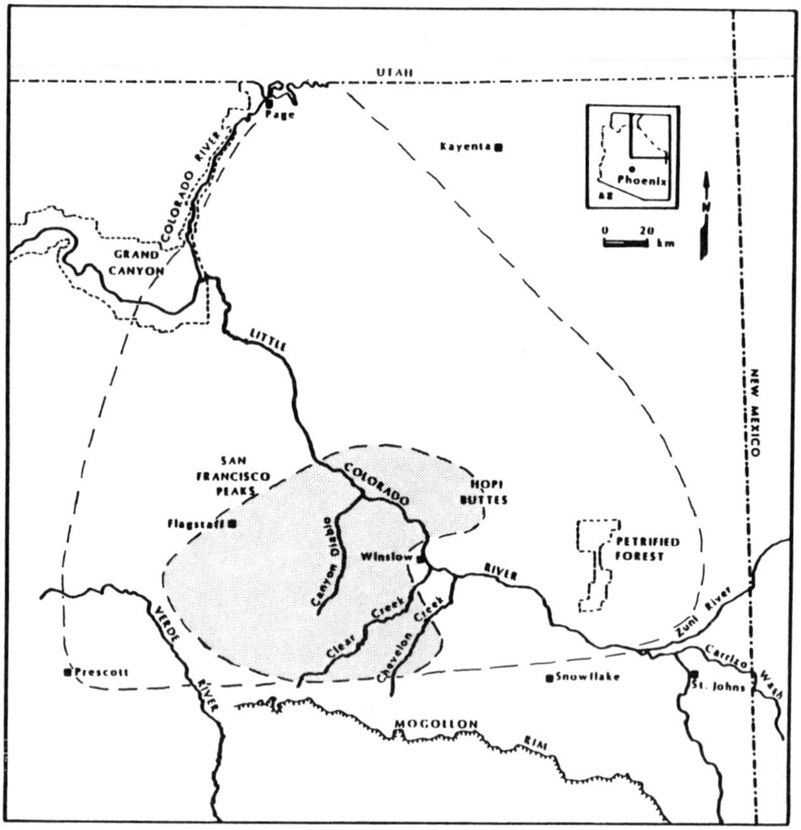

Figure 25. Postulated geographic distribution of Sosi style LCWW. Core area is shaded.

includes the southeastern San Francisco Peaks, the Hopi Buttes, the Chevelon area and the upper Verde Valley (Stebbins et al. 1981). Outside this area, its frequencies drop sharply to 6% or less in such locations as the eastern Grand Canyon, the Homolovi area (Richard C. Lange, personal communication 1987), the Arizona/Utah border (Fiero et al. 1980) and the Prescott area (Ward 1975).

The core area for Walnut Black-on-white is defined herein as the area in which this type is at least 15% of the decorated ceramic assemblage per site (see Figure 26). The core area encompasses the San Francisco Peaks, the Hopi Buttes, the Chevelon area, the Homolovi area (Richard Lange, personal communication 1987), the Petrified Forest (Cosgrove 1951; Jones 1986) and the upper Verde Valley (Caywood and Spicer 1935; Jackson and Van Valkenburgh 1954). Walnut Black-on-white has been found, although in smaller percentages (7% or less), as far north as the Arizona/Utah border northeast of Page (Ambler et al. 1964), in the eastern Grand Canyon (Schwartz 1963; Schwartz et al. 1979), in the Klethla Valley (Ambler and Olson 1977), northwest of Prescott (Barnett 1970), and in the Zuni River drainage (Beeson 1966).

It is virtually impossible to distinguish between the distribution of the Flagstaff and Walnut styles of Walnut Black-on-white in areas for which only written reports are available to me. Through my own observations, I have noted that Walnut style generally is less common than the Flagstaff style wherever it is found. In the San Francisco Peaks area, Walnut is found more commonly in the northern sector within the Wupatki National Monument. Wherever it is found within the San Francisco Peaks, it occurs on later sites such as Wupatki Ruin (Stanislawski 1963) and Turkey Hill, which also possess polychromes

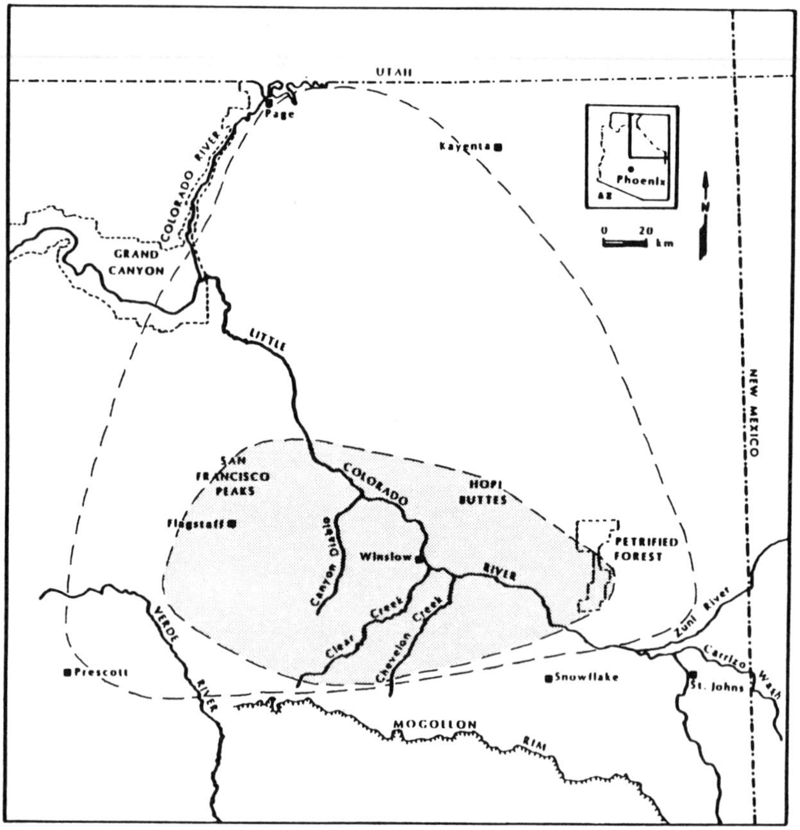

Figure 26. Postulated geographic distribution of Walnut Black-on-white. Core area is shaded.

and such late (post A.D. 1200) black-on-white styles as Wupatki, Kayenta and Tusayan Black-on-white. These associations suggest that the production of the Walnut style began later than the Flagstaff style. However, the Flagstaff style occurs wherever the Walnut style does, suggesting that the former continued to be made throughout the production period of the latter. The Walnut style also occurs in small numbers in the upper Verde Valley. It is extremely rare or absent in the eastern Grand Canyon (Janet Balsom, personal communication 1987) and the Petrified Forest (A. Trinkle Jones, personal communication 1987), where it is superseded by the Flagstaff style.

The Padre style is found almost everywhere that Walnut Black-on-white occurs except for the Zuni River drainage (Beeson 1969) and the Klethla Valley (Ambler and Olson 1977), as shown in Figure 27. Its core area is much more restricted, however, including only the San Francisco Peaks area, the Hopi Buttes, the Chevelon area and the Homolovi area. Padre style sherds occur in frequencies between 4 and 16% of the decorated assemblages in the core area and drop to 2% or below in other areas such as the Petrified Forest (Harrill 1973), the Grand Canyon (Schwartz et al. 1980), the Arizona/Utah border (Fiero et al. 1980), the upper Verde Valley (Alger 1968) and the Prescott area (Ward 1975). The core area percentages might be inflated due to the large size of some of the Padre storage jars, particularly in the Hopi Buttes.

Leupp Black-on-white was not a recognized type until Colton described it in 1955 and therefore does not appear in the earlier reports. However, it is present in the upper Verde Valley and some of the later sites in the San Francisco Peaks area, all of which were excavated prior to this date (see Figure 28). I also noted the presence of this style at sites

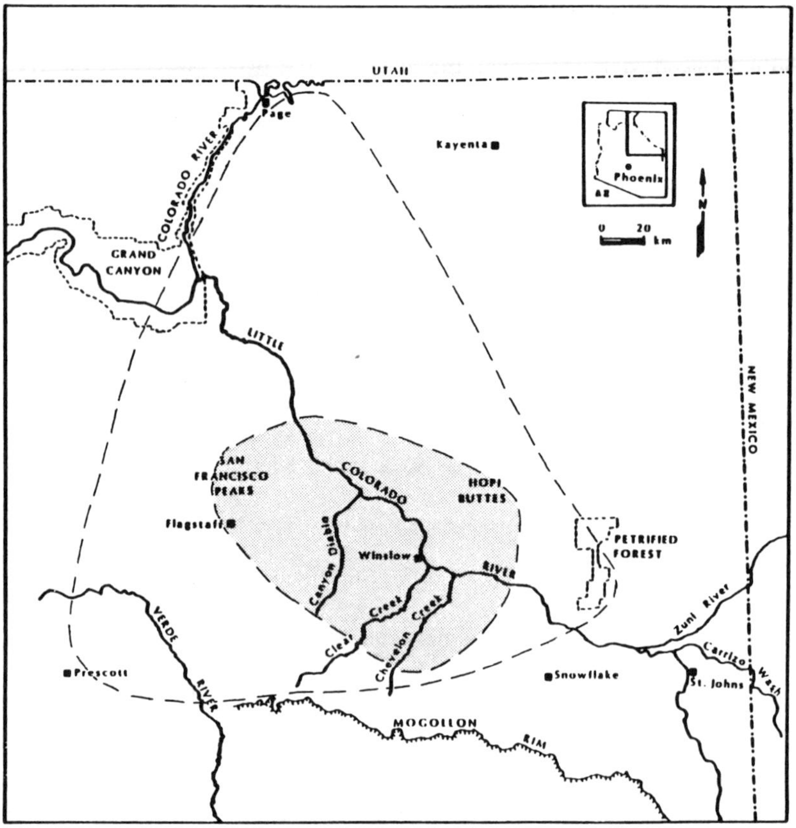

Figure 27. Postulated geographic distribution of Padre style LCWW. Core area is shaded.

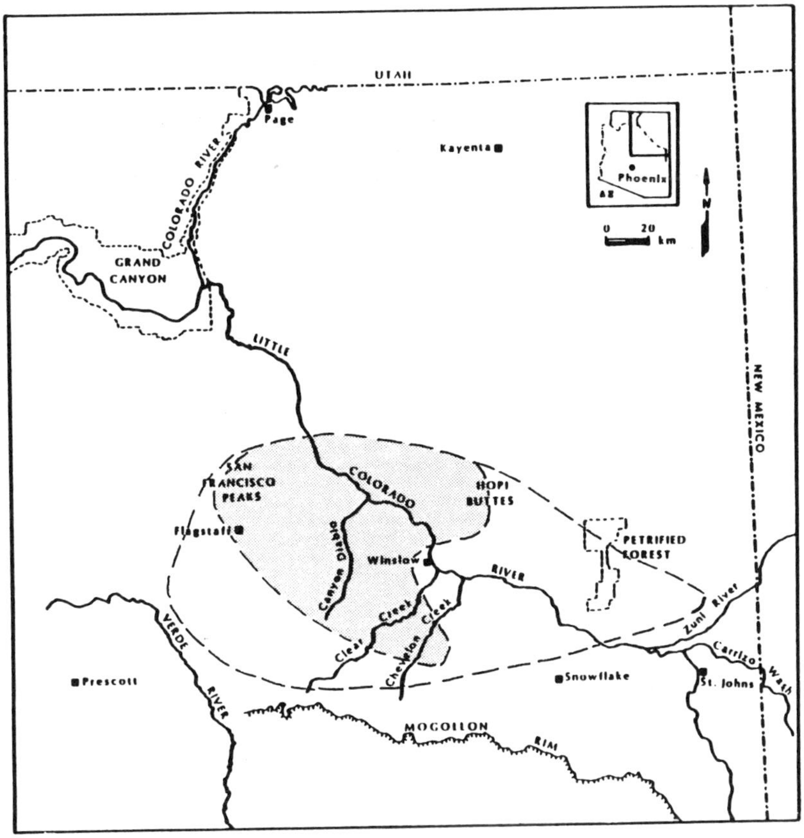

Figure 28. Postulated geographic distribution of Leupp style LCWW. Core area is shaded.

in the Hopi Buttes and the Chevelon area. It has been encountered in the Homolovi area as well (Richard C. Lange, personal communication 1987). I found only one Leupp sherd in my examination of the Beeson (1966) survey collections and one sherd has been reported from a site in the Petrified Forest National Park (Jones 1986:Table 5). Like the Walnut style, Leupp tends to co-occur with later black-on-whites and polychromes, suggesting it was produced toward the later end of the LCWW sequence. It generally occurs in very low frequencies, never exceeding 5% outside the core area. It has not been reported to date in the eastern Grand Canyon (Janet Balsom, personal communication 1987) or the Arizona/Utah border (Ambler et al. 1964; Fiero et al. 1980).

In conclusion, the geographic distributions of the six styles share a core area including the Hopi Buttes, San Francisco Peaks, Homolovi and Chevelon areas. This core area witnessed the most intensive and long-term participation in the LCWW exchange sphere. The data indicate that differences in stylistic distributions outside this core area are a function of shifts in the LCWW exchange network through time, rather than the coexistence of several contemporaneous, yet mutually exclusive networks.

The Black Mesa style is absent in the upper Verde Valley, while it is present in the Zuni River drainage and Petrified Forest. Sosi style sherds occur in all three areas, although they are more common in the upper Verde Valley. The Walnut, Flagstaff and Leupp styles occur in very small frequencies in the Zuni River drainage, while the Flagstaff style is quite prevalent in the upper Verde Valley. In addition, Walnut and Leupp style sherds have been found on late sites in the latter area. These distributions suggest a westward shift through time in the focus of the LCWW exchange sphere away from the upper reaches of the Little Colorado River and toward the upper Verde River valley.

The diminution of LCWW exchange in the upper Little Colorado River drainage may have been prompted by the introduction of Cibola White Ware as a predominant exchange ware in this area. Stephen Plog (1980a:Table 3.3) reports that Cibola White Ware predominates in the Chevelon area after ca. A.D. 1200. Likewise, A. Trinkle Jones (personal communication, 1987) has stated that Cibola White Wares increase in the Petrified Forest National Park at the time that Holbrook Black-on-white is diminishing in numbers, at roughly the same time period. My observations of Beeson's (1969) survey collections revealed that the few Walnut and Leupp sherds that were present co-occurred with relatively high frequencies of Cibola White Ware sherds. Chris Downum (personal communication 1987) feels that the relatively small frequencies of Leupp in the San Francisco Peaks is associated with the intrusion of Cibola White Ware into this area during the thirteenth century.

Similarly, the greater frequencies of Walnut Black-on-white in general, and the Walnut style in particular, on sites post-dating A.D. 1130 in the northern San Francisco Peaks area suggest an increase in LCWW exchange to the north as well. This shift is further indicated by the greater frequencies of Walnut Black-on-white (mostly the Flagstaff style) in the eastern Grand Canyon, as compared to Holbrook Black-on-white (Black Mesa and/or Sosi style). LCWW is found most commonly in the Unkar Delta on sites which have been assigned to the Dox Phase (ca. A.D. 1100 to 1150).

The generally smaller frequencies of the Walnut, Padre and Leupp styles suggest that they might have had more specialized functions which did not require as many vessels, or that they were not in as high a demand as the Flagstaff style. Alternatively, they might reflect a general reduction of LCWW exchange activity by the thirteenth century.

The data used to reach these conclusions are admittedly fragmentary because of the widely accepted practice of lumping styles under the more general typological categories. As a result, my conclusions are somewhat impressionistic and they should be tested by more extensive stylistic analyses of LCWW sherds from areas throughout the exchange sphere.

Function and Vessel Form

Table 29 below shows the distribution of bowls and jars across the six styles of LCWW within the design sample. All the sherds with classifiable design styles were analyzed from each of the sites in the design analysis sample, except in cases where the sherd collection for a particular site was too large. In such cases (e.g., Winona Village, NA 10803 and NA 10779), sherds were selected from the proveniences used in the petrographic analysis. Sherds suspected to be from the same vessel were sorted separately and only one sherd per vessel was analyzed. It is assumed that these figures are generally representative of the frequencies of bowls and jars across LCWW styles. Some bias might have been introduced by the differences in sizes between bowls and jars, however. The effects of such a bias will be discussed below.

Several conclusions can be drawn from the data in Table 29. Black Mesa, Sosi and Leupp styles occur on bowls almost three times as often as they occur on jars. In contrast,

Table 29. Percentages of Bowl and Jar Sherds Across the Six Styles.

Form	Black Mesa	Sosi	Flagstaff	Walnut	Padre	Leupp
Bowl	71.4	72.2	63.7	46.5	44.3	72.8
Jar	28.6	27.8	36.3	53.5	55.7	27.2
Total	100.0	100.0	100.0	100.0	100.0	100.0

jars painted with Walnut and Padre designs are slightly more numerous than bowls displaying these styles. The Flagstaff style is biased toward bowls, but not to the same extent as Black Mesa and Sosi. The less severe bias of Walnut and Padre toward jars on the one hand, and Flagstaff toward bowls on the other, is due at least in part to the fact that more than one style can occur on a single vessel. For example, Walnut can co-occur on bowls with Leupp; Flagstaff and Walnut can appear on the same jar; and Padre can co-occur with Leupp on bowls.

A different picture emerges, however, when these data are broken down by area (refer to Table 30). The Hopi Buttes subsample consistently has a greater proportion of jars than reflected in the figures in Table 29. As a result, the bias toward bowls for Black Mesa, Sosi and Flagstaff is diminished, while the bias toward jars in Walnut and Padre is increased within this area. Only the Leupp bowl-to-jar ratio remains essentially the same as in the pooled sample. It is assumed that the vessel form ratios reflected in the Hopi Buttes subsample approximate the actual proportions of bowls and jars that were manufactured within the production area.

Table 30. Percentages of Bowl and Jar Sherds Across the Six Styles by Area.

Style	Form	Hopi Buttes		San Francisco		Chevelon	
Black Mesa	Bowl	53.8	(21)	78.8	(93)	61.1	(11)
	Jar	46.2	(18)	21.2	(25)	38.9	(7)
Sosi	Bowl	64.1	(25)	81.0	(87)	45.5	(10)
	Jar	35.9	(14)	19.0	(21)	54.5	(12)
Flag.	Bowl	59.8	(199)	74.3	(136)	47.4	(18)
	Jar	40.2	(134)	25.7	(47)	52.6	(20)
Walnut	Bowl	38.2	(34)	66.7	(24)	47.4	(9)
	Jar	61.8	(55)	33.3	(12)	52.6	(10)
Padre	Bowl	40.3	(25)	63.6	(7)	45.8	(11)
	Jar	59.7	(37)	36.4	(4)	54.2	(13)
Leupp	Bowl	72.4	(42)	76.5	(13)	71.4	(20)
	Jar	27.6	(16)	23.5	(4)	28.6	(8)

Note: Raw counts are shown in parentheses.

These figures are interesting in light of Gumerman's and Skinner's (1968:191) observations concerning vessel forms for Holbrook and Walnut Black-on-white at the Plaza Site. They state that the former type (i.e., Black Mesa and Sosi styles) was predominantly large storage jars. One might argue that such large vessels would not have been exported from the production area, thus accounting for the heavier representation of jar sherds in the Hopi Buttes subsample, since larger vessels will break down into more sherds than small vessels. There is some evidence to support this argument. The whole jars I have examined from the San Francisco Peaks consist of small seed jars and pitchers, in contrast to the large storage jars from the Plaza Site.

However, the differences in bowl:jar ratios across subsamples, and across design styles within the Hopi Buttes subsample, cannot be explained away as functions of jar size alone. If jar size in the Flagstaff and Walnut styles were the only distinguishing characteristic between the Hopi Buttes and other two subsamples, then one would expect comparable Black Mesa and Sosi bowl:jar ratios across the three areas, contrary to the figure shown in Table 30. Instead, it would appear that more small Black Mesa and Sosi style jars were manufactured in the Hopi Buttes area than were exchanged to either the San Francisco Peaks or the Chevelon area. Within the Hopi Buttes subsample, one would expect the Flagstaff style to have a bowl:jar ratio comparable to the Walnut style, instead of being biased toward bowls. It would appear that more Flagstaff than Walnut bowls were produced in this area. On the other hand, the greater proportion of Flagstaff and Walnut jars in the Hopi Buttes subsample could be due to larger jar size with respect to these two styles.

The San Francisco subsample has greater proportions of bowls across all six styles in comparison to the Hopi Buttes subsample and the sample as a whole. This characteristic is most notable with respect to Walnut and Padre. The bowl:jar ratios are reversed in the Hopi Buttes and San Francisco samples.

The Chevelon ratios are consistently more even than those for either of the two other subsamples, except with regards to Black Mesa and Leupp. The former style shows a greater bias toward bowls in the Chevelon subsample than its Hopi Buttes counterpart, although the bias is less severe than in the case of the San Francisco sherds. The latter style's bowl:jar ratio is relatively consistent across all three areas. The even distribution of bowls and jars across the majority of styles in the Chevelon subsample might be due to sample bias since I also noted an unusual paucity of rim sherds in the Chevelon collection, which suggests to me that some of the LCWW sherds had been segregated and stored separately. I was not able to find any other boxes with LCWW sherds in them, however.

The differences in the vessel form ratios between the Hopi Buttes and San Francisco Peaks suggest that bowls were exchanged in greater numbers to the latter area than jars, even when a particular style was produced on jars more often than it was on bowls. I have observed a predominance of bowl sherds in the LCWW assemblages of site in the Zuni River drainage and the upper Verde Valley as well.

The bias toward bowls in exchange contexts seems reasonable since jars, whether large or small, cannot be nested and are therefore more clumsy to transport (Whittlesey 1974). It also suggests that LCWW vessels might have been traded into these areas primarily as commodities in and of themselves, not as containers for other goods.

Bowls do not necessarily predominate in all six styles within exchange contexts, however. Surface and subsurface collections from sites north of the Puerco River in the Petrified Forest National Park contained more LCWW jar than bowl sherds, specifically for the Black Mesa and Sosi styles, as well as for Walnut Black-on-white (styles unspecified) (Jones 1986). Surface collections in the Homolovi area have retrieved greater numbers of jar sherds for Walnut Black-on-white (styles unspecified) and the Padre style, while the Black Mesa, Sosi and Leupp styles are more biased toward bowl sherds. However, the total number of bowl sherds is slightly greater than the total number of jar sherds. If the Chevelon collection is indeed representative of the vessel forms in LCWW assemblages in this area, the more even bowl:jar ratio might reflect the importation of a greater number of jars, as compared to the San Francisco Peaks. Alternatively, the greater numbers of jar sherds in Petrified Forest, Homolovi and Chevelon assemblages might be due to the fact that larger jars were imported into these areas than other locations such as the San Francisco Peaks or the Verde Valley. As stated above, larger jars would leave behind proportionately more sherds per vessel than bowls. Whether the variation in jar frequencies is due to the number of jars which were exported or their sizes, the differences in bowl:jar ratios across the LCWW exchange sphere indicate that the function of this trade ware probably varied across space.

With regard to the individual styles, Walnut and Padre seem to have been produced more frequently in jar form than the other styles. Even when they occur primarily in the form of bowl sherds in exchange contexts, their bowl:jar ratios tend to be less heavily biased toward bowls than the other styles. This fact might at least partially explain why the Walnut and Padre styles generally occur in lower frequencies than the other styles, since jars were not used in as large numbers as bowls in many areas. Leupp is the only style that remains consistent with respect to the bowl:jar ratio in both the source area and exchange contexts, indicating a more consistent function.

Conclusion

This chapter has examined the stylistic dimension of LCWW with respect to its mineralogical variability and its distribution across space. A classification of this ware which is based on stylistic criteria was presented as an alternative to the typological scheme set forth by Colton (1955). It incorporates some of his divisions of the types into varieties and modifies others. A broad dating scheme was proposed for the styles which is based on tree-ring dates and ceramic associations. It incorporates a split between the Black Mesa and Sosi styles as "early" on the one hand, and the Flagstaff, Walnut, Padre and Leupp styles as "late" on the other. I have hypothesized that Walnut and Leupp were produced toward the end of the LCWW sequence, based on their association with late Tusayan Black-on-whites and polychrome wares.

It is recognized, however, that a great deal of temporal overlap exists between the styles, which is recognizable at least in part due to the co-occurrence of different styles on the same vessels and the problems of classifying design styles on sherds. I proposed above that the temporal overlap reflects a continuum of change in style characterized by periods of transition from one style of ceramic design to the next, and is not merely an analytical problem.

An examination of the relationship between stylistic and mineralogical variability revealed two important aspects of LCWW production. First, a change in production technology exists between the earlier and the later styles. Specifically, there is a general trend toward less quartz and sherd temper in proportion to the volume of matrix through time. Second, the styles are homogeneous with respect to their basic mineralogy. In addition, all six styles are found throughout the Hopi Buttes. However, given the present level of analysis, it is not possible to establish whether or not the styles were specialized products of different communities or settlement clusters within the source area.

The geographic distributions of the six styles, as they are presently understood, indicate a shift in the intensity of LCWW exchange through time consisting of a movement away from the upper Little Colorado River valley and into the upper Verde River valley sometime around A.D. 1200. This westward shift might have been due to the rise of Cibola White Ware as a predominant exchange good that reached as far west as the San Francisco Peaks at about the same time. In addition, the intensity of LCWW exchange increased to the north in the general area of Wupatki National Monument and the eastern Grand Canyon shortly after A.D. 1100.

The fact that all the LCWW design styles are represented in the core area (the middle Little Colorado River drainage and San Francisco Peaks), and that no area within the LCWW exchange sphere received only one style, indicates that individual styles were not being used to demarcate separate interaction networks. The significant overlapping of the geographic distributions of the six design styles attests to the fact that exchange relationships involving LCWW were relatively stable over several generations in most parts of the exchange sphere, despite the late shift to the west and north.

The differential distribution of bowl and jar sherds between the styles suggests that style might have been associated with vessel function, in addition to being a temporal marker. The functional dimension of style is particularly marked after A.D. 1200 when four styles (Flagstaff, Walnut, Padre and Leupp) appear to overlap temporally while occurring in different frequencies across bowls and jars. However, the functional distinction between these later styles is somewhat obscured by the fact that two styles can co-occur on the same vessel whose form is not necessarily the most common for at least one of the styles in question (e.g., when Walnut co-occurs on a bowl with Leupp). Clearly, function is not the only factor determining the variability in design style during this later period.

As a result, it is not clear what the causes of the increase in stylistic variability late in the LCWW sequence might have been. There are several possibilities which could be investigated further, one or more of which might have been responsible for the observed increase in diversity.

First, increasing variability through time might have been a product of cultural drift (Binford 1963). The process of drift is very difficult to measure archaeologically because it would necessitate being able to isolate the individual communities in which LCWW vessels were produced, and would require a relatively precise dating of the vessels in order to measure changes in style from one generation to the next. Although cultural drift was probably a factor in the increase in stylistic diversity through time, it is doubtful that this random process can account for the appearance of such distinctive design elements as the curvilinear scroll in the Walnut style, for which there is no clear antecedent.

Second, there might have been a shift in the organization of production within the Hopi Buttes area through time, resulting in an increase in the number of potters, and possibly the number of communities, producing this ware. The more potters there are producing designs, the greater the number of individual interpretations of design style, thus introducing greater variability in design layout and the ways in which elements are combined. The variability would be especially marked if the potters resided in different communities which did not interact on a regular basis (Friedrich 1970).

As discussed above, it is not known how many communities or separate localities within the Hopi Buttes were producing this ware at any given point in time. Pinpointing the number of production loci with greater precision would require a more fine-grained examination of the mineralogical and chemical variability of Lower Member Bidahochi clay outcrops and volcanic rocks. Comparable analyses would have to be conducted on sherds representative of each LCWW design style. An attribute-based design analysis would have to be undertaken in order to distinguish between the design repertoires of different communities of potters.

Third, the producers of this ware might have been exposed to a more diverse set of stylistic influences some time during the twelfth century with the influx of Cibola White Ware into the middle Little Colorado River drainage. As Sullivan (1984:74-75) has pointed out, the overlapping geographic distributions of Tusayan White Ware, Cibola White Ware and Little Colorado White Ware would have created a situation in which

> potters would necessarily have a larger set of stylistic alternatives from which to select, thereby increasing the variability observed by the archaeologist.

Cibola White Ware has a Walnut style equivalent to Walnut Black-on-white which is called Roosevelt Black-on-white (Sullivan 1984:Figure 5.2). It is not known, however, if Roosevelt Black-on-white was the source of inspiration for the Walnut style in LCWW, or vice versa. A whole vessel study of Walnut style LCWW and Roosevelt Black-on-white designs comparing various levels of design structure (the types of design elements used, their execution and formal characteristics, their articulation into motifs, and design layouts) would be a productive means of addressing this issue.

Finally, the role of vessel function in accounting for the increase in stylistic variability through time should not be ruled out without further study. It is possible that the cultural contexts within which LCWW vessels were used increased through time, requiring a concomitant diversification of stylistic markers. The functional differences between the six styles cannot be sorted out without a more comprehensive study of existing ceramic collections than is possible in this study. More specific criteria for vessel form and size than the bowl/jar dichotomy should be sought through an examination of whole vessel collections. Field notes and unpublished reports on file in archival records might provide intra-site contextual data pertinent to determining vessel function. However, whole vessel collections tend to be heavily biased toward burial offerings, thus obscuring the earlier stages of such vessels' use lives.

There is also some limited evidence that different areas within the exchange sphere might have been using LCWW vessels for different purposes because of the variation in bowl:jar ratios across space. Again, given the gross division between bowls and jars and the lack of detailed provenience information in many of the site reports, it is difficult to determine precisely what these functional differences might have been.

To summarize, the hypotheses proposed herein with respect to LCWW design styles are preliminary and should be tested with more rigorous data. Several suggestions have been offered concerning the types of research which would shed greater light on the role of design style in the LCWW production-distribution system. Most importantly, information concerning the function of design style within the LCWW exchange sphere, as well as changes in exchange relationships through time, would be enhanced significantly if ceramic analysts would classify this ware according to stylistic criteria. Colton's (1955) types incorporate a great deal of stylistic variability and therefore mask changes in the structure and function of LCWW exchange across both time and space.

CHAPTER IX

CONCLUSION

Traditionally, exchange has remained on the periphery of southwestern archaeological theory building. Prehistoric exchange has not been regarded as a necessary adaptive mechanism or as an agent of culture change until the past decade, even though it has been recognized by southwestern archaeologists for many years (e.g., Colton 1941; McGregor 1941a). The reasons why it has been down-played are two-fold. First, exchange did not figure prominently in the culture area/diffusionist framework within which archaeologists have operated throughout most of the history of the discipline. Within the context of this paradigm, long-distance exchange had the same theoretical outcome as diffusion and migration: the movement of traits across cultural boundaries. Archaeologists were more concerned with the end results of such movements than they were in determining the actual distributional mechanisms which were involved.

Second, the prevailing ethnographic model of Pueblo cultures has led archaeologists to perceive historic and prehistoric puebloan communities as self-sufficient microcosms of the culture at large. As a result, exchange has not been regarded as a necessary component of the subsistence base. Nor has it been perceived as an important mechanism of inter-community interaction or effective political leadership. This model has persisted among archaeologists who have adopted alternative approaches to interpreting the plateau southwestern archaeological record under the "new archeology" (Longacre 1964; Hill 1970).

Methods of compositional analysis have been under-utilized as well, despite their availability, because the documentation of exchange has not been a priority within the context of the diffusionist or "new archeology" paradigms. A few sourcing studies had been conducted (e.g., Shepard 1936, 1939; Warren 1969b). However, their results concerning ceramic exchange were ignored for the most part and they had little impact on the perception that exchange was of little consequence in the larger picture of plateau southwestern prehistory. Many cases of exchange have gone undocumented until recently because the necessary analytical methods were not employed.

The developmental model provides a significantly different way of viewing prehistoric exchange. Within the context of this model, it is seen as an essential adaptive mechanism in a high-risk, high-diversity environment. According to this model, exchange provided a means whereby subsistence goods could be moved between communities who no longer had direct access to the natural resources in many areas due to the colonization of these areas and the shift to a sedentary agricultural lifeway after ca. A.D. 700. In addition, exchange is viewed as an integral part of long-term sociopolitical development because of its "self-serving" role as a source of legitimacy for decision-makers (Upham 1982:122). According to the proponents of the developmental model, exchange became part of a positive feedback cycle which led to the development of multi-tiered, multi-community political systems (Lightfoot 1981; Upham et al. 1981; Lightfoot and Feinman 1982; Upham 1982). This new theoretical orientation has led proponents of the model to question the efficacy of the traditional ethnographic model which does not consider interaction beyond the community as a dynamic mechanism of culture change.

The environmental conditions and cultural trends taking place between A.D. 700 and 1100 conform with the baseline conditions necessary for sociopolitical development, as proposed in the developmental model. Climatic conditions generally were improving throughout this period, promoting a further reliance on agriculture. Population increase was widespread throughout the Colorado Plateaus during these centuries. As a result of the population growth, many agriculturally marginal areas had been colonized on a year-round basis by the twelfth century. The occupation of such areas put greater pressure on subsistence productivity since migratory seasonal rounds were no longer a viable option for reducing subsistence risk.

The presence of diverse types of water and soil control systems throughout the plateau Southwest during this period attests to the increased commitment to an agricultural subsistence base. Settlement patterns were characterized by a great deal of diversity as well, as is to be expected during such a dynamic period of growth. Some areas such as Hay Hollow Valley and the San Francisco Peaks area had begun to develop hierarchical settlement patterns, as predicted by the developmental model, while other areas such as the Petrified Forest and the Hopi Buttes had not.

The centuries between A.D. 1100 and 1400 witnessed the culmination and dissolution of many of the cultural trends which had begun in the earlier period. Population growth was followed by the abandonment of many areas due to adverse climatic conditions for most of the period between A.D. 1150 and 1300. Populations aggregated into the areas which had greater agricultural potential.

More extensive water and soil control systems in these areas attest to greater agricultural intensification than in the earlier period. Settlement hierarchies continued to develop in some parts of the plateau Southwest, exhibiting more levels and greater differentiation between the higher and lower order settlements. However, many of these systems collapsed by the second half of the thirteenth century.

The proponents of the developmental model view the continuation of earlier demographic and subsistence trends, in some parts of the Colorado Plateaus as catalysts of sociopolitical development. The increased volume and complexity of the decision-making pressures created by these trends would have promoted the development of centralized political control, in their view (Upham et al. 1981; Lightfoot and Feinman 1982; Upham 1982). They point to the increasingly complex settlement and water and soil control systems as evidence for the rise of centralized political organization. However, the internal structure of these settlement systems and their degree of complexity has been questioned by some researchers. In addition, it is not clear whether the water and soil control systems grew by accretion over an extended period, or whether they were planned and built as complete systems, thus necessitating managerial supervision (Vivian 1974).

The movement of such goods as lithic raw materials, plainwares and decorated wares has been documented at various geographic scales throughout many parts of the plateau Southwest by at least A.D. 1000, due to the increasing number of compositional analyses which have been conducted in recent years (e.g., Garrett 1979; Crown 1980; Deutchman 1980). As a result, exchange is now being recognized as a prevalent phenomenon, even prior to the better known movements of such decorated ceramics as White Mountain Red

Ware and Jeddito Yellow Ware during the thirteenth and fourteenth centuries. Despite the increased interest in exchange, many issues remain unresolved. Very little is known about the structure and function of long-distance exchange networks pre-dating the thirteenth century. Controversy also surrounds the more documented cases of long-distance exchange between A.D. 1100 and 1400 concerning the degree to which large settlements were controlling the movement of goods within and between settlement systems, and whether or not such control was tied to hierarchical, centralized political organization (Henderson 1980b; Coinman 1984; Downum 1986).

To summarize, many questions remain to be answered concerning the structure of settlement systems, their political organization and the role of long-distance exchange in culture change between A.D. 900 and 1400. Pre-thirteenth century exchange, in particular, remains one of the least understood aspects of plateau southwestern prehistory; yet it is a vital link in the process of political centralization proposed in the developmental model.

This project was undertaken in order to provide a case study of such an exchange system. I have used this case study to test the expectations of the developmental model concerning the development of long-distance prestige exchange. My research was structured according to three basic goals: 1) determining the degree of geographic centralization in LCWW production, 2) determining the basic structure of its regional exchange system, and 3) examining stylistic variability within the production-distribution system.

First, a geographically restricted source area for LCWW was delineated in the northeastern portion of the Hopi Buttes using three complementary techniques of compositional analysis: petrographic analysis of LCWW sherds, x-ray diffraction of LCWW sherds and clay samples, and electron microprobe analysis of augite crystals in LCWW sherds and volcanic rocks. Both the clays and non-plastic inclusions in the paste of this ware closely match the distinctive mineralogy of geologic formations within the Hopi Buttes area. Statistical analyses of the petrographic point count data revealed no significant differences in the mineralogical composition of LCWW which could be attributed to different source areas. It is therefore reasonable to assume that LCWW found in other areas was imported, rather than being locally produced. However, it was not possible to determine if this ware was produced in more than one locality within the Hopi Buttes, given the level of analyses undertaken in this study.

Second, a distance decay study was undertaken on data from sites throughout the Little Colorado River drainage in order to characterize the movement of LCWW across space. Two techniques of exploratory data analysis were employed (Tukey 1977). Resistant line-fitting was used in order to derive a linear model of the fall-off in LCWW exchange intensity with increasing distance from its source. The percentage of LCWW in the decorated ceramic assemblage of each site was plotted against its distance from the Hopi Buttes source area. A best-fit resistant line was achieved after attempting several different transformations of the data. However, its slope was almost horizontal, demonstrating that distance did not have a strong frictional effect on the intensity of LCWW exchange, and that other factors must have been affecting the level of exchange activity throughout various parts of the LCWW system. The residuals of the best-fit resistant line indicate that the eastern San Francisco Peaks and the Grand Canyon were more intensively involved in LCWW exchange than the linear fall-off model would predict, given their distance from the source.

A separate resistant line-fitting was conducted on the San Francisco sites alone, which demonstrated that fall-off in exchange within this area conformed to a simple linear model with no transformation of the variables, suggesting that this area was acting as part of the Hopi Buttes direct access supply zone (Renfrew et al. 1968). Significantly, neither Winona Village nor Juniper Terrace, two postulated distribution centers for LCWW in the San Francisco Peaks, possessed positive residuals in either the sample-wide or San Francisco Peaks resistant line. Therefore, it seems that neither settlement was controlling the distribution of this tradeware within the San Francisco Peaks area, as had been hypothesized.

Smoothing, another technique of exploratory data analysis, was employed in order to delineate the fluctuations in LCWW exchange intensity across space. The smoothed frequencies exhibited a series of marked peaks and troughs, again indicating that distance from the source was not the only factor affecting levels of exchange activity. The peaks, representing areas where LCWW exchange was relatively intense, corresponded to the Hopi Buttes supply zone, the southern and eastern San Francisco Peaks, the Grand Canyon and Beeson's (1966) survey area in the upper Little Colorado River drainage. I have argued that the Chevelon area also was actively involved in LCWW exchange, even though it is represented by a trough in the smoothed frequency pattern, because the sites in the sample post-date the period of most intensive LCWW exchange in this area during the twelfth century.

All the areas represented by peaks in the smoothed data, in addition to the Chevelon area, are characterized by contrasts in topography and vegetation zones. They also incorporate border zones between different cultural groups. These dual characteristics suggest that LCWW may have been functioning within a formalized system of interaction designed to maintain cooperative ties between cultural groups who controlled different natural resources, or whose territories may have been subject to different climatic regimes. Such amicable relationships would facilitate the peaceful exchange of subsistence goods between these groups during periods of subsistence stress. The structure of the LCWW regional exchange sphere is therefore in line with the theory that long-distance exchange was initiated as a risk-minimizing strategy which replaced mobility once a commitment to a sedentary agricultural way of life had been made in the prehistoric plateau Southwest (Braun and Plog 1982).

The troughs in the smoothed pattern correspond to areas which were peripherally involved in LCWW exchange. For the most part, these areas were not located near cultural borders between the eleventh and first half of the thirteenth centuries, and/or lack the variability in vegetation and topography which is characteristic of the peak areas. However, very little archaeological fieldwork has been conducted in the area between the San Francisco Peaks and the Hopi Buttes. As a result, it is not known whether this area was indeed peripheral to the LCWW exchange sphere, or if it appears as a trough in the smoothed pattern because of the paucity of data. The northern San Francisco Peaks settlements were less involved in this exchange system than settlements to the south mostly as a result of their greater distance from the source, as demonstrated by the linear distance decay pattern for this area. It is noteworthy that both Winona Village and Juniper Terrace appear in troughs in the smoothed pattern, again reinforcing the fact that they were not distribution centers controlling the access of surrounding settlements to LCWW vessels.

The results of the distance decay analysis, coupled with an examination of intra-site contextual data, has led me to conclude that LCWW exchange was not hierarchically organized or redistributive, even though it was targeted at specific areas, often overriding the frictional effects of distance. Several of the areas within the LCWW exchange system possessed bimodal settlement patterns by the late twelfth century. Some of these areas incorporated settlements which could have functioned as exchange centers, given that they occupied the highest tier within their respective settlement systems, and that they possessed specialized structures such as ballcourts or great kivas which could have been used as loci of inter-community exchange. However, these settlements did not function as redistribution points for this tradeware, nor were they receiving preferential access to LCWW. It is highly unlikely that LCWW was functioning as a status symbol since it is not differentially distributed across domestic structures or burial populations in sites in the extended sample. Therefore, the expectations derived from the developmental model concerning long-distance exchange are not born out in this case study.

The third goal of the research was approached through a design analysis of LCWW. A classification system which is based on stylistic criteria was presented as an alternative to the widely used typological system introduced by Colton (1955). A broad dating scheme of the six LCWW design styles was proposed which is based on dendrochronological data and contextual associations between different types of decorated ceramics (Breternitz 1966; Chris Downum, personal communication 1987). A split was suggested between the "early" styles of Black Mesa and Sosi on the one hand, and the "late" styles of Flagstaff, Walnut, Padre and Leupp on the other. I have also hypothesized that Walnut and Leupp originated toward the end of the LCWW sequence, based on their association with other thirteenth century decorated wares. This split is somewhat artificial, however, since a great deal of temporal overlap exists between the styles. I have suggested that this overlapping is due at least in part to the occurrence of transition periods during the shift from one stylistic mode to the next, rather than being purely an artifact of the classification system itself.

A comparison of the mineralogical composition of the six design styles revealed that the LCWW system underwent changes in production technology through time. Specifically, there is a general trend toward less quartz and sherd temper in proportion to the volume of matrix between the earlier and later styles. However, all six styles are homogeneous with respect to sourcing diagnostics, such as feldspars, ferromagnesium and volcanic rocks. The analyses conducted during the course of this project are not fine-grained enough to establish whether minute differences between the styles exist in terms of their mineralogical or chemical composition, which might be linked to distinct production loci within the Hopi Buttes source area.

A review of the geographic distributions of the six design styles, as they are presently understood, indicated a shift in the intensity of LCWW exchange further north along the Little Colorado River and southwest into the upper Verde River valley sometime after A.D. 1200. This shift occurred at the same time that LCWW was replaced as a predominant tradeware by Cibola White Ware in east-central Arizona, the Petrified Forest and the Chevelon drainage. Despite this shift in exchange activity through time, the distributions of the styles overlap significantly. The fact that all six LCWW styles are found in the core area of the exchange sphere in the middle Colorado River valley and the San Francisco Peaks indicates that individual styles were not used to demarcate separate interaction networks.

The differential distribution of bowl and jar sherds across style suggests that style might have been associated with vessel function. In addition, there is evidence that various areas within the exchange sphere might have been using LCWW vessels for different purposes because of the variation in bowl:jar ratios across space.

The design analysis also has revealed that LCWW was characterized by greater stylistic diversity during the first half of the thirteenth century. Several possible explanations have been suggested for this increase in variability, such as cultural drift (Binford 1963), a change in the organization of production within the Hopi Buttes area, an increase in stylistic influences due to the westward shift of the Cibola White Ware exchange sphere, and changes in the function of LCWW vessels.

The hypotheses proposed concerning the role of design style within the LCWW exchange system are preliminary and need to be investigated further. Future research on the LCWW production-distribution system would be enhanced if researchers began to classify this ware according to stylistic rather than typological criteria. A more in-depth study of the relationship between design style and vessel form is needed in order to better define the functional dimension of style. More specific criteria for vessel form and size should be developed by examining whole vessels. A comprehensive study of whole designs in terms of their structure and composition on different vessel forms needs to be undertaken.

In addition, a better understanding of the organization of LCWW production could be achieved if fine-grained chemical analyses were conducted on LCWW sherds and the raw materials in order to detect minute differences between the clay and temper deposits within the source area. With such data in hand, it might be possible to determine if separate production loci were in operation within the Hopi Buttes source area.

LCWW is only one long-distance exchange good which was circulating prior to the thirteenth century. It is difficult to generalize beyond this case study since other contemporaneous exchange systems could have been organized along very different lines, for very different purposes. However, if LCWW is representative of long-distance ceramic exchange prior to ca. A.D. 1200, then ceramics were not operating within prestige exchange systems at that time. LCWW can serve as a basis of comparison for studying the distributions and contexts of other pre-thirteenth century exchange goods in future research efforts.

In addition, the present research has implications for the reconstruction of long-distance exchange during the thirteenth century, especially involving decorated ceramics. The results have demonstrated that directional exchange can exist in the absence of centralized political control. The regional distributional patterns of LCWW closely match the distributions of later decorated wares, which have been used by the proponents of the developmental model to argue for the existence of prestige exchange systems. Yet, there is no evidence to suggest that LCWW functioned as a status item.

The existence of prestige exchange during later centuries remains equivocal given currently available data. The present study has highlighted the need to examine independent contextual evidence in order to determine if such directionality is the product of prestige exchange, the movement of goods across environmental and/or cultural boundaries, uneven population densities (and thus demand) across the landscape, or some other factor. If the dynamic model of sociopolitical development outlined in the developmental model is to be tested conclusively, then the issue of equifinality must be resolved through the examination of contextual data at both the inter-site and intra-site levels.

Are observed settlement patterns indeed the result of hierarchical systems made up of contemporaneous centers and smaller satellite villages occupied during the fourteenth century? Is there evidence to suggest that these communities' economies were linked through a common water control system, shared raw material sources and/or agricultural land, or similar assemblages of exchange goods? Are the exchange goods unevenly distributed across these settlements systems, and do the centers possess greater per capita concentrations of these goods than the satellite communities? Are the exchange goods unevenly distributed within settlements, both large and small, being concentrated in certain households, roomblocks or segments of the burial population? Is there corroborative evidence to suggest that those individuals or groups controlling the greatest number of certain exchange goods enjoyed a higher status than the general population within their community and/or settlement system? If most or all of these questions can be answered in the affirmative with a reasonable degree of certainty, then a stronger case can be made for the presence of prestige exchange in the thirteenth century and beyond.

If such a case is made, then it will be necessary to examine whether the function of exchange became purely political, or whether decision-makers also used their political authority to control a pre-existing adaptive strategy. In addition, how did the function of prestige systems, whether purely political or not, affect the types of goods exchanged, the mode of production of those goods, and their distribution across the landscape relative to population densities, cultural boundaries and environmental zones? These and many other questions await answers before the role of exchange in sociopolitical development in particular, and culture change in general, can be understood more clearly.

An important component of future research concerning regional exchange pre- and post-dating A.D. 1200 should be the documentation of the movement of goods both within and across settlement systems. Sourcing studies are an essential first step to such research. Petrographic and/or chemical analyses should be conducted on potential exchange goods in order to distinguish between their source areas and exchange contexts. The lack of data on the frequencies of exchange goods at small, lower order sites is particularly acute. Effective comparisons cannot be made between these sites and higher order centers without such information.

In summary, the present study has made contributions in three areas of research. First, this study can serve as an example of a comprehensive ceramic sourcing analysis with the following characteristics: 1) the use of a ceramic ware, instead of types, as the unit of analysis, 2) the application of complementary compositional analyses to source both the paste and non-plastic inclusions within the ceramic ware, and 3) the use of a relatively large sample of sherds from different areas within the ware's geographic distribution, preferably from the most likely production sources.

Second, the present research has demonstrated that long-distance directional exchange in the plateau Southwest is not necessarily linked to centralized political control. This fact has important implications for the developmental model. Finally, greater insight has been gained into the production-distribution system of LCWW. Its source has been located and its movements throughout the Little Colorado River drainage have been characterized. An alternative system of classifying LCWW has been presented which is based on stylistic criteria. If this system is adopted by other archaeologists, research can continue on the hypotheses concerning the changes in the LCWW exchange sphere through time, and the relationship between style and vessel function offered herein.

REFERENCES

Adams, C.E.

1985 The Archaeology of the Southern Black Mesa to Central Little Colorado River Valley Area. Paper presented at the Fall, 1985 Arizona Archaeological Council Meetings.

Ahlstrom, R.V.N.

1985 *The Interpretation of Archaeological Tree-Ring Dates*. Unpublished Ph.D. dissertation, Department of Anthropology, University of Arizona, Tucson.

Alger, N.T.

1968 Perkins Pueblo and Tuzigoot: A Cultural Comparison of Two Pueblo Sites. Ms. on file, Department of Anthropology, Arizona State University, Tempe.

Allen, W.L., and J.B. Richardson III

1971 The Reconstruction of Kinship from Archaeological Data: The Concepts, the Methods, and the Feasibility. *American Anthropologist* 36:41-53.

Ambler, R.A., and A.P. Olson

1977 *Salvage Archaeology in the Cow Springs Area*. Technical Series No. 15. Museum of Northern Arizona, Flagstaff.

Ambler, R.A., A.J. Lindsay, Jr., and M.A. Stein

1964 Survey and Excavation on Cummings Mesa, Arizona and Utah, 1960-1961. Bulletin No. 39, Glen Canyon Series No. 5. Museum of Northern Arizona, Flagstaff.

Arnold, D.E.

1975 Ceramic Ecology of the Ayacucho Basin, Peru. *Current Anthropology* 16:183-194.

1978 Ethnography of Pottery-Making in the Valley of Guatemala. In *The Ceramics of Kaminaljuyu, Guatemala*, edited by R. Wetherington, pp. 327-400. Pennsylvania Univeristy Press, University Park.

1981 A Model for the Identification of Nonlocal Ceramic Distribution: A View From the Present. In *Production and Distribution: A Ceramic Viewpoint*, edited by H. Howard and E.L. Morris, pp. 31-44. British Archaeological Review, International Series No. 120.

Balsom, J.R.
1984 *Application of Heavy Mineral Analysis to Grand Canyon Ceramics*. Unpublished Masters thesis, Department of Anthropology, Arizona State University, Tempe.

Barnett, F.
1970 *Malti Ranch Ruins: A Report on the Excavation of Five Small Prehistoric Indian Ruins of the Prescott Culture in Arizona*. Technical Series No. 10. Museum of Northern Arizona, Flagstaff.

Barth, F.
1959 *Political Leadership Among the Swat Pathans*. Monographs on Social Anthropology No. 19. London School of Economics.

Beeson, W.J.
1966 Archaeological Survey Near St. Johns, Arizona: A Methodological Study. Unpublished Ph.D. dissertation, Department of Anthropology, University of Arizona, Tucson.

Binford, L.R.
1962 Archaeology as Anthropology. *American Antiquity* 28:217-225.

1963 "Red Ochre" Caches from the Michigan Area: A Possible Case of Cultural Drift. *Southwestern Journal of Anthropology* 19:89-108.

Binford, L.R., and W.J. Chasko, Jr.
1976 Nunamiut Demographic History: A Provocative Case. In *Demographic Anthropology Quantitative Approaches*, edited by E.B.W. Zubrow, pp. 63-143. University of New Mexico Press, Albuquerque.

Birdsell, J.B.
1966 Some Predictions for the Pleistocene Based on Equilibrium Systems Among Recent Hunter-Gatherers. In *Man the Hunter*, edited by R. Lee and I. Devore, pp. 229-240. Aldine, Chicago.

Blanton, R.E., J. Appel, L. Finsten, S. Kowalewski, G. Feinman, and E. Fisch
1979 Regional Evolution in the Valley of Oaxaca, Mexico. *Journal of Field Archaeology* 6:369-390.

Blanton, R.E., and G. Feinman
1984 The Mesoamerican World System. *American Anthropologist* 86:673-682.

Blanton, R.E., S. Kowalewski, G. Feinman, and J. Appel

1981 *Ancient Mesoamerica: A Comparison of Change in Three Regions.* Cambridge University Press, Cambridge, England.

1982 *Monte Alban's Hinterland, Part I: The Prehispanic Settlement Patterns of the Central and Southern Parts of the Valley of Oaxaca, Mexico.* Prehistory and Human Ecology of the Valley of Oaxaca No. 7. Museum of Anthropology Memoirs No. 15. University of Michigan, Ann Arbor.

Bliss, W.L., and P.H. Ezell

1956 The Arizona Section of the San Juan Pipeline. In *Pipeline Archaeology: Reports of Salvage Operations in the Southwest on El Paso Natural Gas Company Projects, 1950-1953*, edited by F. Wendorf, N. Fox and O.L. Lewis, pp. 81-143. Laboratory of Anthropology, Santa Fe and Museum of Northern Arizona, Flagstaff.

Brand, D.D.

1938 Aboriginal Trade Routes for Sea Shells in the Southwest. *Yearbook of the Association of Pacific Coast Geographers* 4:1-10.

Brandt, E.A.

1980 On Secrecy and the Control of Knowledge: Taos Pueblo. In *Secrecy, a Cross-Cultural Perspective*, edited by S.K. Tefft, pp. 123-146. Human Sciences Press, New York.

Braun, D.P., and S. Plog

1982 Evolution of "Tribal" Social Networks: Theory and Prehistoric North American Evidence. *American Antiquity* 47:504-525.

Breternitz, D.A.

1966 *An Appraisal of Tree-Ring Dated Pottery in the Southwest.* Anthropological Paper No. 10. Univeristy of Arizona, Tucson.

Brown, G., and G.W. Brindley

1980 X-ray Diffraction Procedures for Clay Mineral Identification. In *Crystal Structures of Clay Minerals and Their X-ray Identification*, edited by G.W. Brindley and G. Brown, pp. 305-359. Mineralogical Society Monograph No. 5. London.

Brunton, G.

1955 Vapour pressure glycolation of oriented clay minerals. *American Mineralogist* 40:124-126.

Carlson, R.L.
1970 *White Mountain Redware: A Pottery Tradition of East-Central Arizona and Western New Mexico*. Anthropological Paper No. 19. University of Arizona, Tucson.

Cartledge, T.R.
1987 Current Cohonina Concepts. Paper presented at the the Arizona Archaeological Council Meeting, Flagstaff.

Caywood, L.R., and E.H. Spicer
1935 *Tuzigoot: The Excavation and Repair of a Ruin on the Verde River Near Clarkdale, Arizona*. National Park Service, Berkley, Calif.

Chagnon, N.A.
1968 *Yanomamo: The Fierce People*. Holt, Rinehart and Winston, New York.

Charlton, T.H.
1984 Production and Exchange: Variables in the Evolution of a Civilization. In *Trade and Exchange in Early Mesoamerica*, edited by K.G. Hirth, pp. 17-42. University of New Mexico Press, Albuquerque.

Chayes, F.
1956 *Petrographic Modal Analysis: An Elementary Statistical Appraisal*. John Wiley and Sons, New York.

Ciolek-Torrello, R.S.
1978 *A Statistical Analysis of Activity Organization, Grasshopper Pueblo, Arizona*. Unpublished Ph.D. dissertation, Department of Anthropology, University of Arizona, Tucson.

Claeson, C.F.
1968 Distance and Human Interaction. *Geografisker Annaler B* 50:142-161.

Clark, G.A.
1982 Quantifying Archaeological Research. In *Advances in Archaeological Method and Theory, Vol. 5*, edited by M.E. Schiffer, pp. 217-273. Academic Press, New York.

Coe, M.D., and R.A. Diehl
1980 *In the Land of the Olmec, Vol. 2: The People of the River*. University of Texas Press, Austin.

Coinman, N.R.
1984 *Ceramics from the North Pueblo Nuvakwewtaqa (Chavez Pass Ruin).* Unpublished Master's Thesis, Department of Anthropology, Arizona State University, Tempe.

Colton, H.S.
1939 *Prehistoric Culture Units and Their Relationships in Northern Arizona.* Museum of Northern Arizona Bulletin 17, Flagstaff.

1941 Prehistoric Trade in the Southwest. *Scientific Monthly* 52:308-319.

1946 *The Sinagua: A Summary of the Archaeology of the Region of Flagstaff, Arizona.* Museum of Northern Arizona Bulletin 22, Flagstaff.

1955 *Pottery Types of the Southwest.* Museum of Northern Arizona Ceramic Series 3, Flagstaff.

1968 Frontiers of the Sinagua. In *Collected Papers in Honor of Lyndon Hargrave*, edited by A.H. Schroeder, pp 9-16. Papers of the Archaeological Society of New Mexico No. 1. Museum of New Mexico, Albuquerque.

Colton, H.S., and L.L. Hargrave
1937 *Handbook of Northern Arizona Pottery Wares.* Museum of Northern Arizona Bulletin 11, Flagstaff.

Cordell, L.S.
1979 Prehistory: Eastern Anasazi. In *Southwest*, edited by A. Ortiz, pp. 131-151. Handbook of North American Indians, vol. 9, William G. Sturtevant, general editor. Smithsonian Institution, Washington, D.C.

Cordell, L.S., and F. Plog
1979 Escaping the Confines of Normative Thought: A Reevaluation of Puebloan Prehistory. *American Antiquity* 44:405-429.

Cosgrove, C.B., Jr.
1951 Report on Excavation, Repair and Restoration of Agate House and Other Sites. Ms. on file, Western Archaeology and Conservation Center, National Park Service, Tucson.

Cronin, C.
1962 An Analysis of Pottery Design Elements. In *Chapters in the Prehistory of Eastern Arizona I*, edited by P.S. Martin, J.B. Rinaldo, W.A. Longacre, C. Cronin, L.G. Freeman and J. Schoenwetter, pp. 105-114. Fieldiana: Anthropology 53, Chicago.

Crown, P.L.
1980 Understanding Variability in the Utility Wares in the Upper Little Colorado Region. Paper presented at the 45th Annual Meeting of the Society for American Archaeology, Philadelphia.

Crown, P.L., and R.L. Bishop
1987 Convergence in Ceramic Manufacturing Traditions in the Late Prehistoric Southwest. Paper presented at the 52nd Annual Meeting of the Society for American Archaeology, Toronto, Canada.

Dana, J.D.
1959 *Dana's Manual of Mineralogy*. 17th rev. ed. Revised by C.S. Hurlbut, Jr. John Wiley and Sons, New York.

Danson, E.B.
1957 *An Archaeological Survey of West-Central New Mexico and East-Central Arizona*. Papers of the Peabody Museum of Archeology and Ethnology No. 44. Cambridge, Mass.

Danson, E.B., and R.M. Wallace
1956 A Petrographic Study of Gila Polychrome. *American Antiquity* 22:180-183.

David, N., and H. Hennning
1972 *The Ethnography of Pottery: A Fulani Case Seen in Archaeological Perspective*. Modules in Anthropology Vol. 21. Addison-Wesley Press, Reading, Mass.

Dean, J.S.
1970 Aspects of Tsegi Phase Social Organization: A Trial Reconstruction. In *Reconstructing Prehistoric Pueblo Societies*, edited by W.A. Longacre, pp. 140-174. University of New Mexico Press, Albuquerque.

Dean, J.S., R.C. Euler, G.J. Gumerman, F. Plog, R.H. Hevly, and T.N.V. Karlstrom
1985 Human Behavior, Demography, and Paleoenvironment on the Colorado Plateaus. *American Antiquity* 50:537-554.

Dean, J.S., A.J. Lindsay, Jr., and W.J. Robinson
1978 Prehistoric Settlement in Long House Valley, Northeastern Arizona. In *Investigations of the Southwestern Anthropological Research Group; The Proceedings of the 1976 Conference*, edited by R.C. Euler and G.J. Gumerman, pp. 25-44. Museum of Northern Arizona, Flagstaff.

Dean, J.S., and W.J. Robinson
1979 Computer Cartography and the Reconstruction of Dendroclimatic Variability in the Americn Southwest, A.D. 680 to 1970. In *Computer Graphics in Archaeology: Statistical Cartographic Applications to Spatial Analysis in Archaeological Contexts*, edited by S. Upham, pp. 79-94. Anthropological Research Paper No. 15. Arizona State University, Tempe.

Deutchman, H.L.
1980 Chemical Evidence of Ceramic Exchange on Black Mesa. In *Models and Methods in Regional Exchange*, edited by R.E. Fry, pp. 119-133. SAA Papers No. 1. Society for American Archaeology, Washington, D.C.

Di Peso, C.C.
1968 Casas Grandes and the Gran Chichimeca. *El Palacio* 75:45-61.

1974 *Casas Grandes, A Fallen Trading Center of the Gran Chichimeca Vol. 2: The Medio Period.* Amerind Foundation Series No. 9. Dragoon, Arizona.

Dittert, A.E.
1958 First Southwestern Ceramic Seminar: Cibola White Ware. Ms. on file, Department of Anthropology, Arizona State University, Tempe.

Dixon, W.J. (chief editor)
1985 *BMDP Statistical Software*. University of California Press, Berkeley.

Douglass, A.A.
1982 Ceramic Exchange Systems in the Prehistoric Southwest: A Quantitative Analysis of Little Colorado White Ware Distributions. Paper presented at the 27th Annual Meeting of the Arizona-Nevada Academy of Sciences, Flagstaff.

Downum, C.E.
1984 Tree-ring Dated Ceramics and the Estimation of Site Occupation Span. Paper presented at the 49th Annual Meeting of the Society for American Archaeology, Portland.

1986 Potsherds, Provenience and Ports of Trade: A Review of the Evidence from Chavez Pass. Paper presented at the Fourth Mogollon Conference, Tucson, Arizona.

Drennan, R.A., and J.A. Nowack
1984 Exchange and Sociopolitical Development in the Tehuacan Valley. In *Trade and Exchange in Early Mesoamerica*, edited by K.G. Hirth, pp. 147-156. University of New Mexico Press, Albuquerque.

Dumond, D.E.
1977 Science in Archaeology: The Saints Go Marching In. *American Antiquity* 42:330-349.

Earle, T.K.
1982 Prehistoric Economies and the Archaeology of Exchange. In *Contexts for Prehistoric Exchange*, edited by J.E. Ericson and T.K. Earle, pp. 1-12. Academic Press, New York.

Euler, R.C.
1985 Demography and Cultural Dynamics on the Colorado Plateau. Ms. in possession of author.

Euler, R.C., G.J. Gumerman, T.N.V. Karlstrom, J.S. Dean, and R.H. Hevly
1979 The Colorado Plateaus: Cultural Dynamics and Paleoenvironment. *Science* 205:1089-1101.

Fewkes, J.W.
1898 Archaeological Expedition to Arizona in 1895. In *Seventeenth Annual Report of the Bureau of American Ethnology for the Years 1895-1896*, Part 2, by J.W. Powell, pp. 519-742, Washington, D.C.

1904 Two Summers' Work in Pueblo Ruins. In *Twenty Second Annual Report of the Bureau of American Ethnology for the Years 1900-1901*, Part 1, by J.W. Powell, pp. 3-195, Washington, D.C.

1909 Ancient Zuni Pottery. In *Putman Anniversary Volume*, edited by F. Boas, R.B. Dixon, A.L. Kroeber, R.W. Hodge, and H.I. Smith, pp. 43-82. New York.

Fiero, D.C., R.W. Munson, M.T. McClain, S.M. Wilson, and A.H. Zier
1980 *The Navajo Project: Archaeological Investigations Along the Page to Phoenix 500Kv Southern Transmission Line*. Research Paper No. 11. Museum of Northern Arizona, Flagstaff.

Findlow, F.J., and M. Bolognese
1982 Regional Modeling of Obsidian Procurement in the American Southwest. In *Contexts for Prehistoric Exchange*, edited by J.E. Ericson and T.K. Earle, pp. 53-81. Academic Press, New York.

Fish, P., P. Pilles, and S. Fish
1980 Colonies, Traders and Traits: The Hohokam in the North. In *Current Issues in Hohokam Prehistory: Proceedings of a Symposium*, edited by F. Plog and D. Doyel, pp. 151-175. Anthropological Research Paper No. 23. Arizona State University, Tempe.

Flannery, K.V.
1967 The Olmec and the Valley of Oaxaca: A Model of Interregional Interaction in Formative Times. In *Dumbarton Oaks Conference on the Olmec*, edited by B. Meggers. Anthropological Society of Washington, Washington, D.C.

Ford, R.I.
1972a Barter, Gift or Violence: An Analysis of Tewa Intertribal Exchange. *Anthropological Papers* 6:21-45. University of Michigan Museum of Anthropology, Ann Arbor.

1972b An Ecological Perspective on the Eastern Pueblos. In *New Perspectives on the Pueblos*, edited by A. Ortiz, pp. 1-17. Unversity of New Mexico Press, Albuquerque.

Fried, M.
1967 *The Evolution of Political Society*. Random House, New York.

Friedrich, M.
1970 Design Structure and Social Interaction: Archeological Implications of an Ethnographic Analysis. *American Antiquity* 35:332-343.

Garrett, E.
1979 A Petrographic Analysis of Black Mesa Ceramics. Ms. on file, Department of Geology, Western Michigan University, Kalamazoo.

Geib, P.R., and M.M. Callahan
1985 Volcanic Ash Temper and Ceramic Exchange in the Kayenta Anasazi Region. Paper presented at the 50th Annual Meetings of the Society for American Archaeology, Denver.

Gibbs, R.J.
1965 Error Due to Segregation in Quantitative Clay Mineral X-Ray Diffraction Mounting Techniques. *American Mineralogist* 50:741-751.

Gladwin, H.S., and W. Gladwin
1935 *The Eastern Range of the Red-on-Buff Culture*. Medallion Paper No. 16. Gila Pueblo, Globe, Arizona.

Gladwin, H.S., E.W. Haury, E.B. Sayles, and N. Gladwin
1937 *Excavations at Snaketown: Material Culture*. Medallion Paper No. 25. Gila Pueblo, Globe, Arizona.

Gladwin, N.
1937 Petrography of Snaketown Pottery. In *Excavations at Snaketown: Material Culture*, by H.S. Gladwin, E.W. Haury, E.B. Sayles, and N. Gladwin, pp. 230-233. Medallion Paper No. 25. Gila Pueblo, Globe, Arizona.

Gladwin, W., and H.S. Gladwin
1929 *The Red-on-Buff Culture of the Gila Basin*. Medallion Paper No. 3. Gila Pueblo, Globe, Arizona.

1930 *Some Southwestern Pottery Types, Series I*. Medallion Paper No. 8. Gila Pueblo, Globe, Arizona.

1931 *Some Southwestern Pottery Types, Series II*. Medallion Paper No. 10. Gila Pueblo, Globe, Arizona.

1933 *Some Southwestern Pottery Types, Series* III. Medallion Paper No. 13. Gila Pueblo, Globe, Arizona.

Glagolev, A.
1934 Quantitative Analysis with the Microscope by the Point Method. *Engineering and Mining Journal* 135:399.

Goodman, L.A., and W.H. Kruskal
1972 Measures of Association for Cross-classifications, IV: Simplification of Asymptotic Variances. *Journal of the American Statistical Association* 67:415-421.

Gratz, K.E., and P.J. Pilles
1979 Sinagua Settlement Patterns and Organizational Models: A Trial Survey. Paper presented at the 1979 Annual Meeting of the Southwestern Anthropological Association, Santa Barbara.

Graves, M.W., S.J. Holbrook, and W.A. Longacre
1982 Aggregation and Abandonment at Grasshopper Pueblo: Evolutionary Trends in the Late Prehistoric of East-Central Arizona. In *Multidisciplinary Research at Grasshopper Pueblo, Arizona*, edited by W.A. Longacre, S.J. Holbrook, and M.W. Graves, pp. 110-121. Anthropological Papers of the Univeristy of Arizona No. 40. University of Arizona Press, Tucson.

Green, M.
1976 Chipped Stone Raw Material Utilization in the Chevelon Drainage. Ms. on file, Department of Anthropology, Arizona State University, Tempe.

1985 *Chipped Stone Raw Materials and the Study of Interaction in Black Mesa, Arizona*. Occasional Paper No. 11. Southern Illinois University at Carbondale Center for Archaeological Investigations, Carbondale.

Gumerman, G.J.
1969 *The Archaeology of the Hopi Buttes District, Arizona*. Unpublished Ph.D. dissertation, Department of Anthropology, University of Arizona, Tucson.

1975 Alternative Cultural Models for Demographic Change: Southwestern Examples. In *Population Studies in Archaeology and Biological Anthropology: A Symposium*, edited by A. Swedlund, pp. 104-115. SAA Memoir No. 30. Society for American Archaeology, Washington, D.C.

Gumerman, G.J., and R.C. Euler
1976 *Papers on the Archaeology of Black Mesa*. Southern Illinois University Press, Carbondale.

Gumerman, G.J., and S.A. Skinner
1968 A Synthesis of the Prehistory of the Central Little Colorado Valley, Arizona. *American Antiquity* 33:185-199.

Gumerman, G.J., D. Westfall, and C.S. Weed
1972 *Archeological Investigations on Black Mesa: The 1969-1970 Seasons*. Prescott College Studies in Anthropology 4. Prescott College Press, Prescott, Arizona.

Hack, J.T.
1942 The Changing Environment of the Hopi People and Its Effect on Their Agricultural Economy. *Papers of the Peabody Museum of Anthropology and Ethnology* 35:70-80, Cambridge, Mass.

Hantman, J.L.
1983 *Social Networks and Stylistic Distributions in the Prehistoric Plateau Southwest.* Unpublished Ph.D. dissertation, Department of Anthropology, Arizona State University, Tempe.

Hantman, J., and R. Jewett
1978 A Comparative Locational Analysis of Four Regions in East-Central Arizona. In *An Analytical Approach to Cultural Resource Management*, edited by F. Plog, pp. 212-220. Anthropological Research Paper No. 13. Arizona State University, Tempe.

Hantman, J.L., K.G. Lightfoot, S. Upham, F. Plog, S. Plog, and B. Masse
1984 Cibola Whitewares: A Regional Perspective. In *Regional Analysis of Prehistoric Ceramic Variation: Contemporary Studies of Cibola Whitewares*, edited by A.P. Sullivan and J.L. Hantman, pp. 17-35. Anthropological Research Paper No. 31. Arizona State University, Tempe.

Hantman, J.L., and S. Plog
1982 The Relationship of Stylistic Similarity to Patterns of Material Exchange. In *Contexts for Prehistoric Exchange*, edited by J.E. Ericson and T.K. Earle, pp. 237-263. Academic Press, New York.

Hardy, K.D., P.R. Plante, and S. Plog
1980 The Structure of Prehistoric Southwestern U.S. Ceramic Exchange Systems: A Black Mesa Case Study. Paper presented at the 45th Annual Meeting of the Society for American Archaeology, Philadelphia.

Harlow, F.H.
1973 *Matte-Paint Pottery of the Tewa, Keres, and Zuni Pueblos.* Museum of New Mexico, Santa Fe.

Harrill, B.G.
1973 The Dobell Site: Archaeological Salvage Near the Petrified Forest. *The Kiva* 39:35-67.

Harris, M.
1968 *The Rise of Anthropological Theory.* Thomas Y. Crowell, New York.

Hartman, D., S.T. Stebbins, and S.G. Dosh
1985 Archaeological Investigations Along Show Low Creek: Schoens Dam Flood Control Project, Apache-Sitgreaves National Forest, Navajo County, Arizona. Ms. on file, Museum of Northern Arizona, Flagstaff.

Hartwig, F., and B. Dearing
1979 *Exploratory Data Analysis*. Sage Quantitative Applications in the Social Sciences No. 16. Sage Publications, Beverly Hills.

Haury, E.W.
1936 *Some Southwestern Pottery Types, Series V*. Medallion Paper No. 19. Gila Pueblo, Globe, Arizona.

1956 Speculations on Prehistoric Settlement Patterns in the Southwest. In *Prehistoric Settlement Patterns in the New World*, edited by G.R. Willey, pp. 3-10. Publications in Anthropology No. 23. Viking Fund, Washington, D.C.

1962 The Greater American Southwest. In *Courses Toward Urban Life*, edited by R.J. Braidwood adn G.R. Willey, pp. 106-131. Publication in Anthropology No. 32. Viking Fund, Chicago.

1976 *The Hohokam: Desert Farmers and Craftsmen*. University of Arizona Press, Tucson.

Hawley, F.M.
1936 *Field Manual of Prehistoric Southwestern Pottery Types*. Anthropological Series Vol. 1, No. 4. University of New Mexico, Albuquerque.

Haynes, R.
1974 Application of Exponential Distance Decay to Human and Animal Activities. *Geografisker Annaler B* 56.

Henderson, T.K.
1979 Site Aggregation and Settlement System at Chavez Pass, Arizona. Paper presented at the 44th Annual Meeting of the Society for American Archaeology, Vancouver, B.C., Canada.

1980a A Methodology for Developing Time and Space Frameworks in the Chavez Region. Ms. on file, Department of Anthropology, Arizona State University, Tempe.

1980b Social Interaction and Organizational Change: A Diachronic Perspective. Paper presented at the 45th Annual Meeting of the Society for American Archaeology, Philadelphia.

Hill, J.N.
1970 *Broken K Pueblo: Prehistoric Social Organization in the American Southwest*. Anthropological Paper No. 18. University of Arizona, Tucson.

Hirth, K.G.
1984 The Analysis of Prehistoric Economic Systems: A Look to the Future. In *Trade and Exchange in Early Mesoamerica*, edited by K.G. Hirth, pp. 281-302. University of New Mexico Press, Albuquerque.

Hodder, I.
1974 A Regression Analysis of Some Trade and Marketing Patterns. *World Archaeology* 6:172-189.

1978 Social Organization and Human Interaction: The Development of Some Tentative Hypotheses in Terms of Material Culture. In *The Spatial Organization of Culture*, edited by I Hodder, pp. 199-269. University of Pittsburgh Press, Pittsburgh.

1982 Toward a Contextual Approach to Prehistoric Exchange. In *Contexts for Prehistoric Exchange*, edited by J.E. Ericson and T.K. Earle, pp. 199-211. Academic Press, New York.

Hodder, I, and P. Lane
1982 A Contextual Examination of Neolithic Axe Distribution in Britain. In *Contexts for Prehistoric Exchange*, edited by J.E. Ericson and T.K. Earle, pp. 213-235. Academic Press, New York.

Hodder, I., and C. Orton
1976 *Spacial Analysis in Archaeology*. Cambridge University Press, Cambridge.

Hogg, A.H.A.
1971 Some applications of surface fieldwork. In *The Iron Age and Its Hillforts*, edited by M. Jesson and D. Hill, pp. 105-125. University of Southampton Press, Southampton.

Hudgens, B.R.
1974 Turkey Hills community: A Sinagua Settlement Pattern Study. Ms. on file, Museum of Northern Arizona, Flagstaff.

Hudson, L.B.
1978 *A Quantitative Analysis of Prehistoric Exchange in the Southwest United States*. Unpublished Ph.D. dissertation, Department of Anthropology, University of California at Los Angeles.

Jackson, E., and S.P. van Valkenburgh
1954 *Montezuma Castle Archaeology, Part I: Excavations and Conclusions*. Southwest Monuments Association Technical Series, Vol. 3, Globe, Arizona.

Johnson, G.
1978 Information Sources and the Development of Decision-Making Organizations. In *Social Archaeology: Beyond Subsistence and Dating*, edited by C.L. Redman, M. Berman, E. Curtin, W. Langhorne, Jr., N. Versaggi, and J. Wanser, pp. 87-112. Academic Press, New York.

Jones, A.T.
1983 Agricultural Systems at Grand Canyon: Walhalla Glades. Ms. on file, Department of Anthropology, Arizona State University, Tempe.

1986 *Pueblo Period Archaeology at Four Sites, Petrified Forest National Park: Data Recovery Along the Mainline Road*. Publications in Anthropology No. 38. Western Archaeological and Conservation Center, Tucson.

Judd, N.
1954 *The Material Culture of Pueblo Bonito*. Smithsonian Miscellaneous Collections, Vol. 124. Smithsonian Institution Press, Washington, D.C.

Keller, D.
1979 Archaeological Investigations, Bureau of Indian Affairs, Phoenix Area Office, Hopi Indian Agency, Branch of Roads, Hopi Route 2, Navajo Indian Reservation, Coconino County, Arizona. Ms. on file, Museum of Northern Arizona, Flagstaff.

Kelley, J.C., and E.A. Kelley
1975 An Alternative Hypothesis for the Explanation of Anasazi Culture History. In *Collected Papers in Honor of Florence Hawley Ellis*, edited by T.R. Frisbie, pp. 178-223. Papers of the Archaeology Society of New Mexico No. 2, Santa Fe.

Kelley, R.E.
1969 Salvage Excavations at Six Sinagua Sites. *Plateau* 41:112-132.

Kidder, A.V.
1924 *An Introduction to the Study of Southwestern Archaeology*. Publications of the Department of Archaeology of Phillips Academy, Andover, Mass.

Kidder, A.V., and C.A. Amsden
1931 *The Pottery of Pecos I: The Dull Paint Wares*. Papers of the Southwestern Expedition No. 5. Phillips Academy, Andover, Mass.

Kidder, A.V., and A.O. Shepard
1936 *The Pottery of Pecos II: The Glaze Paint and Other Wares*. Yale University Press, New Haven.

Kiersch, G.A., and W.D. Keller
1955 Bleaching Clay Deposits, Sanders-Defiance Plateau District, Navajo County, Arizona. *Economic Geology* 50:469-494.

Kroeber, A.L.
1939 *Cultural and Natural Areas of Native North America*. Publications in American Archaeology and Ethnology, Vol. 38. University of California, Berkeley.

Lamberg-Karlovsky, C.C.
1975 Third Millenium Modes of Exchange and Modes of Production. In *Ancient Civilization and Trade*, edited by J.A. Sabloff and C.C. Lamberg-Karlovsky, pp. 341-368. University of New Mexico Press, Albuquerque.

Laczko, R.M.
1979 *A Preliminary Examination of PIII Settlement Patterns at Mesa Verde National Park, Colorado*. Unpublished M.A. thesis, Department of Anthropology, Hunter College, City University of New York, New York.

Lambert, M.
1966 *Indian Pottery: Materials, Tools and Techniques*. Popular Series Pamphlet No. 5. Museum of New Mexico Press, Santa Fe.

Leach, E.R.
1954 *Political Systems of Highland Burma: A Study of Kachin Social Structure*. Beacon Press, Boston.

LeBlanc, S.A.
1983 Review of Multidisciplinary Research at Grasshopper Pueblo, Arizona. *The Kiva* 48:337-338.

Leinhart, S., and S. Wasserman
1979 Exploratory Data Analysis: An Introduction to Selected Methods. In *Sociological Methodology 1979*, edited by K. Schuessler, pp. 311-372. Jossey-Bass, San Francisco.

Lemoine, C., S. Walker, and M. Picon
1982 Archaeological, Geochemical and Statistical Methods in Ceramic Provenance Studies. In *Archaeological Ceramics*, edited by J.S. Olin and A.D. Franklin, pp. 57-64. Smithsonian Institution Press, Washington, D.C.

Lightfoot, K.G.
1978 Food Redistribution Among Prehistoric Pueblo Groups. *The Kiva* 44:319-339.

1981 *Prehistoric Political Development in the Little Colorado Region, East-Central Arizona.* Unpublished Ph.D. dissertation, Department of Anthropology, Arizona State University, Tempe.

Lightfoot, K.G., and G. Feinman
1982 Social Differentiation and Leadership Development in Early Pithouse Villages in the Mogollon Region of the American Southwest. *American Antiquity* 47:64-86.

Lightfoot, K.G., and R.A. Jewett
1984 Late Prehistoric Distributions in East-Central Arizona: An Examination of Cibola Whiteware, White Mountain Redware, and Salado Redware. In *Regional Analysis of Prehistoric Ceramic Variation: Contemporary Studies of the Cibola Whitewares*, edited by A.P. Sullivan and J.L. Hantman, pp. 36-73. Anthropological Research Paper No. 31. Arizona State University, Tempe.

Lindsay, A.J., Jr.
1961 The Beaver Creek Agricultural Communityon the San Juan River, Utah. *American Antiquity* 27:174-187.

Lipe, W.D.
1970 Anasazi Communities in Red Rock Plateau, Southeastern Utah. In *Reconstructing Prehistoric Pueblo Societies*, edited by W.A. Longacre, pp. 84-139. School of American Research Advanced Seminar Series. University of New Mexico Press, Albuquerque.

Litto, G.
1976 *South American Folk Pottery.* Watson-Guptill, New York.

Longacre, W.A.
1964 Sociological Implications of the Ceramic Analysis. In *Chapters in the Prehistory of Eastern Arizona II*, edited by P.S. Martin, J.B. Rinaldo, W.A. Longacre, L.G. Freeman, J.A. Brown, R.H. Hevly, and M.E. Cooley, pp. 155-170. Fieldiana: Anthropology, Vol. 55. Chicago Natural History Museum, Chicago.

1970 *Archaeology as Anthropology: A Case Study.* Anthropological Paper No. 17. University of Arizona, Tucson.

1981 Kalinga Pottery: An Ethnoarcheological Study. In *Patterns of the Past: Studies in Honour of David Clarke*, edited by I. Hodder, G. Isaac and N. Hammond, pp. 49-66. Cambridge University Press, Cambridge.

Longacre, W.A., S.J. Holbrook, and M.W. Graves
1982 *Multidisciplinary Research at Grasshopper Pueblo, Arizona*. Anthropological Papers of the University of Arizona No. 40. University of Arizona Press, Tucson.

Martin, P.S.
1974 Early Development in Mogollon Research. In *Archaeological Research in Retrospect*, edited by G.R. Willey, pp. 3-29. Winthrop Publishers, Cambridge.

Martin, P.S., J.B. Rinaldo, W.A. Longacre, C. Cronin, L.G. Freeman, and J. Schoenwetter
1962 *Chapters in the Prehistory of Eastern Arizona, I*. Fieldiana: Anthropology, Vol. 53. Chicago Natural History Museum, Chicago.

Martin, P.S., J.B. Rinaldo, W.A. Longacre, L.G. Freeman, J.A. Brown, F.H. Hevly, and M.E. Cooley
1964 *Chapters in the Prehistory of Eastern Arizona, II*. Fieldiana: Anthropology, Vol. 55. Chicago Natural History Museum, Chicago.

Matson, R.G., and W.D. Lipe
1978 Settlement Patterns on Cedar Mesa: Boom and Bust on the Northern Periphery. In *Investigations of the Southwestern Anthropological Research Group: The Proceedings of the 1976 Conference*, edited by R.C. Euler and G.J. Gumerman, pp. 1-12. Museum of Northern Arizona Press, Flagstaff.

Mauss, M.
1954 *The Gift*. Translated by I. Cunnisson. Reprinted. Free Press, New York. Originally published 1924, *L'Annee Sociologique*, Second Series.

Mera, H.P.
1935 *Ceramic Clues to the Prehistory of North Central New Mexico*. Technical Series Bulletin No. 8. Laboratory of Anthropology, Santa Fe.

McGregor, J.C.
1937 *Winona Village: A XIIth Century Settlement with a Ball Court near Flagstaff, Arizona*. Bulletin No. 12. Museum of Northern Arizona, Flagstaff.

1941a *Southwestern Archaeology*. 1st ed. John Wiley, New York.

1941b *Winona and Ridge Ruin*. Bulletin No. 18. Museum of Northern Arizona, Flagstaff.

1965 *Southwestern Archaeology*. 2nd ed. University of Illinois Press, Urbana.

McGuire, R.
1980 The Mesoamerican Connection in the Southwest. *The Kiva* 46:3-38.

McGuire, R., and C.E. Downum
1982 A Preliminary Consideration of Desert-Mountain Trade Relations. In *Mogollon Archaeology: 1980 Conference*, edited by P. Beckett, pp. 111-122. Acoma Books, Ramona, California.

Moore, R.B., G.E. Ulrich, and E.W. Wolfe
1974 Geology of the Eastern and Northern Parts of the San Francisco Volcanic Field, Arizona. In *Geology of Northern Arizona With Notes on Archaeology and Paleoclimate*, edited by T.N.V. Karlstrom, G.A. Swan and R.L. Eastwood, pp. 465-494. Geological Society of America Guidebook for Rocky Mountain Section Meeting, Flagstaff.

Mulvey, T.
1983 The development of Electron-Probe Microanalysis: An Historical Perspective. In *Quatitative Electron-Probe Microanalysis*, edited by V.D. Scott, and G. Love, pp. 15-35. Ellis Horwood, Chichester, Great Britain.

Nelson, N.C.
1916 Chronology of the Tano Ruins, New Mexico. *American Anthropologist* 18:159-180.

Nemenyi, P., S.K. Dixon, N.B. White, Jr., and M.L. Hedstrom
1977 *Statistics From Scratch*. Holden-Day, San Francisco.

Newman, T.M.
1955 Documentary Sources on the Manufacture of Pottery by the Indians of the Central Plains and Middle Missouri. *Plains Anthropologist* 4:13-20.

Nicholson, W.E.
1929 The Potters of Sokoto, Northern Nigeria. *Man* 29:45-50.

Olson, A.P.
1963 The 1959-1960 Transwestern Pipeline Survey: Window Rock to Flagstaff. Ms. on file, Museum of Northern Arizona, Flagstaff.

Patterson, S.H.
1969 Clay in Mineral and Water Resources of Arizona. *Arizona Bureau of Mines Bulletin* 180:324-336.

Peacock, D.P.S.
1981 Archaeology, Ethnology and Ceramic Production. In *Production and Distribution: A Ceramic Viewpoint*, edited by H. Howard and E.L. Morris, pp. 187-194. British Archaeological Review, International Series No. 120.

Pillai, K.C.S.
1960 *Statistical Tables for Tests of Multivariate Hypotheses*. The Statistical Center, University of Phillipines, Manila.

Pilles, P.J.P, Jr.
1969 Habitation and Field Houses Near Winona and Angell, Arizona. *The Kiva* 34:90-102.

1976 The Field House and Sinagua Demography. In *Limited Activity and Occupation Sites: A Collection of Conference Papers*, edited by A.E. Ward, pp. 119-133. Contribution to Anthropological Studies No. 1. Universtiy of Arizona, Tucson.

1987 An Overview of Sinagua Prehistory. Paper presented at the Arizona Archaeological Council Meeting, Flagstaff.

Pires-Ferreira, J.W., and K.V. Flannery
1976 Models for Formative Exchange. In *The Early Mesoamerican Village*, edited by K.V. Flannery, pp. 286-292. Academic Press, New York.

Plog, F.
1974 *The Study of Prehistoric Change*. Academic Press, New York.

1975 Demographic Studies in Southwestern Prehistory. In Population Studies in Archeology and Biological Anthropology: A Symposium, edited by A. Swedlund, pp. 94-103. *SAA Memoir* No. 30. Society for American Archaeology, Washington, D.C.

1976 Ceramic Analysis. In *Chevelon Archaeological Research Project*, edited by F. Plog, J.N. Hill, and D. Read, pp. 58-78. Monograph II of the Archaeological Survey. University of California, Los Angeles.

1978 The Keresan Bridge: An Ecological and Archaeological Account. In *Social Archaeology: Beyond Subsistence and Dating*, edited by C.L. Redman, M. Berman, E. Curtin, W. Langhorne, Jr., N. Versaggi, and J. Wanser, pp. 349-372. Academic Press, New York.

1979 Prehistory: Western Anasazi. In *Southwest*, edited by A. Ortiz, pp. 108-130. Handbook of North American Indians, Vol. 9, W.G. Sturtevant, general editor. Smithsonian Institution, Washington, D.C.

1981 *Cultural Resources Overview: Little Colorado Area, Arizona*. USDA Forest Service, Albuquerque and Bureau of Land Management, Phoenix.

1983 Political and Economic Alliances on the Colorado Plateaus, A.D. 400-1450. In *Advances in World Archaeology*, edited by F. Wendorf and A. Close, pp. 289-330. Academic Press, New York.

1984 Exchange, Tribes and Alliances: The Northern Southwest. *American Archaeology* 4:217-223.

Plog, F., J.N. Hill, and D. Read (editors)
1976 *Chevelon Archaeological Research Project*. Monograph II of the Archaeological Survey. University of California, Los Angeles.

Plog, F., S. Upham, and P. Weigand
1982 A Perspective on Mogollon-Mesoamerican Interaction. In *Mogollon Archaeology: Proceedings of the 1980 Mogollon Conference*, edited by P.A. Beckett, pp. 227-238. Acoma Press, Ramona, California.

Plog, S.
1976 The Inference of Prehistoric Social Organization from Ceramic Design Variability. *Michigan Discussions in Anthropology* 1:1-47. University of Michigan, Ann Arbor.

1980a *Stylistic Variation in Prehistoric Ceramic Design Analysis in the American Southwest*. Cambridge University Press, New York.

1980b Village Autonomy in the American Southwest: An Evaluation of the Evidence. In *Models and Methods in Regional Exchange*, edited by R.A. Fry, pp. 135-146. SAA Papers No. 1. Society for American Arhcaeology, Washington, D.C.

Powell, S.L.
1980 *Material Culture and Behavior: A Prehistoric Example for the American Southwest*. Unpublished Ph.D. dissertation, Department of Anthropology, Arizona State University, Tempe.

Powers, M.C.
1953 A New Roundness Scale for Sedimentary Particles. *Journal of Sedimentary Petrology* 23:117-119.

Price, B.J.
1978 Commerce and Cultural Process in Mesoamerica. In *Mesoamerican Communication Routes and Cultural Contacts*, edited by T.A. Lee, Jr., and C. Navarrete, pp. 231-245. Paper No. 40. New World Archaeological Foundation, Provo, Utah.

Reed, S.J.B.
1975 *Electron Microprobe Analysis*. Cambridge University Press, Cambridge.

Reina, R.E., and R.M. Hill
1978 *The Traditional Pottery of Guatemala*. University of Texas Press, Austin.

Renfrew, C.
1975 Trade as Action at a Distance: Questions of Integration and Communication. In *Ancient Civilization and Trade*, edited by J.A. Sabloff and C.C. Lamberg-Karlovsky, pp. 3-59. University of New Mexico Press, Albuquerque.

1977 Alternative Models for Exchange and Spatial Distribution. In *Exchange Systems in Prehistory*, edited by T.K. Earle and J.E. Ericson, pp. 71-90. Academic Press, New York.

Renfrew, C., J.E. Dixon, and J.R. Cann
1968 Further Analysis of Near Eastern Obsidians. *Proceedings of the Prehistoric Society* 34:319-331.

Reynolds, H.T.
1977 *Analysis of Nominal Data*. Quantitative Applications in the Social Sciences. SAGE Publications, Beverly Hills, Calif.

Ritchie, N.N.
1970 Excavations at Walnut Canyon National Monument, Arizona. Ms. on file, Museum of Northern Arizona, Flagstaff.

Roberts, F.H.H.
1931 *Ruins at Kiatuthlanna, Eastern Arizona.* Bulletin No. 100. Bureau of American Ethnology, Washington, D.C.

Robinson, W.J., B.G. Harrill, and R.L. Warren
1975 *Tree-Ring Dates from Arizona H-I: Flagstaff Area.* Laboratory of Tree-Ring Research, University of Arizona, Tucson.

Rohn, A.H.
1963 Prehistoric Soil and Water Control on Chapin Mesa, Southwestern Colorado. *American Antiquity* 28:441-455.

1977 *Cultural Change and Continuity on Chapin Mesa.* The Regents Press of Kansas, Lawrence.

SAS Institute, Inc.
1985 *SAS User's Guide: Statistics.* 5th ed. Cary, North Carolina.

Sahlins, M.D.
1963 Poor Man, Rich Man, Chief: Political Types in Melaniesa and Polynesia. *Comparative Studies in Society and History* 5:285-303.

Sanders, W.T., and D. Webster
1978 Unilinealism, Multilinealism and the Evolution of Complex Societies. In *Social Archaeology*, edited by C.A. Redman, M. Berman, E. Curtin, W. Langhorne, Jr., N. Versaggi, and J. Wanser, pp. 249-302. Academic Press, New York.

Santley, R.S.
1984 Obsidian Exchange, Economic Stratification, and the Evolution of Complex Society in the Basin of Mexico. In *Trade and Exchange in Early Mesoamerica*, edited by K.G. Hirth, pp. 43-86. University of New Mexico Press, Albuquerque.

Schaefer, P.D.
1969 Prehistoric Trade in the Southwest and the Distribution of Pueblo IV Hopi Jeddito Black-on-Yellow. *The Kroeber Anthropological Society Papers* 41:54-77

Schaller, D.M.
1987 Petrographic Analysis, X-Ray Diffraction and Electron Microprobe Analysis of Little Colorado White Ware. Ms. on file, Department of Anthropology, Arizona State University, Tempe.

Schoenwetter, J., and A.E. Dittert
1968 An Ecological Interpretation of Anasazi Settlement Patterns. In *Anthropological Archaeology of the Americas*, edited by B. Meggers, pp. 41-66. Anthropological Society of Washington, Washington, D.C.

Schneider, J.K.
1974 *Economic Man*. Free Press, New York.

Schultz, L.G.
1963 *Clay Minerals in Triassic Rocks of the Colorado Plateau*. U.S. Geological Survey Bulletin 1147-C.

Schwartz, D.W.
1963 An Archaeological Survey of Nankoweap Canyon, Grand Canyon National Park. *American Antiquity* 28:289-302.

Schwartz, D.W., R.C. Chapman, and J. Kepp
1980 *Archaeology of the Grand Canyon: Unkar Delta*. School of American Research Press, Grand Canyon Archaeological Series, Vol. 2, Santa Fe.

Schwartz, D.W., M.P. Marshall, and J. Kepp
1979 *Archaeology of the Grand Canyon: The Bright Angel Site*. School of American Research Press, Grand Canyon Archaeological Series, Vol. 1, Santa Fe.

Service, E.
1971 *Primitive Social Organization*. 2nd ed. Random House, New York.

Sharrock, F.W., D.S. Dibble, and K.M. Anderson
1961 The Creeping Dune Irrigation Site in Glen Canyon, Utah. *American Antiquity* 27:188-202.

Shepard, A.O.
1936 Petrology of Pecos Pottery. In *The Pottery of Pecos II: The Glaze Paint, Culinary and Other Wares*, by A.V. Kidder and A.O. Shepard. Yale University Press, New Haven.

1939 Technology of La Plata Pottery. In *Archeological Studies in the La Plata District*, by E.H. Morris, pp. 249-287. Publication No. 519. Carnegie Institution of Washington, Washington, D.C.

1942 *Rio Grande Glaze Paint Ware*. Publication No. 528, Contribution No. 39. Carnegie Institution of Washington, Wahington D.C.

1965 Rio Grande Glaze Paint Pottery: A Test of Petrographic Analysis. In *Ceramics and Man*, edited by F.R. Matson, pp. 62-87. Publication in Anthropology, No. 41. Viking Fund, Chicago.

1980 *Ceramics for the Archaeologist*. Publication No. 609. Carnegie Institution, Washington, D.C. Reprinted by Braun-Bumfield, Ann Arbor.

Smith, W.
1952 *Excavations in Big Hawk Valley, Wupatki National Monument, Arizona*. Museum of Northern Arizona Bulletin 24. Flagstaff.

South, S.
1972 Evolution and Horizon as Revealed in the Ceramic Analysis in Historical Archaeology. *The Conference on Historic Site Archaeology Papers* 6:1:71-106. Institute of Archeology and Anthropology, University of South Carolina, Columbia.

Spence, M.W.
1982 The Social Context of Production and Exchange. In *Contexts for Prehistoric Exchange*, edited by J.E. Ericson and T.K. Earle, pp. 173-197. Academic Press, New York.

Spier, L.
1917 *Chronology of the Zuni Ruins*. Anthropological Papers Vol. 18. American Museum of Natural History, New York.

Stanislawski, M.
1963 *Wupatki Pueblo: A Study in Cultural Fusion and Change in Sinagua and Hopi Territory*. Unpublished Ph.D. dissertation, Department of Anthropology, University of Arizona, Tucson.

1973 Review of Archaeology as Anthropology: A Case Study. *American Antiquity* 38:117-121.

Stark, B.L.
1986 Perspectives on the Peripheries of Mesoamerica. In *Ripples in the Chichimec Sea: New Considerations of Southwestern-Mesoamerican Interactions*, edited by F.J. Mathien and R.H. McGuire, pp. 270-290. Southern Illinois University Press, Carbondale.

Starkey, H.C., P.D. Blackmon, and P.L. Hauff
1984 *The Routine Mineralogical Analysis of Clay-Bearing Samples*. U.S. Geological Survey Bulletin No. 1563.

Stebbins, S., D.E. Weaver, Jr., and S.G. Dosh
1981 *Archaeology at the Confluence of the Verde River and West Clear Creek.* Research Paper No. 24. Museum of Northern Arizona, Flagstaff.

Sullivan, A.P.
1984 Design Styles and Cibola Whiteware: Examples from the Grasshopper Area, East-Central Arizona. In *Regional Analysis of Prehistoric Ceramic Variation: Contemporary Studies of the Cibola Whitewares*, edited by A.P. Sullivan and J.L. Hantman, pp. 74-93. Anthropological Research Paper No. 31. Arizona State University, Tempe.

Sussman, R.
1972 Child Transport, Family Size and Increase in Human Population During the Neolithic. *Current Anthropology* 13:258-259.

Swarthout, J., and A.P. Dulaney
1978 The Great Cibola Typological Consensus Test. Paper presented at the 2nd Cibola White Ware Conference, Museum of Northern Arizona, Flagstaff.

Tagg, M.D., and R.W. Layhe
1985 *Archaeological Excavations at AZ I:10:30 (ASM), a Sinagua Settlement: Townsend-Divide Unit I, U.S. Highway 89, Coconino County, Arizona. Archaeological Series No. 169.* Cultural Resource Management Division, Arizona State Museum, University of Arizona, Tucson.

Toll, H.W., T.C. Windes, and P.J. Mckenna
1980 Late Ceramic Patterns in Chaco Canyon: The Pragmatics of Modeling Ceramic Exchange. In *Models and Methods in Regional Exchange*, edited by R.A. Fry, pp. 95-117. SAA Papers No. 1. Society for American Archaeology, Washington, D.C.

Tower, D.B.
1945 *The Use of Marine Mollusca and Their Value in Reconstructing Prehistoric Trade Routes in the American Southwest.* Papers of the Excavators' Club No. 2, Cambridge, Mass.

Trott, J.J., and G. McPherson
1984 Bureau of Indian Affairs, Branch of Roads Route N15 (6), (9), and (10), Leupp to Dilkon, Navajo Indian Reservation, Land Districts 5 and 7, Navajo County, Arizona. Ms. on file, Museum of Northern Arizona, Flagstaff.

Tuggle, H.D.
1970 *Prehistoric Community Relationships in East Central Arizona.* Unpublished Ph.D. dissertation, Department of Anthropology, University of Arizona, Tucson.

Tukey, J.
1977 *Exploratory Data Analysis.* Addison-Wesley, Reading, Mass.

Upham, S.
1978 *Final Report on Arhaeological Investigations at Chavez Pass Ruin, Coconino National Forest, Arizona: The 1978 Field Season.* Report submitted to the U.S. Department of Agriculture, Forest Service, Coconino National Forest, Flagstaff.

1982 *Polities and Power: An Economic and Political History of the Western Pueblo.* Academic Press, New York.

Upham, S., K.G. Lightfoot, and G.M. Feinman
1981 Explaining Socially Determined Ceramic Distributions in the Prehistoric Plateau Southwest. *American Antiquity* 46:822-833.

Ulrich, G.E., G.H. Billingsley, R. Hereford, E.W. Wolfe, L.D. Nealey, and R.L. Sutton
1984 Map Showing Geology, Structure, and Uranium Deposits of the Flagstaff 1°x 2° Quadrangle. *U.S. Geological Survey Miscellaneous Geological Investigations Map I-1446, scale 1:250,000.*

van der Leuuw, S.
1977 Towards a Study of the Economics of Pottery Making. *El Horreo*, Cingvla IV. Albert Egges van Giffen Institute of Prehistory, University of Amsterdam.

van der Plas, L., and A.C. Tobi
1965 A Chart for Judging the Reliability of Point Counting Results. *American Journal of Science* 263:87-90.

Velleman, P.F., and D.C. Hoaglin
1981 *Applications, Basics and Computing of Exploratory Data Analysis.* Duxbury Press, Boston.

Vivian, G.R.
1970 An Inquiry Into Prehistoric Social Organization in Chaco Canyon, New Mexico. In *Reconstructing Prehistoric Pueblo Societies*, edited by W.A. Longacre, pp. 59-83. University of New Mexico Press, Albuquerque.

1974 Conservation and Diversion: Water-Control Systems in the Anasazi Southwest. In *Irrigation's Impact on Society*, edited by T.E. Downing and M. Gibson, pp. 95-112. Anthropological Paper No. 25. University of Arizona, Tucson.

Vivian, G.R., and T. Mathews
1965 *Kin Kletso, a Pueblo III community in Chaco Canyon, New Mexico*. Technical Series No. 6. Southwest Monuments Association, Globe, Arizona.

Vivian, G.R., and P. Reiter
1960 *The Great Kivas of Chaco Canyon and Their Relationships*. Monograph No. 22. School of American Research, Santa Fe.

Ward, A.E.
1969 Tse Tlani: A 12th Century Sinagua Village. *Plateau* 41:77-104.

1975 The PC Ruin: Archaeological Investigations in the Prescott Tradition. *The Kiva* 40:131-164.

Warren, A.H.
1968 Petrographic Notes on Glaze Paint Pottery. In *The Cochiti Dam Archeological Salvage Project, Part I: Report on the 1963 Season*, edited by C.H. Lange, pp. 184-197. Research Record No. 6. Museum of New Mexico, Santa Fe.

1969a Report on Petrographic Analysis of Unkar Delta Ceramic Materials. Unpublished ms. on file at the School of American Research, Santa Fe.

1969b Tonque Pueblo: One Pueblo's Glaze Pottery Dominated the Middle Rio Grande Commerce. *El Palacio* 76:36-42.

1980 Appendix E: Descriptions of Temper Types Identified in Ceramics from Unkar Delta. In *Archaeology of the Grand Canyon: Unkar Delta*, edited by D.W. Schwartz, R.C. Chapman and J. Kepp, pp. 345-353. School of American Research Press, Grand Canyon Archaeological Series, Vol. 2, Santa Fe.

Wasley, W.W.
1959 *Cultural Implications of Style Trends in Southwestern Prehistoric Pottery: Basketmaker III to Pueblo II in West Central New Mexico*. Unpublished Ph.D. dissertation, Department of Anthropology, University of Arizona.

Weigand, P.C., G. Harbottle, and E.V. Sayre
1977 Turquoise Sources and Source Analysis: Mesoamerica and the Southwestern U.S.A. In *Exchange Systems in Prehistory*, edited by T.K. Earle and J.E. Ericson, pp. 15-34. Academic Press, New York.

Wendorf, F.W.
1953 Archeological Studies in the Petrified Forest National Monument. *Museum of Northern Arizona Bulletin* 27, Flagstaff.

Wentworth, C.K.
1922 A Scale of Grade or Class Terms for Clastic Sediments. *Journal of Geology* 30:377-392.

White, C.
1974 Lower Colorado River Area Aboriginal Warfare and Alliance Dynamics. In *ANTAP, California Indian Political and Economic Organization*, edited by L.J. Bean and T.F. King, pp. 113-135. Ballena Press, Ramona, California.

Whittlesey, S.M.
1974 Identification of Imported Ceramics Through Functional Analysis of Attributes. *The Kiva* 40:101-112.

1978 *Status and Death at Grasshopper Pueblo: Experiments Toward an Archaeological Theory of Correlates*. Unpublished Ph.D. dissertation, Department of Anthropology, University of Arizona, Tucson.

Wilcox, D.R.
1981 Changing Perspectives on the Protohistoric Pueblos, A.D. 1450-1700. In *The Protohistoric Period in the North American Southwest, A.D. 1450-1700*, edited by D.R. Wilcox and W.B. Masse, pp. 378-409. Anthropological Research Papers No. 24. Arizona State University, Tempe.

Williams, H.
1936 Pliocene Volcanoes of the Navajo-Hopi Country. *Geological Society of America Bulletin* 47:111-172.

Williams, J.L.W., and D.A. Jenkins
1976 The Use of Petrographic, Heavy Mineral and Arc Spectographic Techniques in Assessing the Provenience of Sediments Used in Ceramics. In *Geochronology: Earth Science and the Past*, edited by D.A. Davidson and M. Shackley, pp. 115-134. Westview, Boulder, Co.

Wilson, J.P.
1969 *The Sinagua and Their Neighbors.* Unpublished Ph.D. dissertation, Department of Anthropology, Harvard University, Cambridge, Mass.

Wilson, R.F.
1974 Mesozoic Stratigraphy of Northeastern Arizona. In *Geology of Northern Arizona with Notes on Archaeology and Paleoclimate, Part 1*, edited by T.N.V. Karlstrom, G.A. Swann and R.L. Eastwood, pp. 192-207. Regional Studies: Geological Society of America Guidebook for Rocky Mountain Section Meeting, Flagstaff.

Wissler, C.
1917 *The American Indian: An Introduction to the Anthropology of the New World.* D.C. McCurtrie, New York.

1926 *The Relation of Nature to Man in Aboriginal America.* Oxford Universtiy Press, New York.

Wobst, H.M.
1977 Stylistic Behavior and Information Exchange. In *Papers for the Director*, edited by C. Cleland, pp. 317-342. Museum of Anthropology Paper No. 61. University of Michigan, Ann Arbor.

Woodbury, R.
1961 Prehistoric Agriculture at Point of Pines, Arizona. *SAA Memoir No. 17.* Society for American Archaeology, Washington, D.C.

Woosley, A.I.
1980 Agricultural Diversity in the Prehistoric Southwest. *The Kiva* 45:317-335.

Wright, G.A.
1970 On Trade and Culture Process in Prehistory. *Current Anthropology* 11:171-173.

APPENDIX A

DATING WINONA VILLAGE PITHOUSE CLUSTERS AND TRASH MOUNDS

Winona Village is composed of seven pithouse clusters and a ball court. These features were assigned six different NA site numbers during excavations in the 1930s and subsequently have been given Coconino National Forest numbers (refer to Figure 29). All but two of the pithouse clusters (NA 2135 and the southern cluster of NA 2133) are associated with trash mounds. NA 2131 also includes a three-room masonry structure. The tree-ring dates that were derived from wooden beams excavated out of the pithouses show that not all the houses within a single cluster were occupied contemporaneously, although more than one pithouse probably was occupied at any given point in time. Each cluster therefore represents the history of shifting occupation and trash accumulation of a small group of households.

The bulk of the Winona Village ceramic collection at the Museum of Northern Arizona is composed of sherds which were excavated from the trash mounds. Although sherds were excavated from pithouses in relatively large quantities (Colton 1946), portions of the pithouse assemblages were discarded after being tabulated. In addition, the museum's records indicate that an undetermined number of sherds were reburied at the site in NA 2135C. Of those pithouse assemblages which originally had LCWW sherds, some have disappeared altogether while others are incomplete and no longer contain this ware. As a result, it was not possible to use sherds in the sourcing study and stylistic analysis which were derived from well dated contexts such as pithouse floors.

However, it was desirable to estimate dates for the trash mounds and pithouses so that assessments concerning the impact of change through time on compositional and stylistic variability could be made when comparing the LCWW sherds samples from Winona

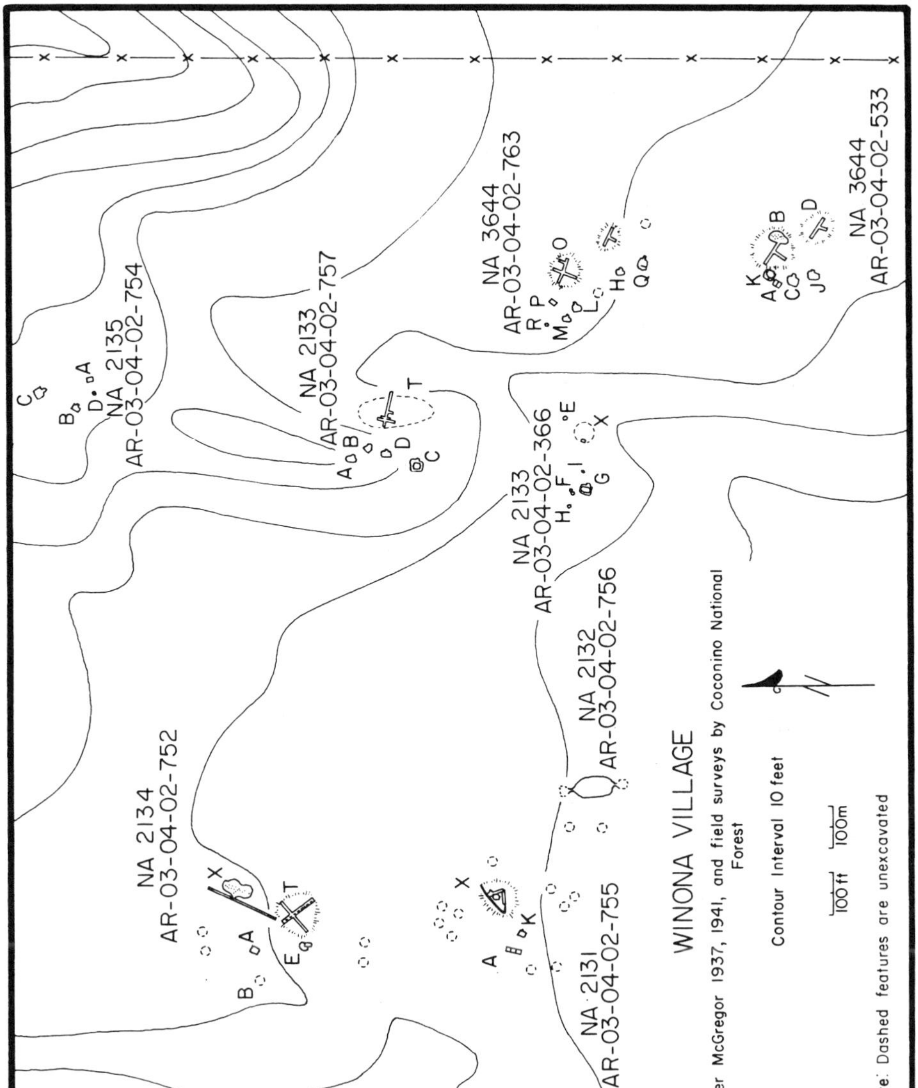

Figure 29. Plan view of Winona Village.

Village, Juniper Terrace and the Plaza Site, the three potential production/exchange centers included in this study.

It is reasonable to assume that a midden associated with a particular pithouse cluster represents the accumulation of trash throughout the life history of that cluster. Therefore, the dates of each trash mound should be bracketed by the earliest construction date and the latest date of abandonment for the pithouses in its associated cluster. This somewhat simplistic model is compromised by the fact that the two NA 3644 clusters each possess two middens. It is not clear at this time whether the middens represent different episodes of trash accumulation, or whether each midden within a cluster was used contemporaneously by different households. The midden designated NA 3644I is associated with pithouses NA 3644H and Q, while NA 3644O is adjacent to pithouses NA 3644L, M, P and R. The date ranges I have assigned these trash mounds reflect their positioning relative to the pithouses in the northern NA 3644 cluster. In contrast, middens NA 3644B and D are not associated with separate subgroups of pithouses. As a result, I have assigned them date ranges for the southern NA 3644 cluster as a whole.

The occupation spans listed in Table 31 were estimated for the dated pithouses at Winona Village by interpreting sequences of the published tree-ring dates (Robinson et al 1975) according to three guidelines. First, a strong cluster of cutting dates or near cutting dates (i.e., where only a few outer rings are missing) at the beginning of a sequence is assumed to be associated with the construction of the pithouse. Second, a maximum pithouse occupation period of 15 years was used in order to determine the beginning or ending date, depending on which end of the sequence was left open. Third, a maximum of

Table 31. Postulated Date Ranges for Winona Village Features.

Trash Mound	Pithouse	Interpreted Occupation Span
	NA 2133A	A.D. 1086 to 1101
	NA 2133B	A.D. 1072 to 1087
		A.D. 1082 to 1097
	NA 2133D	A.D. 1091 to 1106
NA 2133T		*A.D. 1072 to 1106*
		A.D. 1082 to 1106
	NA 2134A	A.D. 1130 to 1145
	NA 2134B	A.D. 1080 to 1095
		A.D. 1090 to 1105
	NA 2135E.1	A.D. 1076 to 1091
NA 2134T		*A.D. 1076 to 1145*
	NA 3644A	not interpretable
	NA 3644C	*A.D. 1110 to 1125*
	NA 3644J	*A.D. 1083 to 1098*
	NA 3644K	A.D. 1076 to 1091
		A.D. 1051 to 1076
NA 3644B		*A.D. 1076 to 1125*
		A.D. 1051 to 1125
NA 3644D		A.D. 1076 to 1125
		A.D. 1051 to 1125
	NA 3644M	A.D. 1097 to 1112
	NA 3644P	A.D. 1107 to 1122
	NA 3644Q, room 1	A.D. 1060 to 1075
		A.D. 1070 to 1081
NA 3644I		A.D. 1060 to 1075
		A.D. 1070 to 1081
NA 3644O		A.D. 1097 to 1122

Note: Proveniences used in the petrographic and design analyses are shown in *italics*.

five years from the last repair episode to the abandonment of the pithouse was assumed. The last two assumptions were derived from observations of the patterning of ree-ring date sequences from well-dated pithouse structures throughout the Colorado Plateaus (Chris Downum, personal communication 1985). Only the dated pithouses associated with trash mounds are included in the table. Proveniences used in this study are italicized.

NA 2133A can serve as an example of how these guidelines were operationalized in estimating the occupation spans of the pithouses listed above. The dates of the outermost rings for tree-ring samples from NA 2133A are as follows (cutting dates are italicized):

106	4
107	3 4 4 5 6 6 7 9
108	0 0 2 2 3 4 4 4 4 5 5 *5* 6 6 6 6 6 *6 6 6 6 6* 7 8
109	5

The cluster of cutting dates suggests that the pithouse was constructed ca. A.D. 1086. The later dates probably represent one or more repair episodes. The pithouse burned some time after A.D. 1095. If this structure was occupied for the maximum span of 15 years, it would have been abandoned ca. A.D. 1101. This terminal date also corresponds closely with a maximum five year interval between the final repair episode (ca. A.D. 1095) and abandonment (Chris Downum, personal communication 1985).

Some pithouses have no clear cluster of construction dates. In such cases, it was necessary to work backward from the last date of repair or abandonment. For example, NA 2133D has a final non-cutting date of A.D. 1101 which has been interpreted as the last date of repair. Given a maximum use life of 15 years and a maximum period of occupation without repair of 5 years, the construction date would have been ca. A.D. 1091.

Finally, a few of the pithouses are associated with only a single non-cutting date. In such cases, both the beginning and ending dates of the estimated occupation span are floating and are therefore suspect. However, such dates provide at least a rough estimate which, together with better dated pithouses, can be used to bracket the periods of trash accumulation in the middens.

For example, NA 2133B has one non-cutting date of A.D. 1082. All that can be said for certain is that the structure burned some time after this date. If A.D. 1082 is assumed to be the last date of repair, then the structure would have been abandoned no later than A.D. 1087. If it were occupied for the 15 year maximum, then it would have been built ca. A.D. 1072. If A.D. 1082 represents the construction episode, then the pithouse would have been abandoned no later than A.D. 1097. Alternatively, the single date may represent a repair episode in the middle of the structure's use life. I have employed the two extreme cases in order to present the most divergent date ranges possible, given the data.

Several structures across the site remain unexcavated or undated and their chronological positions within the life history of their respective clusters cannot be determined at this time. The postulated date ranges for the clusters, and hence the trash mounds, potentially could be extended at one or both ends if more dates were available. As a result, the dates probably are conservative estimates. Most of the tree-ring samples have non-cutting dates and the estimated date ranges are therefore too early in most cases. Unfortunately, it is not possible to determine how skewed they are.

In conclusion, the dendrochronological data suggest a maximum date range of A.D. 1051 to 1145. However, the construction date of A.D. 1051 postulated for NA 3644K is probably too early since it is anomalous with respect to other construction dates within its respective cluster and across the site as a whole. The single non-cutting date of A.D. 1082 from this structure probably is a construction date, instead of a repair date, thus shifting the occupation span of NA 3644K later in time.

The bulk of the construction of pithouses at Winona Village seems to have occurred in the fourth quarter of the eleventh century. NA 2133 (both clusters) and NA 2135 were abandoned sometime during the first decade of the twelfth century. NA 2134 and NA 3644 (both clusters), however, were still occupied during at least the second quarter of the twelfth century. They may have been occupied even later since the terminal dates associated with the pithouses in these clusters are non-cutting dates. The chronological placement of NA 2131 in the occupation of Winona Village remains unknown since no tree-ring dates have been obtained from its structures. The LCWW sherd sample used in this study spans the occupation of the site. The sherds from NA 2134T and NA 3644B and C are roughly contemporaneous with the Juniper Terrace sample, and possibly the Plaza Site.

APPENDIX B

THE PETROGRAPHIC DATA

Table 32. Petrographic Point Count Data.

Thinsec. #	S	F	Clay	Qtz.	Sherd	U.F.	A.F.	C.F.	V.R.	Ferro.	Op.	Cryp.	Sec.
9400.01	1	2	269	18	10	1	0	0	0	0	0	1	1
9400.02	4	2	256	21	14	3	1	0	0	0	0	2	3
9400.03	4	1	249	24	11	5	1	1	2	1	1	1	4
9400.04	1	1	277	10	8	2	1	0	0	0	0	0	2
9400.05	1	1	249	32	13	4	0	0	0	0	0	0	2
9400.06	3	2	258	24	5	4	0	0	1	0	0	3	5
9400.07	3	2	275	15	3	2	1	1	0	0	0	1	2
9400.08	3	2	268	15	12	1	0	1	0	1	0	0	2
9400.09	3	2	258	18	15	3	0	0	0	2	2	1	1
9400.10	4	2	273	16	1	1	1	0	0	0	0	2	6
9400.11	4	2	277	16	5	1	0	1	0	0	0	0	0
9400.12	4	2	271	19	2	3	3	0	0	0	0	1	1
9400.13	4	2	240	23	33	1	1	0	0	0	0	0	2
9400.14	4	1	274	18	1	3	0	0	4	0	0	0	0
9400.15	4	2	252	35	4	3	1	0	0	0	1	3	1
9400.16	2	1	275	12	6	7	0	0	0	0	0	0	0
9400.17	2	1	229	49	1	8	1	0	0	0	0	0	12
9400.18	5	2	259	27	0	0	2	0	7	0	1	1	3
9400.19	5	1	283	6	10	0	0	0	0	0	0	0	1
9400.20	5	1	260	15	15	2	1	1	1	1	1	0	3
9400.21	3	2	284	6	1	1	0	0	0	0	0	0	8
9400.22	2	2	270	20	4	3	0	0	0	0	0	1	1
9400.23	1	2	271	18	2	2	0	0	0	0	0	1	7
9400.24	3	2	238	16	36	0	0	0	4	1	0	1	4
9400.25	2	2	249	19	25	3	1	0	0	0	0	2	1
9400.26	2	2	251	21	23	1	1	0	0	0	0	2	1
9400.27	3	1	263	29	3	1	1	0	1	0	0	2	0
9400.28	5	2	286	7	2	1	0	0	0	0	1	2	1
9400.29	3	2	273	10	12	1	1	0	0	0	0	2	1
9400.30	5	1	256	14	23	4	0	0	0	0	0	0	3
9400.31	1	1	258	24	11	2	0	0	0	0	0	3	2
9400.32	1	1	264	16	11	2	1	1	0	0	2	1	2
9400.33	2	1	244	12	38	3	0	0	1	0	0	1	1
9400.34	5	1	274	9	11	2	1	0	1	2	0	0	0
9400.35	5	2	263	26	4	0	1	0	0	0	2	1	3

Table 32. Petrographic Point Count Data (Continued).

Thinsec. #	S	F	Clay	Qtz.	Sherd	U.F.	A.F.	C.F.	V.R.	Ferro.	Op.	Cryp.	Sec.
9400.36	1	2	278	17	1	1	0	0	0	1	0	2	0
9400.37	1	2	238	24	20	4	1	0	0	0	0	2	11
9400.38	1	1	250	27	3	6	0	0	0	1	0	0	13
9400.39	1	2	245	26	19	3	1	0	1	0	0	2	3
9400.40	4	1	270	15	15	0	0	0	0	0	0	0	0
9400.41	4	1	265	2	10	1	0	0	1	0	0	1	1
9400.42	3	1	267	9	20	1	0	0	1	0	0	1	1
9400.43	3	1	286	6	5	1	1	0	0	0	0	0	1
9400.44	5	1	282	10	5	2	0	1	0	0	0	0	0
9400.45	5	2	241	13	38	0	0	0	2	2	0	2	2
9400.46	5	2	284	9	5	1	0	0	0	0	0	0	1
9400.47	1	1	229	46	0	21	0	3	0	0	0	1	0
9400.48	2	1	274	16	10	1	0	0	0	0	0	0	0
9400.49	2	2	216	45	15	8	1	1	0	0	0	1	13
9400.50	2	2	219	40	35	2	1	0	1	0	0	2	0
2134T.01	1	2	251	25	16	4	1	0	1	1	0	0	1
2134T.02	1	2	271	13	11	2	0	0	0	0	0	0	3
2134T.03	1	2	249	23	17	6	0	1	1	0	0	2	1
2134T.04	1	2	258	17	21	0	1	0	0	0	1	2	0
2134T.05	1	2	249	16	27	2	1	1	0	0	1	2	1
2134T.06	1	2	248	9	41	0	0	1	0	0	0	1	0
2134T.07	1	2	243	17	37	2	0	0	0	0	0	0	1
2134T.08	1	2	248	11	34	1	1	0	0	2	1	1	1
2134T.09	2	1	260	16	18	0	1	0	1	0	1	3	0
2134T.10	1	1	256	12	27	1	0	0	1	0	1	1	1
2134T.11	4	1	234	15	48	2	0	0	1	0	0	0	0
2134T.13	2	1	258	11	28	1	0	0	0	0	1	1	0
2134T.14	1	1	265	3	26	3	1	0	1	1	0	0	0
2133T.01	1	1	233	40	0	8	0	2	0	0	0	1	16
2133T.02	1	2	250	9	37	3	0	0	0	0	0	1	0
2133T.03	1	1	237	31	2	8	2	3	0	0	0	3	14
2133T.04	1	1	241	35	0	7	1	2	0	0	0	1	13
2133T.05	1	1	225	10	61	2	1	0	0	0	1	0	0
2132.01	3	1	229	24	35	1	2	1	3	1	0	2	2
3644B.01	1	1	204	70	2	10	1	1	2	1	3	6	0

Table 32. Petrographic Point Count Data (Continued).

Thinsec. #	S	F	Clay	Qtz.	Sherd	U.F.	A.F.	C.F.	V.R.	Ferro.	Op.	Cryp.	Sec.
3644B.02	2	2	257	25	11	5	0	0	0	0	1	0	1
3644B.03	4	1	273	12	8	4	1	0	1	0	0	1	0
3644B.04	2	1	275	7	17	0	0	0	0	0	0	1	0
3644B.05	1	1	232	36	15	12	0	0	0	0	0	5	0
3644B.06	1	2	234	36	26	2	0	0	1	0	0	0	1
3644B.07	1	2	231	22	37	2	2	0	0	1	1	1	3
3644B.08	1	2	237	29	20	7	0	0	3	0	0	1	3
3644C.01	3	1	288	5	6	0	0	0	0	0	0	1	0
3644C.02	4	1	256	23	17	3	1	0	0	0	0	0	0
3644J.01	2	1	277	13	9	1	0	0	0	0	0	0	0
1814A.01	2	1	256	21	15	5	0	0	1	0	1	1	0
1814A.02	3	2	235	40	12	7	0	1	0	0	3	1	1
1814A.03	4	2	272	5	21	2	0	0	0	0	0	0	1
1814A.04	6	2	240	26	24	4	1	0	1	1	1	2	0
1814A.05	4	2	262	11	19	2	0	1	0	1	1	3	0
1814A.06	5	2	249	28	8	10	3	0	0	0	1	0	2
1814A.07	2	1	287	11	1	0	0	0	0	0	0	0	1
1814A.08	2	1	248	18	31	2	0	0	0	0	1	0	0
1814A.09	1	2	263	10	23	1	0	1	1	1	0	1	0
1814A.10	5	2	282	8	5	1	1	1	0	0	0	2	0
1814A.11	2	1	262	16	19	1	0	0	0	1	0	1	0
1814A.12	4	2	263	16	13	5	2	0	0	0	0	0	1
1814A.13	3	1	282	10	4	3	0	0	0	0	1	0	0
1814A.14	3	1	250	17	29	2	0	0	0	0	1	1	0
1814A.15	4	1	268	14	14	3	0	0	0	0	0	1	1
1814A.16	1	1	280	16	2	2	0	0	0	0	0	0	0
1814A.17	3	2	237	28	26	3	2	0	0	1	0	2	1
1814A.18	2	1	260	18	16	0	2	1	1	0	0	0	2
1814A.19	5	1	259	6	27	1	0	0	3	1	0	1	2
1814A.20	3	2	281	3	13	0	0	0	0	0	0	1	2
1814A.21	4	1	241	45	0	8	0	1	0	0	0	5	0
1814A.22	2	1	265	16	14	2	1	0	0	1	0	1	0
1814A.23	3	2	252	15	29	0	0	0	1	3	0	0	0
1814A.24	4	1	277	10	8	1	0	0	1	0	0	2	1
1814A.25	3	1	290	6	3	1	0	0	0	0	0	0	0

Table 32. Petrographic Point Count Data (Continued).

Thinsec. #	S	F	Clay	Qtz.	Sherd	U.F.	A.F.	C.F.	V.R.	Ferro.	Op.	Cryp.	Sec.
1814A.26	2	1	259	19	16	4	0	1	0	1	0	0	0
1814A.27	3	2	272	12	14	0	0	0	1	0	1	0	0
1814A.28	3	1	269	25	2	3	0	0	0	0	1	0	0
1814A.29	4	1	245	21	0	15	3	1	1	0	1	0	13
1814A.30	4	1	244	39	7	8	1	0	0	0	0	1	0
680.01	3	1	270	13	15	0	0	0	1	1	0	0	2
680.02	3	1	269	8	18	2	0	0	1	0	0	2	4
680.03	3	1	277	13	10	0	0	0	0	0	0	0	3
680.04	4	1	277	12	7	2	0	0	0	1	0	0	6
680.05	3	1	276	10	9	1	0	0	0	1	2	0	3
680.06	3	2	269	15	7	4	0	0	0	1	1	1	5
680.07	5	2	259	19	14	1	1	0	1	0	0	2	6
680.08	4	1	263	15	14	1	0	0	0	1	0	0	7
680.09	5	1	267	11	19	0	0	0	0	1	0	1	3
680.10	2	1	281	13	4	2	0	0	0	0	0	0	0
680.11	2	1	282	8	8	1	0	1	0	0	1	0	1
680.12	4	2	282	5	11	0	0	0	0	0	0	0	2
680.13	4	2	282	7	5	2	0	0	0	0	0	0	7
680.14	1	2	240	31	23	3	1	0	1	0	0	1	2
680.15	2	1	266	10	11	7	1	1	0	2	1	1	1
680.16	2	1	268	15	12	1	0	0	0	1	0	1	4
680.17	1	2	267	16	17	0	0	0	0	0	0	0	0
680.18	6	1	234	23	27	4	1	0	0	0	1	1	11
680.20	2	1	272	18	3	2	1	1	2	1	0	0	0
680.21	3	1	278	11	9	1	0	0	0	1	0	0	3
9183.01	4	2	276	1	22	0	0	0	0	0	0	0	2
9183.02	6	1	271	16	11	1	0	0	0	0	0	1	2
9183.03	2	2	279	8	10	2	0	0	0	0	0	0	5
9183.04	4	2	276	19	1	0	0	0	0	1	0	1	3
9183.05	1	1	282	13	5	0	0	0	0	0	0	0	0
9183.06	3	1	286	10	3	1	0	0	0	0	0	0	0
9183.07	3	2	265	15	16	2	1	0	0	0	0	0	1
9183.08	5	2	273	22	3	0	0	0	0	0	0	0	2
9183.09	3	2	271	12	14	1	0	0	0	0	0	0	2
9183.10	4	2	273	11	12	2	1	0	1	0	0	0	4

Table 32. Petrographic Point Count Data (Continued).

Thinsec. #	S	F	Clay	Qtz.	Sherd	U.F.	A.F.	C.F.	V.R.	Ferro.	Op.	Cryp.	Sec.
9183.11	2	1	277	8	9	0	0	0	0	0	0	0	9
9183.12	1	1	255	28	16	1	0	0	0	0	0	0	0
9183.13	5	1	270	9	14	2	0	0	3	0	0	0	2
9183.14	3	2	260	9	27	1	0	0	0	0	0	0	3
9183.15	5	1	267	18	8	0	0	0	1	0	1	0	6
9183.16	5	2	285	6	8	0	0	0	0	0	0	0	1
9183.17	4	1	253	7	40	0	0	0	0	0	0	0	0
9183.18	3	1	267	10	18	1	1	0	0	0	0	0	3
9183.19	2	1	255	16	24	1	0	1	0	0	0	0	3
10779.01	3	1	277	8	11	1	2	0	0	0	0	1	0
10779.02	3	2	258	19	20	1	0	0	0	0	1	1	1
10779.03	1	1	263	12	21	3	0	0	0	0	0	0	2
10779.04	1	1	282	5	12	0	0	0	0	1	0	0	0
10779.05	2	2	270	12	13	3	0	0	1	0	1	0	0
10779.06	2	2	257	19	20	2	0	0	1	0	1	0	1
10779.07	2	1	257	15	26	0	0	0	1	1	0	0	0
10779.08	2	2	253	17	27	1	0	0	0	0	0	0	4
10779.09	1	1	270	22	4	2	0	0	0	1	1	0	1
10779.10	1	1	262	26	10	2	0	0	0	0	0	0	2
10779.11	2	1	233	11	55	0	0	0	0	1	0	0	1
10779.12	2	1	276	14	8	1	0	0	0	1	0	0	2
10779.13	1	1	270	6	23	0	0	0	1	0	0	0	0
10779.14	1	1	269	5	25	1	0	0	0	0	0	0	3
10779.15	3	2	233	35	28	2	0	0	1	1	0	0	3
10779.16	3	2	254	2	43	0	0	0	0	1	0	0	1
10779.17	3	1	277	11	7	1	2	0	1	0	0	0	3
10779.18	6	1	235	19	45	1	0	0	0	0	0	0	3
10779.19	4	1	286	7	3	2	1	0	0	1	0	0	0
10779.20	3	1	276	16	7	1	0	0	0	0	0	0	2
10757.01	3	1	274	14	10	0	1	0	0	0	0	1	1
10757.02	6	1	257	20	20	2	0	0	0	0	1	0	1
10757.03	3	1	285	2	12	0	0	0	1	0	0	0	1
10757.04	3	2	279	8	10	0	0	0	0	0	0	0	3
10757.05	4	2	287	4	8	0	0	0	0	0	0	1	0
10757.06	2	1	254	9	36	0	0	0	0	0	0	1	1

Table 32. Petrographic Point Count Data (Continued).

Thisec. #	S	F	Clay	Qtz.	Sherd	U.F.	A.F.	C.F.	V.R.	Ferro.	Op.	Cryp.	Sec.
10757.07	2	2	260	22	17	0	0	0	0	0	0	0	3
10757.08	1	2	258	26	13	0	0	0	0	1	0	0	4
10757.09	2	1	277	6	13	1	0	0	1	2	0	0	1
10757.10	1	1	271	11	16	1	0	0	0	0	0	0	3
10757.11	3	1	276	12	6	0	0	0	0	0	0	0	7
10757.12	1	1	279	16	3	2	0	0	0	0	0	0	0
10757.13	4	2	244	19	35	0	0	0	0	0	0	2	3
10757.14	5	2	280	14	3	0	0	0	0	0	1	0	4
10757.15	1	1	270	11	18	1	0	0	0	0	0	0	0
10757.16	3	2	276	6	11	3	1	1	1	0	0	0	2
10757.17	5	1	262	15	18	3	1	0	0	0	0	0	3
10757.18	4	1	287	5	7	0	0	0	0	0	1	0	1
10757.19	2	1	271	15	12	1	0	0	1	0	0	0	5
10757.20	6	1	256	20	21	0	0	0	1	2	0	0	3
10757.21	4	2	283	12	5	0	0	0	0	0	0	0	3
10757.22	4	1	241	22	29	5	0	0	1	1	0	1	0
10803.01	1	1	247	39	0	11	0	2	0	0	0	1	0
10803.02	2	2	256	10	32	2	0	0	0	0	0	0	0
10803.03	1	1	267	15	8	9	0	1	0	0	0	0	3
10803.04	1	2	243	18	36	0	0	0	1	2	0	0	2
10803.05	1	1	252	14	31	1	0	0	0	1	0	1	2
10803.06	1	1	250	43	0	4	0	0	1	0	0	1	2
10803.07	1	1	236	41	20	1	0	0	0	1	0	1	1
10803.08	2	1	233	21	43	0	0	0	2	0	1	0	2
10803.09	2	2	274	14	12	0	0	0	0	0	0	0	0
10803.10	2	1	232	28	34	1	2	0	0	1	1	1	4
10803.11	2	2	250	12	35	1	0	0	1	1	0	0	3
10803.12	2	1	266	15	15	4	0	0	0	0	0	0	3
10803.13	2	1	227	15	5	2	1	0	0	0	0	0	4
10803.14	2	1	260	23	16	0	1	0	0	0	0	0	4
10803.15	1	1	267	32	0	0	0	0	0	0	0	1	1
10803.16	1	1	242	22	35	0	0	1	0	0	0	0	1
10803.17	2	1	280	13	0	2	0	0	3	0	1	1	1
10803.18	1	2	275	14	9	1	0	0	0	0	0	0	3
10803.19	3	1	270	13	15	0	1	0	0	1	0	0	1

Table 32. Petrographic Point Count Data (Continued).

Thinsec. #	S	F	Clay	Qtz.	Sherd	U.F.	A.F.	C.F.	V.R.	Ferro.	Op.	Cryp.	Sec.
10803.20	2	1	282	10	8	0	0	0	0	0	0	0	0
10803.21	2	1	248	44	0	1	1	0	2	0	0	2	6
7806.01	4	2	269	9	22	0	0	0	0	0	0	0	1
7806.02	4	2	259	23	13	1	0	0	0	1	0	0	5
7806.03	4	2	287	12	1	0	0	0	0	0	0	0	1
7806.04	4	1	260	15	17	5	0	0	1	0	0	0	3
7806.05	4	1	267	19	5	1	1	0	4	0	0	1	2
7806.06	4	2	251	21	25	2	0	0	0	0	0	0	5
7806.07	5	2	278	13	7	0	0	0	0	0	0	0	5
7806.08	5	1	277	2	21	0	0	0	0	0	0	0	0
7806.09	5	1	256	5	29	3	0	0	0	1	0	1	7
7806.10	5	1	261	9	29	0	0	0	0	0	0	1	1
7806.11	5	2	274	15	9	0	0	0	0	0	0	0	3
7806.12	3	2	261	16	21	1	0	0	1	0	0	0	0
7806.13	3	1	289	8	2	0	0	0	0	0	0	1	0
7806.14	3	1	277	20	3	0	0	0	0	0	0	0	3
7806.15	3	2	257	31	0	5	1	0	0	0	1	2	5
7806.16	3	2	295	3	2	0	0	0	0	0	0	0	1
7806.17	6	2	275	13	10	0	0	1	0	0	1	0	2
7806.18	6	1	267	12	18	0	0	0	0	0	0	0	5
7806.19	6	1	275	15	9	1	0	0	0	0	0	0	2
7806.20	6	1	286	6	7	0	0	0	0	0	0	0	3
7432.01	1	1	281	11	1	0	0	0	0	0	0	0	8
7432.02	2	1	285	8	5	1	0	0	1	0	0	0	0
7432.03	4	1	275	14	10	0	0	0	0	0	0	0	2
7432.04	1	1	260	17	21	0	0	0	1	1	0	0	2
7432.05	1	1	285	11	4	0	0	0	0	0	0	0	1
7432.06	5	1	264	7	23	2	0	0	1	3	0	0	0
7432.07	3	2	280	16	3	1	0	0	0	0	0	0	2
7432.08	3	2	252	19	27	1	0	0	0	0	0	1	1
7432.09	1	1	273	12	13	1	0	0	0	0	0	0	1
7432.10	1	1	249	45	5	1	0	0	0	0	0	0	1
7432.11	1	1	282	8	8	0	0	0	0	0	0	2	0
7432.12	3	1	256	19	16	1	0	2	2	3	0	0	4
7432.13	2	2	262	28	7	1	0	0	1	1	0	0	0

Table 32. Petrographic Point Count Data (Continued).

Thinsec. #	S	F	Clay	Qtz.	Sherd	U.F	A.F.	C.F.	V.R.	Ferro.	Op.	Cryp.	Sec.
7432.14	2	1	261	15	19	0	0	1	3	1	0	0	2
7432.16	2	2	255	15	26	1	1	1	0	0	1	0	0
7432.17	2	1	272	16	11	1	0	0	0	0	0	0	1
7432.18	3	1	284	10	5	0	0	0	0	0	0	0	2
7432.19	3	1	288	10	1	1	0	0	0	0	0	0	0
7432.20	3	1	272	21	1	1	0	1	0	1	0	0	5
2403.01	3	1	278	12	7	0	0	0	0	0	0	0	5
2403.02	2	2	274	13	8	2	1	0	0	0	1	1	1
2403.03	3	1	266	20	8	0	0	0	1	0	0	2	4
2403.04	3	1	230	60	0	8	0	0	0	0	1	1	0
2403.05	3	1	292	5	1	0	0	0	0	0	0	0	2
2403.06	3	2	260	15	19	5	0	0	0	0	0	1	2
2403.07	3	2	265	15	15	1	0	0	0	0	0	0	5
2403.08	3	1	266	21	7	2	1	0	0	0	0	1	4
2403.09	6	1	248	18	28	1	0	0	0	1	0	2	5
2403.10	6	2	279	15	5	1	0	0	0	0	0	0	0
2403.11	6	1	278	4	3	0	0	0	0	0	0	0	16
2403.12	1	1	266	16	13	0	0	1	1	2	1	0	2
2403.13	5	1	294	2	1	1	0	0	0	0	0	0	2
2403.14	4	2	244	24	28	0	0	0	0	0	0	4	2
2403.15	3	2	210	47	0	35	1	4	0	0	0	2	3
2403.16	3	1	281	16	0	0	1	1	0	0	0	1	0
2403.17	3	2	255	23	19	3	0	0	0	0	0	0	3
2403.18	6	[illegible]	262	20	0	5	1	0	0	0	0	4	8

Key:

S: Style
1. Black Mesa
2. Sosi
3. Flagstaff
4. Walnut
5. Padre
6. Leupp

Qtz.: Quartz
U.F.: Untwinned Feldspar
A.F.: Albite-twinned Feldspar
C.F.: Cross-twinned Feldspar
V.R.: Volcanic Rock
Ferro.: Ferromagnesium
Op.: Opaques

Cryp: Cryptocrystalline Quartz
Sec: Secondary/Other Minerals

F: Vessel Form
1. Bowl
2. Jar

APPENDIX C

LCWW DESIGN STYLES

This appendix contains descriptions of the six designs styles which occur on LCWW. These descriptions are based on my design analysis of 2400 LCWW sherds and examinations of whole vessels housed at the Museum of Northern Arizona, as well as the whole vessels from the Turkey Hill site which are housed at the Arizona State Museum. Histograms, frequencies and descriptive statistics of stylistic variables such as the types of elements present, their composition, their articulation with each other and line widths were used to generate the descriptions and comments. No statistical correlations or multivariate analyses have been employed on the stylistic data. A key to terms used to describe design element articulation in this appendix can be found in Figure 30.

My objective in writing this appendix is to provide researchers with an alternative to the typological criteria presently being used to classify LCWW. Issues such as the changes in LCWW design styles through time, its spatial distribution at different points in time and the use of this ware as a means of dating archaeological assemblages can be addressed more effectively if the stylistic criteria set forth in the following pages are used on a regular basis.

The format of this appendix has been adopted from Colton (1955) because of researchers' familiarity with it. All references to ceramic types are derived from Colton as well. The descriptions suffer from the same limitations as Colton's type descriptions, limitations which are inherent in any attempts to set forth a classification scheme based on qualitative criteria. It is difficult to incorporate the full range of variability into the descriptions and draw clear demarcations between the styles. Determining when a particular trait is "common," versus one that occurs "occasionally" or is "rare" can be problematic.

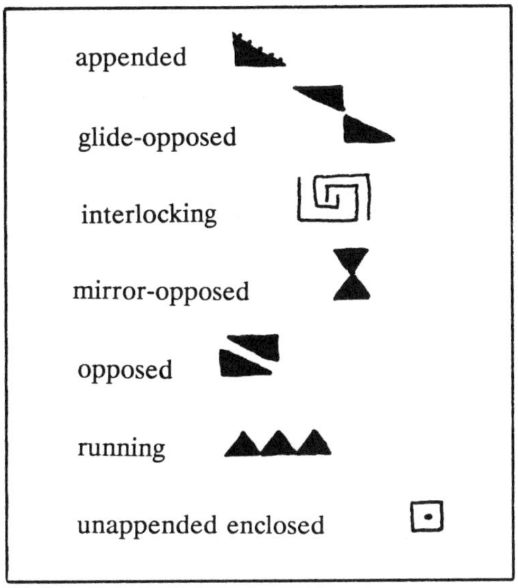

Figure 30. Illustrations of terms used to describe design element articulation.

The date estimates for the styles are based on occurrences of LCWW sherds or whole vessels in tree-ring dated contexts, or their contextual association with other types which have been tree-ring dated. The dendrochronological data are from the San Francisco Peaks area. Dates from the Hopi Buttes production area and other exchange loci are lacking at this time. Therefore, the dates are spatially biased. In addition, the dates from the San Francisco Peaks area are only approximations since the direct association of LCWW with tree-ring dates is relatively rare, even in this area. For both of these reasons, these date estimates should be employed with caution.

This appendix is intended as a guide for LCWW design analysis but it is recognized that the descriptions presented herein are subject to change, particularly as whole vessels are studied systematically. My design analysis was heavily biased toward sherds. As a result, data on design layout and differences in the function of lines within whole designs are incomplete.

BLACK MESA

LCWW TYPE EQUIVALENT: Holbrook Black-on-white, Variety A.

DATE ESTIMATE: A.D. 1050-1150.

DESCRIPTION: elements are generally large and solid, thus rendering a bold effect to the design; right triangles with appended dots along the hypotenuse are common; obtuse triangles are less common; also stepped and rectangular elements; isosceles triangles in running, mirror-opposed series forming open diamonds; curvilinear scrolls are relatively rare; in some cases, curvilinear scrolls are filled in with a checkerboard pattern of alternating solid and open squares; generally, lines are intermediary in width between Sosi style lines on the one hand, and Flagstaff and Walnut style lines on the other, averaging 3.57 mm; lines run parallel to each other or intersect at acute/obtuse angles; elements are often appended to each other in an asymmetric configuration.

TUSAYAN WHITE WARE COUNTERPART: Black Mesa Black-on-white.

COMMENTS: It is often difficult to distinguish the Black Mesa and Sosi styles on sherds unless triangles with appended dots are present. The line work is very similar in both styles and there is a significant amount of overlap in the width of their lines. Black Mesa elements are often incomplete on sherds because of their relatively large size, making precise element identification impossible in many cases. Appended dots and tics can occur on triangles in later Walnut and Flagstaff style designs. The revival of such secondary elements can lead to problems in design classification, unless enough of the design is present to distinguish between the distinctive motifs and line work of the earlier and later styles. Walnut style curvilinear scrolls are sometimes filled in with a checkerboard pattern similar to the Black Mesa motif. However, the open checkerboard squares usually have unappended enclosed dots in them; the squares are smaller and the line work is generally thinner in the Walnut counterpart.

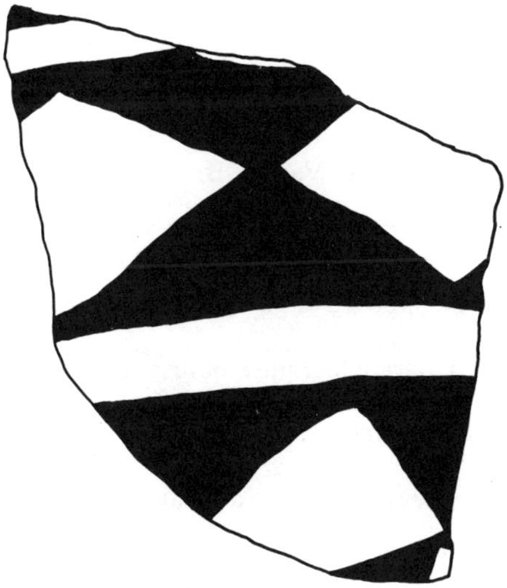

NA 9183

NA 9400

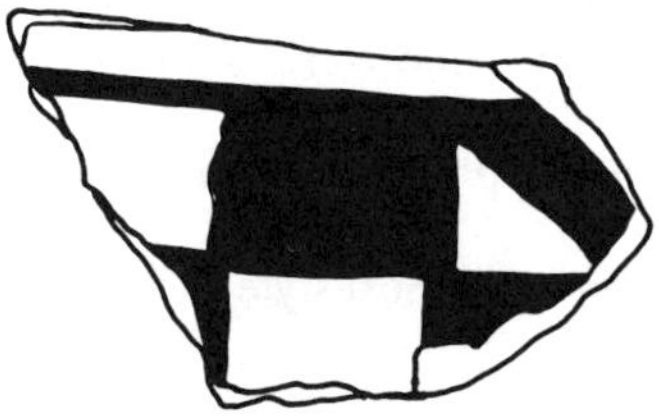

NA 10803

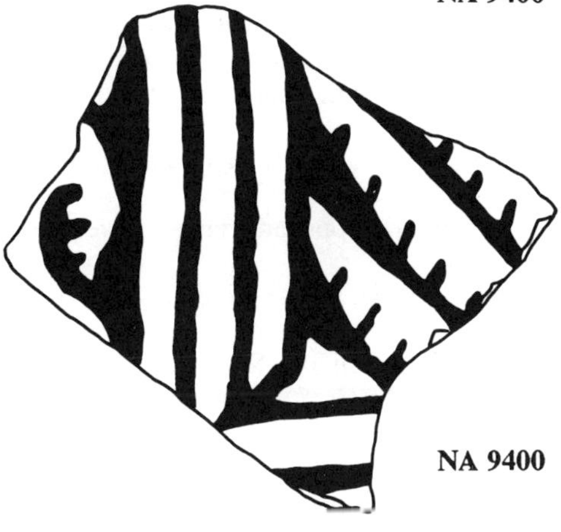

NA 9400

Figure 31. Sherds with Black Mesa style designs.

SOSI

LCWW TYPE EQUIVALENT: Holbrook Black-on-white, Variety B.

DATE ESTIMATE: A.D. 1050-1150.

DESCRIPTION: solid right triangles in running and opposed or glide-opposed series; glide-opposed triangles occasionally grade into parallelograms; obtuse triangles, and rectangular and stepped elements less common; lines average 4.68 mm in thickness; lines run in concentric bands around the vessel or intersect at acute/obtuse angles.

TUSAYAN WHITE WARE COUNTERPART: Sosi Black-on-white.

COMMENTS: It is often difficult to distinguish the Black Mesa and Sosi styles on sherds unless triangles with appended dots are present. The line work is very similar in both styles and there is a significant amount of overlap in the width of their lines. The running and opposed triangle series are bolder in the Sosi style than they are in the Flagstaff style, whose triangle series appear more like barbed lines. There is an intergrade between the Sosi and Flagstaff styles, however, in which running and opposed triangles have appended and interlocking flags or hooks. Lines generally occupy a greater proportion of the design area and the lines intersect in more complex patterns in the Flagstaff style.

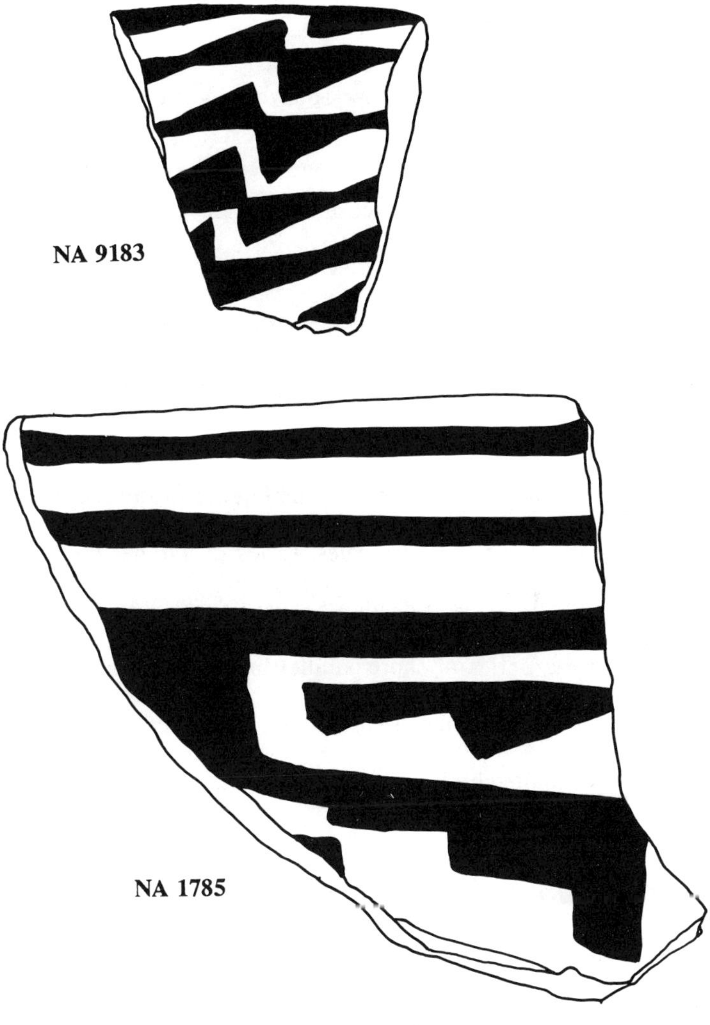

Figure 32. Sherds with Sosi style designs. The sherd from NA 1785 was copied from type sherd illustrations in Colton 1955, Ware 9B, Type 2.

FLAGSTAFF

LCWW TYPE EQUIVALENT: Walnut Black-on-white, Variety A.

DATE ESTIMATE: A.D. 1100-1250.

DESCRIPTION: series of running, opposed and/or glide-opposed solid right or obtuse triangles which create a barbed line effect, sometimes found in conjunction with zig-zag lines; running and opposed obtuse triangles with appended flags or steps which interlock with one another; pairs of interlocking rectilinear scrolls or hooks, often terminating in solid stepped elements which are opposed to one another; running series of solid diamonds encircling the circumference of the vessel; mirror-opposed triangles with dots in the open triangles; series of parallel lines which merge at acute/obtuse angles often act as dividers between panels; lines are relatively narrow, averaging 2.97 mm; series of short parallel lines intersecting at right angles and enclosed in bands encircling the circumference of the vessel create a pattern which is reminiscent of a plaited basketry weave; cross-hatching with unappended enclosed dots in the open squares is relatively rare.

TUSAYAN WHITE WARE COUNTERPART: Flagstaff Black-on-white.

COMMENTS: The running and opposed triangle series are bolder in the Sosi style than they are in the Flagstaff style, whose triangle series appear more like barbed lines. However, it can be difficult to distinguish between Sosi and Flagstaff style designs when only partially visible on sherds. In addition, there is an intergrade between the Sosi and Flagstaff styles, in which running and opposed triangles have appended and interlocking flags or hooks. Lines generally occupy a greater proportion of the design area and the lines intersect in more complex patterns in the Flagstaff style. The "plaited" line work also occurs in the Walnut style. There is a transitional type of the Flagstaff style which grades into a bolder, more negative type of design reminiscent of the Leupp style. It is composed of rows of running and opposed obtuse triangles with appended flags which are separated by bands of parallel lines. The triangles are generally larger and better executed than in the true Flagstaff or Sosi styles. Their sides are straighter and terminate in sharp angles, unlike the rounded corners of triangles in the latter two styles. A few Flagstaff designs have ticked lines reminiscent of the Kana'a style. However, the Flagstaff style ticking occurs on wider lines than in the earlier style. Flagstaff designs can be found on the same vessel with Walnut designs, as in the case where barbed lines co-occur with curvilinear scrolls.

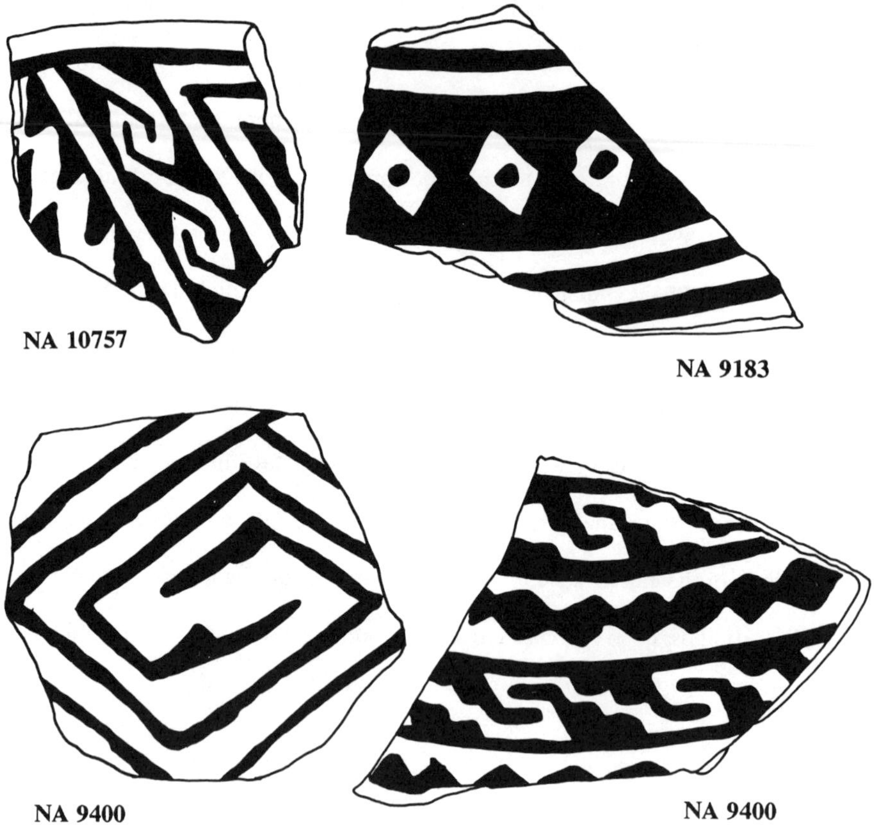

Figure 33. Sherds with Flagstaff style designs.

WALNUT

LCWW TYPE EQUIVALENT: Walnut Black-on-white, Variety B.

DATE ESTIMATE: A.D. 1200-1250.

DESCRIPTION: interlocking pairs of curvilinear scrolls; solid equilateral or isosceles triangles in running series, creating a wavy line effect; these "wavy" lines often run parallel to one another, appended at an angle to curvilinear scrolls; in addition, they can occur within triangular panels; bands of curvilinear scrolls and "wavy" lines are often separated by bands of concentric lines; lines are relatively narrow, averaging 3.06 mm in thickness; the bases of the curvilinear scrolls are occasionally filled in to form a solid triangle; series of short parallel lines intersecting at right angles and enclosed in bands encircling the circumference of the vessel create a pattern which is reminiscent of a plaited basketry weave; cross-hatching with unappended enclosed dots in the open squares is relatively rare.

TUSAYAN WHITE WARE COUNTERPART: none.

COMMENTS: Walnut style designs can occur on the same vessel with Leupp, Padre or Flagstaff style designs. The Walnut and Flagstaff styles cannot be distinguished from one another on sherds if only lines are present. Walnut style curvilinear scrolls are sometimes filled in with a checkerboard pattern similar to the Black Mesa motif. However, the open checkerboard squares usually have unappended enclosed dots in them, the squares are smaller and the line work is generally thinner in the Walnut counterpart. In other cases, Walnut scrolls are filled in with cross-hatching with dots enclosed in the open spaces. A few Walnut designs have ticked lines reminiscent of the Kana'a style. However, the Walnut style ticking occurs on wider lines than in the earlier style.

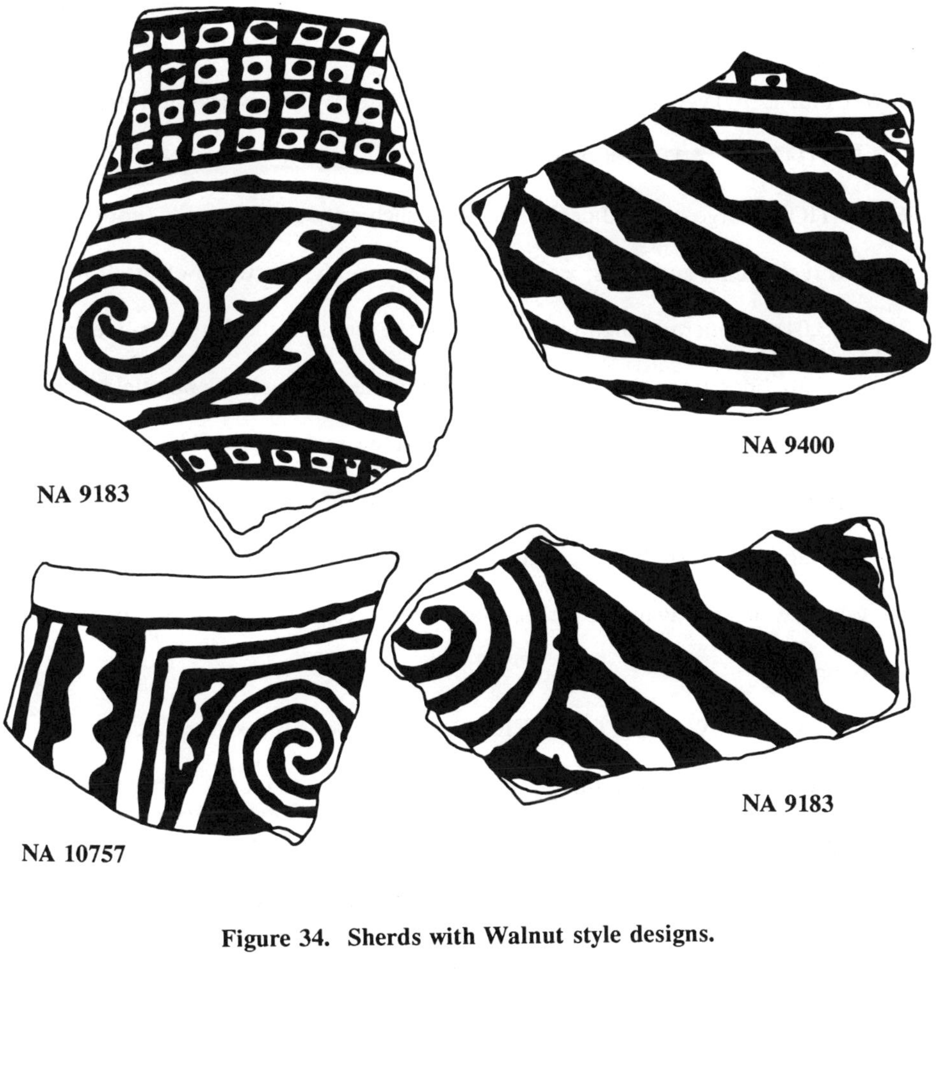

Figure 34. Sherds with Walnut style designs.

PADRE

LCWW TYPE EQUIVALENT: Padre Black-on-white, Walnut Black-on-white, Variety C.

DATE ESTIMATE: A.D. 1100-1250.

DESCRIPTION: large hatched design elements such as triangles, scrolls (both curvilinear and rectilinear) and steps; zigzags occur only rarely; the width of the framing lines (x=3.04) is generally slightly greater than the width of the hatchure lines (x=2.35); hatchure lines are most commonly oblique to the framing lines; parallel hatching and cross-hatching are relatively uncommon; in a few rare cases, solid lines are combined with hatched elements in a manner reminiscent of the Tularosa style, although the lines are narrower than the hatched elements; design elements on the few whole vessels which are available for study are interlocking, mirror-opposed or running and opposed.

TUSAYAN WHITE WARE COUNTERPART: Dogoszhi Black-on-white.

COMMENTS: In many cases, the design elements are incomplete on sherds due to their relatively large size, making it difficult to identify them or determine their articulation with one another. Padre style designs can co-occur on jars with Walnut style designs, the former covering the body in a wide band and the latter encircling the neck of the vessel.

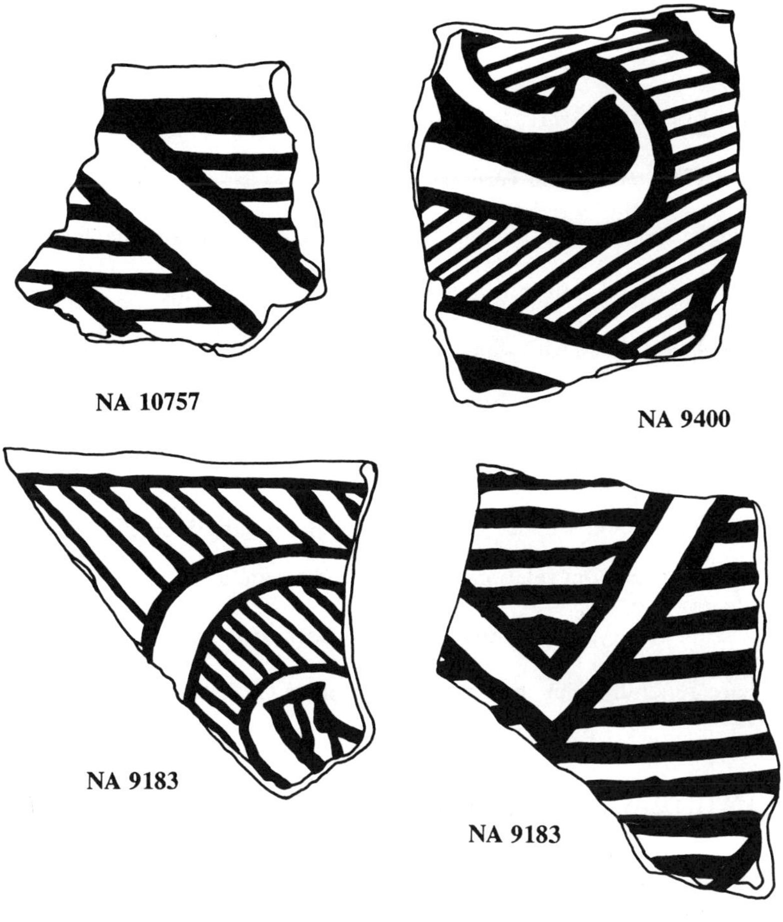

Figure 35. Sherds with Padre style designs.

LEUPP

LCWW TYPE EQUIVALENT: Leupp Black-on-white.

DATE ESTIMATE: A.D. 1200-1250.

DESCRIPTION: the overall predominance of the black paint over the white background creates a negative effect on the design; "mosquito bars," or rectangular cross-hatchures are framed with wide lines, forming triangular or rectangular panels; small dots enclosed within the squares formed by the cross-hatching are common; large solid triangles, sometimes terminating in, or enclosing, curvilinear scrolls; series of running brush strokes, resembling diamonds or parallelograms, in parallel lines oriented diagonally in relationship to the rim create a "saw-toothed effect" (Colton 1955, Ware 8B, Type 9); also parallel lines with diagonal tics drawn through them; lines are generally thick in comparison to other LCWW styles, averaging 5.18 mm; layouts are offset quartered on bowls and encircling bands on bowls and jars.

TUSAYAN WHITE WARE COUNTERPART: Kayenta Black-on-white.

COMMENTS: Leupp and Walnut style designs can co-occur on the same vessel. There is a transitional type of the Flagstaff style which grades into a bolder, more negative type of design reminiscent of the Leupp style. It is composed of rows of running and opposed obtuse triangles with appended flags which are separated by bands of parallel lines. The triangles are generally larger and better executed than in the true Flagstaff or Sosi styles. Their sides are straighter and terminate in sharp angles, unlike the rounded corners of triangles in the latter two styles.

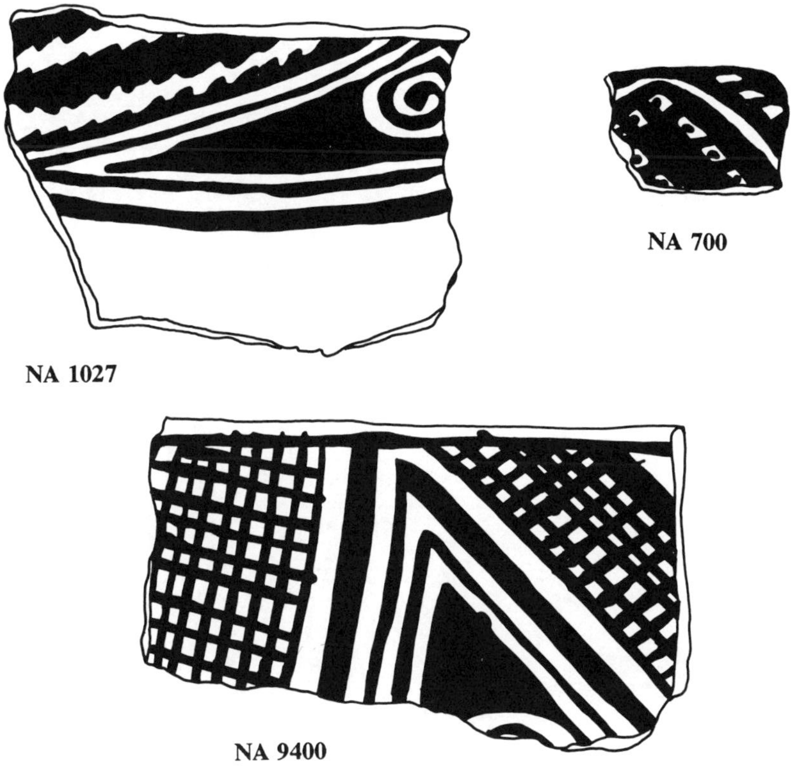

Figure 36. Sherds with Leupp style designs. The sherds from NA 700 and NA 1027 were copied from type sherd illustrations in Colton 1955, Ware 9B, Type 6.